# SHORT-CYCLE HIGHER EDUCATION

## A search for identity

ORGANISATION FOR ECONOMIC CO-OPERATION AND DEVELOPMENT

*The Organisation for Economic Co-operation and Development (OECD), which was set up under a Convention signed in Paris on 14th December, 1960, provides that the OECD shall promote policies designed:*

- *to achieve the highest sustainable economic growth and employment and a rising standard of living in Member countries, while maintaining financial stability, and thus to contribute to the development of the world economy;*
- *to contribute to sound economic expansion in Member as well as non-member countries in the process of economic development;*
- *to contribute to the expansion of world trade on a multilateral, non-discriminatory basis in accordance with international obligations.*

*The Members of OECD are: Australia, Austria, Belgium, Canada, Denmark, Finland, France, the Federal Republic of Germany, Greece, Iceland, Ireland, Italy, Japan, Luxembourg, the Netherlands, Norway, Portugal, Spain, Sweden, Switzerland, Turkey, the United Kingdom and the United States.*

# FOREWORD

A crucial problem facing OECD Member countries in the reform of their higher education systems is the development of new types of programmes and institutions representing a diversity of meaningful educational opportunities corresponding to the increasing diversity of students entering post-secondary studies.

Although strategies of diversification differ from country to country, some common trends and preoccupations can be discerned. In particular, these strategies try to develop types of education which have so far been neglected, or not represented at all, in most of the existing universities. For the majority of OECD countries this has meant setting up institutions or courses offering post-secondary education of shorter duration and with a strong vocational component, generally grouped under the "non-university sector" of higher education.

It is in this framework that an analysis in depth was undertaken of the various problems facing "short-cycle institutions" and their place in the systems of higher education. The present volume is a synthesis of this work.

Part One offers a general conceptual framework for defining and analysing short-cycle higher education and presents the main issues arising in the planning and reform of this type of education, with particular reference to their linkages and relations with the university sector.

Part Two deals with four different types of short-cycle higher education institutions in different Member countries and with a number of specific issues which short-cycle or non-university establishments are facing almost everywhere : status and role of teachers, structure and content of studies, employment of short-cycle higher education graduates and the new functions which these institutions are called upon to perform. These texts represent a selection of papers which were presented as background and discussion documents to an international

Meeting on Short-Cycle Higher Education organised by the Secretariat at Grenoble, France on 15, 16 and 17 November 1971.

The conclusions reached at that meeting, together with a number of documents relating to its discussions and proceedings, are presented in Part Three.

The Secretariat would like to express its sincere thanks to all participants at the Grenoble meeting and in particular to those who contributed either by presenting papers on that occasion, or by facilitating the preliminary investigations and studies in their respective Member countries. Special thanks are due to the University of Social Sciences of Grenoble, which served as host to the meeting, and to the French Ministry of Education, which granted a subsidy for its organisation.

Within the OECD Secretariat, the main responsibility for preparing the Grenoble Meeting and the general direction of the activities and studies concerning short-cycle higher education were with Dorotea Furth and Ladislav Cerych. Dorotea Furth has also edited the present volume.

# CONTENTS

Foreword ........................................ 5

Part One

SHORT-CYCLE HIGHER EDUCATION: SOME BASIC CONSIDERATIONS
by Dorotea Furth, Directorate for Scientific Affairs

I. Introduction ........................................ 13

II. Existing types of short-cycle institutions ........................................ 15

III. Objectives and motivations behind the development and reform of short-cycle institutions ........................................ 21

IV. Issues and dilemmas ........................................ 23

Annex. Note on terminology ........................................ 41

Part Two

SOME NATIONAL EXPERIENCES AND KEY ISSUES

I. The Norwegian Regional Colleges
by Ingjald Ø Sørheim, Head, Regional College Section, Ministry of Education (Norway) ........................................ 45

II. Community-Junior Colleges in the United States
by S. V. Martorana, Vice-Chancellor for Two-Year Colleges, State University of New York (United States) ........................................ 83

III. Development of Two-Year Post-Secondary Schools in Yugoslavia, by the Department for Research in Higher Education, Institute for Social Research, University of Zagreb (Yugoslavia) .......... 149

IV. Place and Role of University Institutes of Technology (IUT) in the new French Universities, by Jean-Louis Quermonne, Président, Université des Sciences sociales, Grenoble (France) .......... 211

V. Teachers in Non-University Higher Education: a British Case Study, by Gareth Williams, Associate Director, and Alice Crampin, Research Officer, Higher Education Research Unit, London School of Economics and Political Science (United-Kingdom) .......... 235

VI. Teaching Learning Approaches in Short-Cycle Higher Education, by Guy Berger, Professeur, Université de Vincennes (France) .......... 263

VII. Problems of Employment for Graduates of Short-Cycle Higher Education and French Experience with University Institutes of Technology (IUTs), by Michel-Yves Bernard, Professeur au Conservatoire national des Arts et Métiers, Paris, and Conseiller technique au Ministère de l'Education nationale (France) .......... 283

VIII. Outreach Programmes in the United States Community Colleges, by Dr. R. E. Schultz, Director, International Office, The American Association of Junior Colleges (United States) .......... 313

Part Three

GENERAL REPORT
of the International Meeting on Short-Cycle Higher Education, Grenoble (France), 15-17 November 1971

- The Grenoble Meeting .......... 343

- Guidelines for discussion .............................. 345

I. The Place and Role of SCIs in the Global System of Post-Secondary Education .............................. 345

II. Problems of the Teaching Staff .............................. 353

III. Structure and Content of Studies .............................. 359

IV. Employment Problems of Graduates .............................. 365

V. Summary Considerations .............................. 371

- Reports of the Working Groups .............................. 373

I. Problems of the Teaching Staff .............................. 373

II. Structure and Content of Studies .............................. 377

III. Problems of Employment of SCI Graduates .............................. 385

- Some Comments on the Grenoble Meeting by Professor Burton Clark, University of Yale (United States) .............................. 389

Annexes

I. Statistics on Short-Cycle Higher Education .............................. 393

II. List of Participants .............................. 405

III. List of Documents .............................. 413

## Part One

# SHORT-CYCLE HIGHER EDUCATION: SOME BASIC CONSIDERATIONS

by

Dorotea Furth
Directorate for Scientific Affairs

# I

## INTRODUCTION

The rapid and almost universal expansion of higher education during the last 15 to 20 years has made most European countries realize that major structural reforms of their post secondary systems are an essential condition for the fulfilment of a variety of new functions which contemporary societies are increasingly assigning them.

The crises characterizing the late sixties can be considered largely as the ultimate expression of the breakdown of a deeply rooted tradition of higher education for an élite; it could be argued that the seventies will represent for most European countries a critical transition period between elitist and mass higher education. Should this be the case, it is clear that past policies for higher education based on "more of the same" strategies will be insufficient and ineffective for the future: traditional universities will have to undergo major changes, and, equally important, new types of higher education will have to be developed to deal with increasing numbers, a more diversified student body and the rapidly changing manpower needs of highly industrialized societies.

Although differences in country traditions, in existing educational systems and governmental policies will inevitably give rise to different structures of mass higher education, the work undertaken within the OECD on this subject points to the existence of certain common trends. The most important seems to be the search for greater diversification and better articulation of post-secondary education. This means that within all structures solutions are being sought to provide a greater variety of educational offerings (patterns of study, degrees and ways in which to obtain them) and that at the same time emphasis is being given to closer co-ordination and complementarity between the different types of institution: flows of students, teachers and financial resources are being facilitated and comprehensive plans for the total systems are being developed.

The majority of OECD Member countries are envisaging, as one of their main strategies, a wider diversification of their post-secondary systems, the development of a variety of extra or non-university institutions and programmes originally created to provide terminal and, for the most part, vocationally oriented post-secondary education. For want of a better term they are referred to in this volume as short-cycle institutions (SCIs) or short-cycle higher education (SCHE). *

The present analysis focuses primarily on the problems faced by those institutions whose present extra or non-university status puts them in the position of having to establish their respectability without losing sight of one of the main functions for which they were created, i. e. to offer education and degrees of a terminal and vocationally oriented character. **

This limitation of subject means chiefly that the analysis will focus essentially on the problems of the non-university sector of higher education. In some cases this term might have been more appropriate, as certain institutions to be discussed here offer courses of the same duration as a normal university degree course (in particular the British polytechnics) whereas short-cycle higher education provided in few instances inside universities is not analysed in the present context. However, the term short-cycle higher education was preferred mainly because it is expected that in the not-so-distant future the distinction between university and non-university institutions will become increasingly blurred. ***

* See Note on terminology, in Annex to Part One of this volume.

** In this context the term short-cycle higher education should be distinguished from first-cycle higher education which designates essentially (at least, at the present time) the first period (usually two years) or normal full university study. In the future this distinction might (or should) disappear.

*** In addition, the term non-university may in some cases be more misleading than the term short-cycle. In France, for example, non-university higher education stricto sensu includes the Grandes Ecoles but not the IUTs; however, the present study intends to examine the latter and not the former.

# II

## EXISTING TYPES OF SHORT-CYCLE INSTITUTIONS

Before defining some of the main issues considered of utmost importance in the development of short-cycle higher education institutions (SCIs), it may be useful to give a brief, synoptic classification and analysis of the existing systems of SCI and to identify the main general motivations and objectives behind their development and/or reform.

### i) The multipurpose model

The prototype of the multipurpose model is the American Junior or Community College. Its development was a direct consequence of mass comprehensive secondary education such as characterized the United States, Canada and Japan. * Consequently, the main factors behind this development have been the pressure of numbers and the resulting changes in the composition of the student body.

The basic characteristics of the "multipurpose" model are:

a) The respective SCIs have a fairly close link with university education, not usually from the administrative point of view but because some of their courses can be assimilated to the first two years of full university study, thus allowing transfer of students and inter-institutional mobility.

b) They are multi-functional institutions with highly diversified curricula ranging from purely academic programmes which prepare for continuation of studies at university to various types of general and vocational training of a terminal nature.

* The Junior College system in Japan, although based on the American model, underwent fundamental changes when introduced into the Japanese context. Given its actual characteristics it is perhaps nearer to the United Kingdom type.

c) Institutions of this model are geared to meet local or regional needs and less concerned with problems of national standards. They constitute a highly decentralized system with a considerable degree of institutional autonomy.

The main SCIs which can be classified under the multipurpose model are the Junior Colleges of some of the Western provinces of Canada and, in the same country, the CEGEPs (Collèges d'enseignement général et professionnel) of Quebec. The latter have an even closer link to universities because the first cycle of university studies is to be provided exclusively in these colleges along with courses of a terminal and vocational nature (the CEGEPs are less autonomous, however, and subject to greater central control).

In Europe, two countries have tried to build up an SCI system, introducing some of the characteristics of the multipurpose model. In Yugoslavia the Više Škole (two-year post-secondary schools) in the early sixties offered transfer as well as terminal courses, and represented the first European experience of relatively autonomous institutions outside the universities providing two-year courses considered equivalent to the first two years of university study. The two-year-old Norwegian District Colleges also represent a departure from the old European tradition and the adoption of some of the main characteristics of this model.

ii) The specialized model

The development of a "specialized type" of SCI was mainly the result of efforts to provide post-secondary education to students from the non-academic streams of secondary schools who were, therefore, not admitted to the university sector. In this respect they were the continuation of a streaming process begun at secondary level.

This model has the following basic characteristics:

a) The links with universities are very loose or almost non-existent. As these institutions provide mainly terminal, vocationally oriented courses, the organisation of their studies is completely independent of the university sector.

b) Each institution provides a limited number of programmes and specializes in one or a few areas of study or training, e.g. various technical fields, teacher training, social assistance, paramedical professions, etc.

c) Inter-institutional differentiation tends to be small owing to low institutional autonomy. The institutions are centrally administered either by regional or national authorities; on the one hand this favours the existence of a co-ordinated system (at least between institutions of the same specialization) but, on the other, pressures to conform to national standards counteract institutional initiative which would reflect local or regional needs.

Until the early sixties almost all continental European countries had an SCI system with roughly these characteristics, in particular, Belgium, Denmark, France, Germany, the Netherlands, Portugal, Spain and Turkey. * During the late sixties, however, many European countries began introducing far-reaching reforms, significant examples of which are: the reform of the "enseignement technique supérieur" in Belgium, the creation of IUTs in France, the reorganisation of Fachhochschulen (formerly Ingenieurschulen and Höhere Fachschulen) in Germany, the polytechnics planned in Portugal, and an overall reform of the higher education system in Spain. Some of the characteristics of the new patterns will be analysed below.

iii) The binary model

In the OECD area this model concerns almost exclusively the United Kingdom, where post-secondary education is divided into two separate sectors which have been developing independently of each other: the university or autonomous sector and the advanced further education sector. The institutions included in the latter** operate on the following principles:

a) the separation from universities is even more marked than in continental Europe, *** as the two sectors operate under different administrative bodies;
b) like SCIs of the "multipurpose model", the United Kingdom institutions are highly diversified, not only in the type and level of studies provided, but also in the development of various patterns of study, e. g. sandwich courses, part-time day and evening courses, etc.;
c) some institutions in this sector (at present, mainly the polytechnics) offer, independently of the universities, degree-level and post-graduate courses. Even so they represent a

* A few European countries (e.g. Austria and Italy) did not have institutions of this type.

** As already mentioned, the term SCI should not be applied here. The duration of study in these institutions is not shorter than in universities.

*** A recent exception to this pattern is found in the relations which have been established between some teacher training establishments and universities.

specialized and professionally oriented sector as opposed to the more theoretical academic orientation of the universities. And even if, in principle, their degrees are of the same level as those awarded by universities, they are far from carrying the same social prestige.

Post-secondary technical education in the United Kingdom seems to have influenced the development of the Ontario CAATs (Colleges of Applied Arts and Technology) in Canada. The main function of these colleges, which are strongly community oriented, is to provide highly diversified terminal programmes of technical education thus reducing to a minimum student transfer to universities.

The above classification of SCI systems represents an obvious over-simplification and should serve only as an analytical framework in which to identify the mixed or totally new models which are emerging in response to the deficiencies in existing systems. Probably the fundamental weakness, common to all three "historical models", is that they imply a distinction between the "noble" and "less noble" parts of higher education. It is this distinction which is at the root of the present search for appropriate reforms.

It is proposed that the three models be examined in greater detail in a later study, especially in regard to their dynamics i. e. their mechanisms of change and development. At this stage only two general trends will be mentioned.

First, it appears that during the past 15 to 20 years short-cycle and, in general, non-university higher education institutions grew at roughly the same rate as universities. * If, in a few countries, the former expanded much faster than the latter (e. g. Junior Colleges in the United States and two-year post-secondary schools in Yugoslavia), the dichotomic nature of the system was in no way altered. Thus, the drawbacks which these dichotomies generated were often perpetuated and even strengthened.

Second, most countries have witnessed in all parts of their post-secondary education systems what might be called an institutional upgrading trend. In this respect the SCIs occupied a special position: on the one hand the status of many of them (sometimes the entire sector) is the result of an upgrading of secondary schools and, on the other, many strive to gain university status and often succeed. The sector is therefore a perpetually changing one with an inflow of institutions from below and an outflow above which implies, in fact, an escape from the

* See Development of Higher Education, 1950-1967, Analytical Report, OECD, 1971.

"less noble" position. Moreover, it often happens that, when an SCI becomes a university status institution, it no longer fulfills some of the main functions for which it was created (e. g. part-time education, courses oriented to local needs). Significant examples of this are the British CATs, some American Junior Colleges, and in a certain sense also those European SCIs which, when unable to become full universities, often add one or two years to the duration of their course of studies so that they may be considered of university level.

# III

## OBJECTIVES AND MOTIVATIONS BEHIND THE DEVELOPMENT AND REFORM OF SHORT-CYCLE INSTITUTIONS

The new types of SCIs which have emerged in recent years in the various Member countries must be viewed in the light of the changing functions and objectives which these institutions are expected to fulfill. These functions can be grouped under four headings: 1) to respond to the increasing pressure of individual demand for higher education; 2) to contribute to the equalization of educational opportunities; 3) to respond to growing needs for a wide and diversified range of qualified manpower; and 4) to generate or facilitate innovation in the post-secondary system by assuming a number of functions which traditional universities are often reluctant to accept.

i) Pressure of numbers

In the past, this factor played a more important role in the development of the United Kingdom and American systems than in the continental European one where SCIs were often more selective than universities. But the rapid expansion of university education during the past two decades, the high number of drop-outs and in general the changing nature of the higher education clientele make the development of SCIs in Europe also an urgent necessity. This would relieve the pressure on universities and at the same time provide a diversity of educational forms at the post-secondary school level.

ii) Equality of opportunity

The unequal representation of various groups and social classes in university enrolments is a well-known phenomenon. Under certain conditions SCIs, through their wider geographic distribution, shorter duration of study, and courses more closely adapted to aptitudes and motivations of the less privileged social strata, might provide the means of easier access to higher education for those excluded in the past.

iii) Response to manpower needs

The main economic rationale of SCIs is that they provide qualifications and skills for which university education is of too high and theoretical a level and secondary education insufficient. In addition, SCIs appear to be more capable than universities of offering the variety of courses and methods of study increasingly required for economic and technological development. Unlike the American Junior Colleges, where the "catering function" prevailed, the manpower supply function has always dominated the European SCIs. However, an even wider implementation and further diversification of these institutions seem to be urgently needed everywhere.

iv) Agent of innovation

It has often been shown that innovations are more likely to succeed through the creation of new institutions than through transformation of the old. Furthermore, even if the creation of these institutions proceeds on a small scale or only on an experimental basis, the success may have a powerful "demonstration" effect on the rest of the system.

This observation applies to many aspects of higher education, the most important probably being the various new functions which higher education institutions are expected to assume, namely, provision of continuing education (retraining, adult education), participation in regional development, the offer of various kinds of services to the community, etc. No less essential are innovations concerning some of the new basic principles of higher learning: individualized education, combining education and work, more diversified curricula corresponding to the wider range of abilities, education for "self-fulfilment" or "individual development". All these innovations apply obviously to the whole of higher education, universities and SCIs alike, but their implementation through the latter appears in some countries to be the easiest or best way to initiate a process of change. This may be true for any of several reasons: they are newly created, or at least they have no secular tradition; they might have greater built-in flexibility; they are closer to local needs and interests; and they perhaps reflect more accurately the nature of the new higher education clientele.

To what extent the new or reformed SCIs can meet, or at least help to meet, the four types of objectives outlined above, remains to be seen. In a future study the OECD Secretariat will try to develop a number of indicators which should permit at least a rough evaluation of the results achieved in this respect.

# IV

## ISSUES AND DILEMMAS

All types of SCI face in their development a number of important issues and dilemmas, some of which will be identified in this sector.

### I. ACCESS AND ADMISSION

#### i) Open access versus selection

One finds in the various systems of higher education different balances between selective and open institutions. Within each system, the SCIs are assigned a particular role which may differ from one system to another.

In the multipurpose (United States, Canada, Yugoslavia) and binary (United Kingdom) systems, where universities are characterized by selective admission, SCIs constitute the open part of the system. In the United States and Canada the existence of mass secondary school education (more than 70% of the age group complete this level) is a significant factor in the increasing demand for access to higher education by students coming from the less privileged levels of society. The SCIs, having open access, are the institutions which receive the heaviest impact of this increasing demand.

However some important drawbacks must also be noted: the coexistence of free and open access to SCIs and selection at universities may easily lead to a certain pseudo-democratization of the system by the reinforcement of institutional status differences. If, in the division of labour within the American system, Community Colleges are assigned the role of "serving both the lower socio-economic strata and the lower ability youth", * clearly, they might at the same time also serve to isolate these groups from other, selective parts of the system. Relieved of this pressure, four-year institutions of high standard can "make place" for youth from middle- and upper-class strata and upper ability groups. An important compensatory mechanism for this discrimination is the provision for Community College students to transfer at the end of their two-year studies (or even before) to four-year colleges or universities. But statistics show that only a relatively small proportion actually benefit from this provision. In fact, American junior colleges operate to a large extent as a selection - or, to use Burton Clark's term, "cooling out" - mechanism for full higher education, yielding heavy drop-outs of which the underprivileged classes may be precisely the main victims. Thus, in the American system, the degree of equality of opportunity is relatively high upon admission into the system and during the first year of study but much lower at the level of graduation; in other words, equality of opportunity in access does not lead automatically to equality of achievement.

All this implies that the principle of open access to SCIs in the American transfer model may create as many problems as it solves unless, of course, new patterns such as reforms of content, diversification of programmes, new types of linkage between community colleges and universities, etc. are introduced. The search for innovation in this respect is now being actively pursued throughout the United States. **

In the United Kingdom system the non-university sector is also open (compared to British universities) but to a lesser degree than in America, and it definitely plays a role in providing access to higher education to less favoured levels of society. In addition, it offers the possibility of study leading to a degree of university (and even post-graduate) level outside the university sector.

However, the large British non-university sector is a stratified system in itself, composed of a variety of institutions with different levels and patterns of study and, accordingly, different conditions of access. Admission requirements for degree-level courses in polytechnics - the élite institutions of the non-university sector - are slightly lower than for universities, but much higher than for higher diploma and certificate courses. The inequality of education opportunity is particularly aggravated by the limitations of student mobility between

* "Planning of New Structures of Post-Secondary Education, Country Statement, United States of America", OECD Document, 1970.

** According to the latest figures the social composition of the student body in Junior Colleges is changing, i.e. middle and even upper classes are now more represented than in the past.

different courses of study. Although policies are slowly being changed, those students who have entered the non-university sector may still only in very exceptional circumstances transfer to universities. In the United Kingdom, unlike America, the real selection process takes place during secondary schooling (see following section).

The situation and role of continental European SCIs with respect to the mix of open access and selection is very different from the two preceding cases. These institutions are influenced mainly by economic and manpower considerations, and tend to respond less to social demand and the equality-of-opportunity objective than their American counterparts. There are, however, two important reasons why SCIs in Europe were able, to some extent, to neglect the need for an open sector and be less sensitive to the pressure of numbers.

Firstly, a very powerful tradition of open universities prevails in the majority of countries. It is precisely the universities - particularly some fields of study - which represent the open sector and which, consequently, are suffering the strongest impact from the quantitative expansion of recent years. Hence in some European countries selective SCIs coexist with open universities, and in a few cases, for example in France, students who have been refused admission to short-cycle technical institutes are admitted to university study.

Secondly, in Europe the pressure of numbers is due fundamentally to the expansion of the general academic streams of secondary schools which prepare students for university study, thereby creating a much greater demand for long-cycle institutions than for SCIs.

Nevertheless, the SCIs, by providing access to post-secondary study for students coming from the non-academic streams, and to whom therefore the universities were not open, have played an important role in providing educational opportunity to less privileged groups.

ii) Linkages with upper secondary schools

While almost everywhere in Europe (including the United Kingdom), the role of secondary schools as a selection mechanism for streaming students into the different types of higher education institution is of primary importance, in the United States, Canada and Japan streaming takes place, at least formally, only upon admission to higher education. Recent and expected developments in Europe point in the same direction, chiefly because of the sometimes radical reforms of upper secondary education already launched or in preparation. The main idea behind these reforms is comprehensiveness and possibility of access to all forms of higher education (including university) for graduates of all types of upper secondary education. This implies the elimination of hierarchy among the different types of secondary school (should a single comprehensive or integrated type not be established) and a diversification based solely on the various fields of study available. Curricula changes - introduction of common core subjects for various disciplines, more vocationally and practically oriented courses in academic streams and more courses of general studies in technical disciplines - would be the basic strategy by which to diminish the traditional hierarchical differences.

Following the above considerations, future SCIs will have to face a number of new problems:

- If, in the near future, graduates from all types of secondary school have access to long-cycle university studies which have more prestige and usually lead to a better position and higher salaries in industry and administration, the SCIs might risk losing part of their potential clientele, while the pressure on universities will be further increased.
- Should SCIs compete for the same clientele as universities or should they cater for students whose interests and abilities do not correspond to the requirements of theoretical, academic education?
- Will a great number of students, dropping out of universities, seek admission to SCIs? What effect would this have on the status and prestige of these institutions?
- For what type of students will SCIs constitute a first choice of studies? What will be the importance of educational background in the admission process for these institutions? And what significance will the concept of "equivalent standard" vis-à-vis formal secondary qualifications have in admission to SCIs? Will there be educational opportunity for those without a formal secondary school diploma but with sufficient professional qualifications ("second route" to higher education)?
- To what extent will it be possible to organise access to higher education as a flexible and reversible process rather than an irreversible one?

To some extent the solution to these questions could be found in a better articulation between upper secondary studies and the first years of higher education. An efficient and developed system of information and guidance at both levels of study (whose importance is recognized more often in theory than in practice) could greatly contribute to this end and help improve the image of SCIs. Such a system should serve as a means by which admission to different parts of post-secondary education is determined by more objective criteria than educational background (and social origin). But what are these criteria? How can orientation become an integral and institutionalized part of the admission process without violating the principle of freedom of choice of studies? Can a common obligatory "orientation year" contribute to more rational decision-making on the part of students and improved admission policies on the part of institutions?

## II. TRANSFER VERSUS TERMINAL PROGRAMMES: A SEARCH FOR COMPATIBILITY

Probably the most important and difficult problem which both old and new SCIs are facing is striking an appropriate balance among the four categories of objectives enumerated in Chapter III above. More specifically, the problem could be formulated as follows: the SCIs must respond to the increasing pressure of social demand for higher education and offer real equality of opportunity, i. e. provide the possibility of transfer to university for students capable of and wishing to continue their studies; they must, at the same time, continue to assume their main role as agents of diversification and innovation by providing vocationally and practically oriented studies. The first requirement tends to force SCIs towards a certain isomorphism with universities (and dependence upon them), and hence to a neglect of some of their original functions; the second might weaken their "respectability" and distort their role as "equalizers of educational opportunity". This search for compatibility between transfer and terminal courses will be examined from the point of view of structural as well as curricula implications.

### i) Structural aspects

The problems involved in emphasizing transfer work too heavily can best be illustrated by the example of the American Community Colleges. Without any doubt, they have contributed to develop a flexible system and provided students who otherwise would have been unable to benefit from long-cycle education with an opportunity for access to four-year institutions. But by giving so much emphasis to this "transfer" function (often not of their own volition but under the pressure of student demand for these types of course) they often neglected other important objectives and sometimes became academically subordinated to surrounding universities whose recognition they needed for their programmes, or even became "bad copies" of these universities when they attempted to be upgraded to the status of four-year colleges. This problem confronts all other multipurpose institutions, especially the junior colleges of Alberta and the CEGEPs of Quebec. District colleges of Norway and CAATs of Ontario which intend to introduce transfer courses in the near future are highly conscious of the need to find an equilibrium, but it is too early to know whether and how they will succeed.

The specialized SCIs in continental Europe, on the contrary, by heavily stressing their economic objectives, have emphasized the terminal nature of the education provided and thus become "blind alleys" for graduates from these institutions. The most recent reforms deal with this problem by introducing so-called "passerelles", "cursos puente", "permeability" or similar measures aimed at permitting or facilitating transfer "subject to certain conditions". An important element of these measures is that transfer is envisaged as a two-way process not only allowing SCI graduates to enrol in long-cycle studies but also - perhaps to a greater extent - permitting potential university drop-outs to enrol in SCIs. Unsuccessful or discouraged students could in this way be recuperated by the system and given the possibility of finishing short-cycle studies.

The practical issues which follow from the above considerations concern especially:

a) the optimum or maximum volume of SCI-university transfer which should be aimed at;

b) the conditions to be fulfilled by students desiring to transfer (in terms of additional examinations and duration of study); and

c) the type of measure by which the rate of transfer can be regulated without unduly limiting the freedom of choice of studies.

ii) Curriculum aspects

The problem of appropriate curricula and of conceptual and pedagogical linkages between practically and theoretically oriented studies probably represents the core of the search for compatibility between transfer and terminal courses. Ideally, this problem would be resolved if equivalence could be established between the first part (first cycle) of long university studies and courses provided in SCIs. In practice no real solutions have yet been found, and many have failed. Of these, at least conceptually the most interesting was the Yugoslav essay in "curriculum inversion". According to this scheme, the practically and vocationally oriented courses were to come at the beginning of post-secondary studies and the more theoretical afterwards. This would have allowed a complete equivalence between short-cycle technical (vocational) higher education offered by the "Viša Škola" and the first two years of regular long-cycle university education, students in both institutions having at the end of their first two years the choice of either continuing their studies or entering the labour force with a recognized intermediary degree. The scheme was not successful, partly because neither its pedagogical nor its conceptual implications were really solved and partly because it resulted in too high a transfer rate of students from the non-university vocationally oriented sector to the university sector. As a consequence Yugoslavia is today probably the only country where the trend is towards an increasing separation between SCIs and universities and where student mobility between the two sectors is being reduced to a minimum.

Whether the idea of "curriculum inversion" can be taken up again and more successfully implemented in different conditions remains to be seen: certainly the traditional sequence of courses in university studies often proves to be inefficient and ineffective. For example, it is claimed that students of medicine or engineering who spend their first one or two years on purely theoretical studies have almost forgotten what they have learned, several years later, that is precisely, at a time when they could evaluate better the relevance of basic sciences for their field.

Even though "curriculum inversion" may, for the moment, be considered unrealistic, most approaches to the problem of curriculum reform in SCIs and to linkages with the curriculum in long-cycle higher education represent a search for types of course common to various fields of study and to institutions providing education of different levels and orientations. Substantial progress has already been made in finding common courses directed towards related or neighbouring fields of study (e.g. medicine, pharmacy, various fields of engineering) but usually these courses are of the same educational level or institutional type. Much less has been done towards finding such common courses ("<u>tronc commun</u>") for medical and paramedical studies, for long-cycle social science and short-cycle courses for social assistants, for engineering and short-cycle technical studies, etc.

Related to the issue of common inter-level and inter-institutional courses (which seems to imply considerable improvement in the use of scarce physical and personnel resources) is undoubtedly the problem of interdisciplinarity. Again, this question should be considered with reference to the linkages between SCIs and universities.

iii) <u>Towards a "student-centred" higher education system</u>

The combination of a new approach to curricula problems and the simultaneous development of a credit point system to cover all higher education institutions would be the most powerful method of achieving an organic linkage of SCIs to other forms of higher education while preserving, and even developing, its diversity. The credits would correspond to small "learning units" or "modules" transferable between fields and levels of study and between the various types of institution. Many features of such a system have already been introduced in the United States but their implementation in Europe is a fairly new phenomenon and mostly limited to single institutions or institutions of one category. Recent proposals have attempted to widen the scope of transferability of credits, for example the French concept of "unités capitalisables" and the German "Baukastensystem". A further step is the Swedish idea of eliminating all types and levels of degree and replacing them by certificates indicating the number and subject content of points acquired. This would allow students to terminate their studies whenever they wish and whenever their number of points is considered sufficient for a particular job.

The practical problems which will have to be solved are numerous. In particular, appropriate criteria must be drawn up for transferability of points between fields and levels of study and between institutions. Transferability obviously cannot be absolute: two years in a nursing school cannot be equivalent to the first two years of medical studies, and a set of conversion keys for different subject and level combinations will have to be defined. Curriculum content and analysis should be the main points of reference, but it is precisely in this area that information is extremely insufficient.

The ideas contained in the curricula and structural reforms represent more than tools or devices facilitating student transfer and mobility: they are, in fact, the expression of a trend towards a student-centred rather than an institution-centred higher education.

## III. STATUS OF TEACHERS AND STUDENTS IN SHORT-CYCLE INSTITUTIONS

### i) Teachers

The often marginal status of SCIs is clearly reflected in some of the present conflicts affecting the teachers in these institutions. Although for some time they have been assuming the responsibilities corresponding to higher education, this has frequently not been recognized in their formal status. In many countries they are still more easily assimilated to secondary school teachers, both salary- and status-wise, and thus denied the rank of professor which is usually reserved for the teaching staff of universities. Further indicators of this situation are the number of teaching hours, degree of academic freedom, possibilities of research, etc., which bear a much closer resemblance to secondary school patterns than to those of higher education.

As always, the whole problem has at least two aspects. On the one hand it is said that teachers in SCIs are not sufficiently qualified to be ranked (and paid) on a par with university professors, while on the other it is argued that the only way of raising the educational standards and prestige of the SCIs is by providing attractive working conditions and adequate status to highly qualified staff.

To a great extent this problem has been solved where new SCIs were created. Thus, in the French IUTs as well as in the Norwegian District Colleges, the teaching staffs have the same status as those in universities, although at slightly lower levels in the scale (a full professor in a District College has the status of an assistant professor in a university). Other countries, such as Germany and Belgium, are following the same trend. But the reverse is true in the United Kingdom, where the teaching staff of polytechnics do not have the status of university professors in spite of the fact that polytechnics are considered as institutions of university level.

If SCI professors are gradually required to have the same level of qualifications as university professors, what incentives will there be to attract good teachers to the so-called "less noble" institutions? In the case of new institutions, the prospect of working in a context which opens up great possibilities for innovation might provide such an incentive. In other cases, where nothing more than reforms of existing institutions take place, alternative solutions must be found. An important step might be to provide research facilities, and time for research, even when the particular SCI represents dominantly or exclusively a teaching institution. In practical terms this can probably best be done where some organisational or administrative link is established with neighbouring universities, as is intended in the idea of the German Gesamthochschulen and Danish University Centres, in French IUTs, Belgian technical education, etc.

Another favourable solution might be for the SCIs to enrol large numbers of students (e.g. more than 3,000) covering a wide range of fields of study as do the United Kingdom polytechnics. The existence of an important multidisciplinary teaching staff may indeed help to develop a more stimulating academic atmosphere than that of the former isolated specialized institutions.

But, to what extent is it desirable to have highly academically-minded professors teaching and directing SCIs? And what are the risks of recruiting a large proportion of those who have not (or not yet) been able to "make it" at universities? With their minds directed to the institutions traditionally of high repute will they not be tempted to distort some of the main functions of SCIs and try to develop bad replicas of universities? And will they not, in a sense, "contaminate" the attitudes and aspirations of other teachers in SCIs? Significantly enough, in the United States, where junior colleges have been integrated into higher education for a longer time, some investigations show that 60% of the faculty members of these schools would prefer to teach in four-year institutions rather than in junior colleges. * How can any of these teachers convince students that these are not second or third class institutions?

ii) Students

As in the case of teachers, the problem is often one of material conditions. The situation must obviously be avoided in which students attending SCIs - many of them from the lower social classes - benefit less from financial assistance and other relevant facilities (use of libraries, restaurants, cultural activities, etc.) than the students enrolled at universities, who are more likely to come from middle or upper class social backgrounds. The situation is slowly changing; this is particularly true in some of the new SCIs (e.g. Norwegian District Colleges, IUTs) where students are entitled to exactly the same scholarship schemes and facilities as university students. The question is whether in certain circumstances they should not in fact receive additional advantages, partly to help compensate for the material and cultural disadvantages resulting from their social backgrounds, partly (when necessary) as a means of strengthening the powers of attraction of SCIs.

## IV. AUTONOMY AND GOVERNMENTAL CONTROL

Although administratively SCIs are gradually being granted higher education status and even considered of "university level", in many countries they are not simultaneously accorded the degree and type of autonomy usually associated with traditional higher education institutions. Hence, the SCIs, and the non-university sector in general, are under much tighter governmental control than universities. However, the extent to which this control should be exercised is at present a highly controversial issue.

The pressures towards increasing autonomy come mainly from the SCIs concerned. They argue that in order to fulfil some of their basic functions they must have more independence in financial, administrative and academic matters. It is being said that an appropriate adaptation to technical and scientific developments, rapid response to local or regional needs and sufficient flexibility to introduce innovations and contribute to the diversification of the system as a whole, cannot

* Hodgkinson, H.L. Institutions in Transition, Carnegie Commission on Higher Education, Berkeley, California, 1970.

be achieved in a situation characterized by the slow and complicated decision-making process which typifies centralized administrations.

Governmental representatives perceive another aspect of the problem. According to them, if SCIs were granted a wide margin of independence, they would be tempted to follow the up-grading trend and concentrate essentially on policies with a view to obtaining university status. In this way SCIs would neglect their main role within the system and, consequently, their responsibilities towards society.

The solution to the issue of autonomy versus governmental control will depend to a great extent on the national context. If control is vested in local or regional authorities it might, on the one hand, facilitate the desired integration of all post-secondary institutions at this level but, on the other, make national coordination more difficult. The reverse can happen if control is exercised by central authorities. The problem also varies according to the degree of autonomy prevailing in universities. When it is very high, the demand for more autonomy on the part of SCIs will at least in part reflect their search for more "respectability" (e. g. United Kingdom polytechnics); when it is low, the SCI will probably support more easily the already-existing limits to their autonomy.

In any case, a certain overall trend can be observed: SCIs and especially the new or reformed establishments, are in general gaining a greater degree of autonomy than was accorded to the old institutions of the non-university sector. At the same time universities tend to be subjected to more central control (especially financial) than in the past.*

## V. LOCATION, REGIONAL DEVELOPMENT AND SERVICE TO THE COMMUNITY

### i) Location of SCI

For some countries this is a very important issue. A wider geographic distribution and location of SCIs in areas which have up to now been lacking in higher education facilities is often considered both as a means of equalizing educational opportunity and as a contribution to regional development. Clearly, this also applies to universities where there is a very strong trend towards geographic decentralization and the breaking up of oversized institutions situated in the capital or in a few centres in the most highly populated parts of the country (e. g.

* This does not apply in countries such as France where, in the past, universities were under rigid central control.

affiliated universities in Sweden, "collegios universitarios" in Spain, the creation of new campuses of the big American universities, etc.).

However, the problems of location of new SCIs are of a special nature. As, originally, they were often physically located close to secondary schools - sometimes under the same roof - a wide range of rather small and specialized establishments emerged. This dispersion was enhanced by the creation of various types of SCIs, particularly those where unit costs were low and which responded to political pressures rather than to systematic planning.

The upgrading of these schools to higher education institutions has generated strong pressures towards a regional concentration of their activities. The widely dispersed local-oriented institutions are gradually being replaced by rather large regional-oriented establishments. The main pressure behind this trend is probably the necessity for finding a "critical mass" without which SCIs cannot fulfil their functions and, even less, improve their prestige and attractiveness. Higher education establishments do indeed require a greater concentration of resources in terms of buildings, equipment, teaching staff, etc. which small communities cannot provide or afford. Thus, the first solution is usually an integration - or at least co-operation- of different local schools which are considered constituent units of bigger regional establishments, or the upgrading of certain institutions strategically well located. In addition, the need for closer regional collaboration with universities - usually located in large urban centres - may also play an important role in the location of new or reformed SCIs.

However, some counter-trends or at least a number of opposing forces to this process of concentration of SCIs are also apparent: distances between the constituent units might represent an important obstacle to real integration; political and social pressures from communities where the schools to be integrated are situated; attitudes of authorities of individual institutions who want their establishments to be upgraded and who resist the loss of autonomy.

Practically all SCI systems - of whatever type - are subject to these conflicting pressures. The British polytechnics, German Fachhochschulen, Norwegian District Colleges, Ontario CAATs and Quebec CEGEPs present interesting examples of the difficulties involved in integrating existing local institutions into large regional establishments.

Yet, in general, the trend is clear: decentralization of universities on the one hand and concentration of SCIs on the other. This process, however desirable and understandable for the achievement of certain objectives, may carry with it some danger of the geographic location of

SCIs being chosen on the basis of similar criteria to those for university institutions. If this should happen, SCIs would be less able to fulfil one of their important functions, namely to bring higher education closer to the numerous potential students for whom geographic distance may represent a fundamental reason for abstaining from further studies. In the new situation, students may either still feel unable to enter a higher education institution because it is too remote from their place of residence, or register immediately at a university which carries more prestige and is geographically no further away than an SCI.

In other words, the shift from local- to regional-oriented SCIs could create a gap in the institutional map of post-secondary education, a gap to be filled by the creation of a new type of locally-centred institution, such as most of the junior colleges in the United States which do not undergo the regional concentration process. This seems particularly important for underprivileged areas - economically declining regions or "poverty pockets" - and in any consideration of mass higher education.

ii) Regional development

SCIs, as all higher education establishments, have an important role to play as agents or poles of regional development. They do this not only by their direct contribution to the economic, social and cultural needs of the area in which they are situated - by training qualified manpower and providing other specific services - but also by the sheer economic mass which they represent, especially if they have reached a certain size: the buying power of their employees (teachers, administrators), the services which this concentration generates (shops, restaurants, transport); employment opportunities created by requirements for new buildings; often significant changes in the urban landscape; and sometimes quite a strong attraction to new industries for whom the proximity of sources of qualified manpower and knowledge may be more important than proximity to sources of raw materials or to consumers.

An exploration of all these aspects has hardly started but it can already be said that the creation and/or development of higher education establishments in general, and SCIs in particular (because they are often more closely connected with the surrounding community), is or should be an important element in the whole conception of comprehensive regional planning ("aménagement du territoire").

As far as the direct contribution of SCIs to regional development is concerned, it is subject to various interpretations; and in some cases conflicts arising from the different points of view have greatly affected the development of SCIs. The central issue under debate is the degree and type of collaboration which should be established between the SCIs and the various sectors of economy represented in the region. The following problems arise:

- To what extent should the curricula and programme of studies be adapted to specific regional needs in an increasingly mobile society?
- What are the conditions under which closer co-operation with, and service to, the surrounding enterprises can be established without risking a situation of control or of a dependent relationship?
- How can SCIs respond, on the one hand to the national standards of education set for them and, on the other to the immediate manpower needs of regions with very different levels of development?

iii) Service to the community

Some issues related to the service function of SCIs already emerge from the two preceding sections; in addition there are the problems of part-time studies, adult and permanent education and extension services of all kinds. It should be recalled that, in this respect, SCIs are often expected to play a more important role than universities, largely because universities have not always been willing or ready to assume these types of responsibility.

Part-time education, adult education and extension services have been traditionally more generalized in Anglo-Saxon higher education systems (including universities), but even there the proportion of part-time students has been steadily declining during recent years. In continental Europe these forms of education are in most cases being provided in special institutions outside the formal educational system. It should also be borne in mind that some SCIs consider part-time education - if it were to concern a large proportion of their students - as a symbol of lower institutional status and might even resist it on those grounds.

The extent to which newly reformed SCIs will be assuming important responsibilities for these "additional" functions in the near future is not very clear. However, some signs of a change of attitude are being observed in several new SCIs, such as District Colleges, CEGEPs and IUTs, where special programmes are being developed along these lines. Significant progress would certainly be achieved if an idea, formulated with regard to the French IUTs*, could be implemented. According to the concept the SCIs should assume, to a certain extent at least, the responsibility for providing a permanent service to their graduates in the form of retraining or refresher courses, re-orientation programmes, etc. This could be a first and important step towards the re-organisation of studies on the basis of a system of recurrent education.

## VI. COST AND FINANCING

This issue is obviously connected with all those mentioned so far. It represents a central part of another study to be undertaken by the Secretariat within the framework of the programme on planning new structures of post-secondary education; it will therefore not be raised in the context of the present paper. Probably the main questions to be answered - but certainly not the only ones - are whether the costs of creating and operating SCIs - in particular with respect to unit costs - are significantly different from those of full university education; which are the major components of these costs - compared to the cost structure of universities; and what methods and sources of financing can be envisaged with particular reference to SCIs? A comparative cost/benefit analysis of short-cycle versus long-cycle education would undoubtedly represent an important contribution to policy formulations concerning SCIs and the higher education system as a whole.

## VII. EMPLOYMENT OF SHORT-CYCLE GRADUATES

To a great extent the status and prestige of SCIs will depend on the conditions under which their graduates enter the labour market and on their prospects of a satisfactory professional career. Responsibilities must certainly be shared. On the one hand it is up to the educational system and especially the SCIs to train high quality graduates able to fulfil requirements of the economy. On the other hand, conditions have to be provided which facilitate the integration of SCI graduates in the labour force in a way which improves their salary conditions and status, particularly in relation to university graduates. This condition is often not fulfilled. For example, job classification and corresponding salary scales in the administration and civil service of many countries do not foresee any specific positions for graduates of short-cycle institutions (or of uncompleted long-cycle studies).

Quite often in the past, SCI graduates were able to get working conditions similar to those of university graduates immediately after

* Michel-Yves Bernard, <u>Les instituts universitaires de technologie</u>, Dunod, Paris, 1970.

graduation when entering their first employment. However, their possibilities of promotion in the course of their professional career were much more limited. The question which arises is whether these limitations to professional advancement can be attributed mainly to the specific type of training received or to certain attitudes prevailing among employers - and in the labour market in general - which act as constraints to the upward mobility of this type of graduate.

Promotion policies based on work performance rather than on the type of degree obtained will most likely help to reduce these disparities. Not less important is the opening-up of better possibilities for further education (continuing education, retraining, university education, etc.). This, in fact, probably represents the key measure towards improving the professional status of SCI graduates, and consequently an essential contribution to the "ennoblement" of SCIs in general.

## VIII. A SEARCH FOR IDENTITY: THE UNDERLYING ISSUE

It is interesting to note that the integration of SCIs into higher education has not necessarily contributed to the increase of their prestige within the context of the overall system. SCIs are still in the process of finding their place and their role in a structure which often seems highly resistant to the incorporation of new members. Conceptually this can be explained fairly simply: as they become, or are becoming, recognized members of the higher education group, they are judged and judge themselves by comparison with the traditionally most prestigeful members of this group, namely the universities.

In the past they did not have this preoccupation, neither did society in general - or at least they had it to a much lesser extent. In spite of many disadvantages, their place and their functions were relatively clearly defined, whether as secondary school institutions or as part of a post-secondary sector considered separate and independent of universities, and their prestige per se was more or less established. But this situation is in a process of change as old universities increasingly become a frame of reference for the new or reformed SCIs. This process implies, in fact, the adoption of a value scale which places highest pure research, development of knowledge for its own sake and theoretical and abstract disciplines, while technically, vocationally and practically-oriented studies are placed on the lowest echelons. Such a value scale is obviously unsuited to the present needs of society and even less so to the emerging system of mass higher education which, on the contrary, requires a wide institutional diversification without, or with a minimum of, institutional hierarchy.

The present problem seems to be that structures of higher education, although evolving slowly, have still changed more rapidly than the value systems prevailing in them. Thus, while the incorporation of SCIs into the system is progressively taking place, the very powerful and traditional norms emanating from universities makes it difficult, if not impossible, for the new members to acquire sufficient prestige and parity of esteem without following these norms and thereby rejecting their own specific functions.

It is possible that the whole problem can only find a real solution in the context of recurrent education which would make any distinction between short- and long-cycle higher education meaningless. But a full, or even a partial implementation of such an ideal probably cannot be expected anywhere within the near future. In the meantime SCIs are faced with a basic dilemma: whether to pursue their objectives through a gradual integration with the university sector or through a more or less independent and parallel development.

While separate development may contribute to reinforcing even more the dichotomic nature of the system by widening the gap between "noble" and "less noble" institutions, it may also contribute to the development of such a large and widely diversified system offering all types, levels and patterns of study that, sooner or later, the traditional university sector would represent only a minority in the overall system and gradually lose its dominant position*; "integration among equals" could then be envisaged as a realistic possibility.

On the other hand, integration with the university sector may imply that SCIs will increasingly orient all their activities in a sense corresponding to the traditional university image and thus to a dangerous uniformisation of the system; or it may bring about a radical change in the philosophy, objectives, functions and methods of university education and consequently a new definition and concept of university institutions and higher education in general.

To a great extent the attitude of universities will constitute the main criterion for a decision between these two alternatives. Will they accept the SCIs as equal partners with all the consequences that such an acceptance would imply? Or will they prefer to keep their traditional (even if superficially revised) value structure?

If universities assume the second of these two attitudes, a parallel development of SCIs would probably constitute, in the short term, a

* There seem to be some elements of such a development in the United Kingdom binary system.

more efficient strategy. If, on the contrary, universities take the first attitude, their integration with various types of SCIs will contribute to the development of a system where unity could be achieved without uniformity, and diversity could exist with a minimum of institutional hierarchy.

## Annex

# NOTE ON TERMINOLOGY

For the clarity of discussion it is important to distinguish between:

1. Short-cycle higher education
2. First-cycle higher education
3. Short-cycle higher education institutions (SCIs)
4. University branches

1. Short-cycle higher education may be defined as post-secondary education of a mainly terminal character designed to train students for middle-level manpower positions. Although in the majority of cases it is provided in institutions established outside universities (SCIs), it should be noted that in a few countries the universities offer a certain number of such short-cycle programmes, while in others this training is the responsibility of secondary level establishments (technical training in Sweden, teacher training in France).

2. First-cycle higher education consists of the first (usually two) years of long-cycle university studies. While in the USA and parts of Canada, SCIs (Junior Colleges) share this function with four-year colleges and universities, in Europe this task is considered to be the sole responsibility of universities (notable exceptions: Yugoslavia and recent developments in Norway).

3. Short-cycle higher education institutions (SCIs) are defined as all types of post-secondary schools established outside universities. In the case of the United Kingdom, all institutions of the Further Education sector providing advanced courses (in spite of the fact that they might not be of shorter duration and that they might lead to degrees of the same level as those provided in universities) are included in this category. Thus the common denominator of SCIs as defined here is the

extra- or non-university character of these establishments which poses for all of them a problem of identity and of appropriate recognition within the overall system of higher education. In some cases, these institutions have already legally acquired university status (e. g. French IUTs), but because of the functions which they assume (i. e. providing short-cycle vocationally oriented higher education) and of the way in which they operate, they presently share, to a large extent, the problems of SCIs and of the non-university sector in other countries.

4. University branches are institutions under direct control of universities, usually set up outside large urban centres for purposes of decentralization. They provide the first years of university studies and are subject to the same regulations as the parent institution.

# Part Two

## SOME NATIONAL EXPERIENCES AND KEY ISSUES

# I

## The Norwegian Regional Colleges

by

Ingjald Ø Sørheim,

Head, Regional College Section, Ministry of Education

(Norway)

## CONTENTS

I. INTRODUCTION. PURPOSE OF THE PAPER ...... 49

II. THE INSTITUTIONAL MAP OF HIGHER EDUCATION IN NORWAY BEFORE THE ESTABLISHMENT OF THE REGIONAL COLLEGES ........................ 51

1. Two disconnected sectors: universities and specialized SCIs ........................ 51
2. Open universities, closed SCIs: insufficient access and transfer mechanisms. Negative consequences of this system ........................ 52
3. The place of the non-university sector in the post-secondary system ........................ 53
4. Other problems of the traditional post-secondary system ........................ 56

III. ARGUMENTS FOR THE CREATION OF REGIONAL COLLEGES AND STRATEGIES FOR LAUNCHING THEM ........................ 59

1. General points ........................ 59
2. Goals of the RCs ........................ 59
3. Planning mechanisms for the development of the RCs ........................ 60
4. Present planning (after establishment) ............ 62
5. Regional Colleges as instruments for innovation in the post-secondary system ........................ 63
6. Pressure groups intervening in the process of establishing the RCs ........................ 67

IV. LINKAGES WITH THE UNIVERSITIES .................. 69

1. Introduction ........................................ 69
2. General strategy: independent institutions with practical co-operation in several fields ............. 69
3. Types and levels of courses ........................ 70
4. The teaching staff .................................. 72
5. The students ........................................ 73
6. Participation in planning ........................... 74
7. Participation at examinations ....................... 75
8. Financing ........................................... 75

V. LINKAGES WITH THE NON-UNIVERSITY SECTOR ...... 77

1. Integration undecided ............................... 77
2. Towards a Regional College system ................... 78

VI. PERSONAL ASSESSMENT. SUMMARY ................ 79

1. Quantitative developments, applications for admission, employment .......................... 79
2. The key factor: the teaching staff and policies for its development .............................. 80
3. Summary: diversification/striking a balance ........ 81

# I

## INTRODUCTION - PURPOSE OF THE PAPER

The purpose of this paper is to discuss the development of a new type of post-secondary institution which has emerged on the Norwegian higher education scene, namely the Regional Colleges. * The basic framework used for the analysis of the characteristics of these new institutions and particularly of their articulation and co-ordination with other higher education establishments is the OECD report on Short-Cycle Higher Education. **

This document states at the very beginning: "It is realized that with the present trend towards a comprehensive system of higher education the concept of short-cycle higher education and the existence of special institutions for this purpose may, in the future, become inappropriate or obsolete". And the report continues: "But before this stage in the development of higher education is reached (and perhaps so that it is reached more easily) many countries see as an indispensable step the development of suitable forms of short-cycle higher education and the building-up of special institutions to allow a wider diversification".

This objective was one of the main reasons for the elaboration of a new scheme of post-secondary Regional Colleges in Norway, the first started in 1969. The Royal Commission that proposed the creation of these new institutions stressed that they should be an integral part of a comprehensive system of higher education. "Integral" was not thought of in terms of organisation. The Regional Colleges were planned, and are now operating, as autonomous institutions. An integrated system then would mean a system with easy transfer of students, teachers and money between institutions and various lines of study.

* In previous OECD papers the term "District Colleges" was used when referring to this type of institution.

** See Part One.

The development of Regional Colleges, as post-secondary institutions outside the universities (but on the undergraduate university level with regard to teachers and students), poses in the Norwegian context the basic dilemma, namely how they can establish their respectability without losing sight of the important "alternative" functions for which they were created. Due to historical and sociological factors, the risks that Regional Colleges assume an inferior position vis-à-vis the universities (or even become poor replicas or bad copies of them) may be considerably smaller than in other countries, but some risks certainly exist. It is therefore considered that the strategy followed in the course of their first years of existence will be crucial to the whole future of Norwegian higher education.

# II

## THE INSTITUTIONAL MAP OF HIGHER EDUCATION IN NORWAY BEFORE THE ESTABLISHMENT OF THE REGIONAL COLLEGES

### 1. Two disconnected sectors: universities and specialized SCIs*

Up to the late 1960s Norwegian higher education was very close to the "specialized model": on the one hand, the universities provided a limited number of choices in the traditional academic fields while on the other the SCIs offered mainly terminal, vocationally oriented courses which had practically no linkage with the universities, transfers either way being quite exceptional. Each of the different types of SCIs provided a limited number of programmes, specializing mainly in one field: teacher training, social workers, engineering, etc. Each individual institution was very small: enrolments in teacher training colleges varied from 275 to 550, while some schools for social workers had less than 100 registered students. The SCIs in Norway also resembled the "specialized model"; they were centrally administered and had very little autonomy.

The situation in 1970 expressed in numbers:

| | |
|---|---|
| Universities (3 in operation and one in Tromsø in the planning stage, which, situated on the 70th parallel, will become the world's northernmost university) | 30,000 |
| SCIs, approximately 50 institutions (including 6,000 students in 17 teacher training colleges) | 10,000 |

* Short-cycle institutions.

2. <u>Open universities, closed SCIs: insufficient access and transfer mechanisms. Negative consequences of this system.</u>

The tradition of open university studies, combined with the "numerus clausus" policy in practically all SCIs, has to a certain extent prevented SCIs from being given the "less noble" label, when compared to universities. A significant example frequently mentioned in Norway is that a student who is not accepted at a teacher training college (training elementary school teachers) may take a long-cycle study course at one of the university faculties and eventually come back as a teacher at the teacher training college where he was originally refused access as a student. An important reason behind the "numerus clausus" was lack of resources, but labour market considerations, too, have sometimes limited enrolment in the SCIs.

The situation with open universities and limited access to most SCIs had unfortunate consequences, as it often forced students to make a second choice. A considerable number went to the universities, and it has been argued that lack of motivation and ability among many of these students may have contributed to the large number of university drop-outs.

Another unplanned development was the rapid increase in the number of secondary school graduates entering vocational training at the secondary level. The consequence was that these graduates pushed out the students graduating from elementary schools for whom the vocational schools were originally intended, and vocational schools started introducing "numerus clausus" measures for a large number of courses.

The access system was fairly rigid both for the universities and most SCIs, only graduates from the theoretical secondary schools (gymnasium) being admitted. The exceptions to this rule were rare; some of the SCIs (especially teacher training and engineering schools) provided a "second route" for students without upper secondary education (although these needed more time than the secondary graduates to obtain the same professional qualifications). As secondary education became universal and more diversified (present policies aiming at giving 90% of each age group three years of schooling after the compulsory 9-year elementary school introduced during the 1960s), their rigid access system became subject to growing pressure.

Transfer between SCIs and the university sector was also highly unsatisfactory, most SCI studies constituting "blind alleys" which were given no credit in the university system. Criticism of this system received strong support by the very positive experiences of the few students allowed to transfer: graduates from technical schools taken into the second or third year of the technical university in Trondheim performed considerably better than the gymnasium graduates, although the latter were selected students with the very best results in the gymnasium (technical universities belonging to the 25% of the university sector subjected to "numerus clausus"). The beginning of systematic adult education and recurrent education also strengthened the attack on the rigid entrance and transfer practices.

## 3. The place of the non-university sector in the post-secondary system

The Royal Commission on Higher Education, which proposed the establishment of Regional Colleges, presented statistical material showing clearly the increasing attraction of SCIs. It was found that approximately 90% of the graduates from secondary schools went on to further education. The distribution of these was:

In percentage

| | UNIVERSITIES | OTHER POST-SECONDARY INSTITUTIONS (SCIs) | OTHER EDUCATION (MOSTLY VOCATIONAL AT THE SECONDARY LEVEL) |
|---|---|---|---|
| 1963 ................ | 53 | 35 | 12[1] |
| 1969 ................ | 39.5 | 39 | 21.5 |

1. In absolute numbers: 3,450 to other education in 1969 as compared to 1,100 in 1963.

The trend in favour of the SCIs would probably have been even more marked if the SCIs had not been closed institutions. The number of students refused access to the SCIs has grown rapidly during the last few years, and there are indications that open university studies quite often represent the second choice. *

The teacher training colleges (which had more than 50% of the SCI enrolment before the establishment of the Regional Colleges) accepted 65% of the applicants in 1960 and 45% in 1969. In the same period it was the university faculties offering teacher training (for secondary

* Research now being conducted will give more precise information.

schools and the upper level of primary schools) which had the largest increase in student numbers.

Schools for social workers accepted more than half of the applicants in 1960 but only 32% in 1969. In the same period, the faculties of Social Science increased their annual intake from 163 in 1960 to 835 in 1969 (511%) whereas the total annual intake of all universities increased from 2,314 in 1960 to 4,333 in 1969 (187%).

The trebling of admissions (other vocational secondary level) also indicates the growth potential of the post-secondary SCIs. It is clearly more rational to expand vocational courses at the post-secondary level, adjusted to the students' backgrounds, than to send them back to the secondary level where they have to repeat much of the curriculum they have already been through.

There are several factors that could explain the increasing attraction of the SCIs:

i) The most important is perhaps the relatively egalitarian nature of Norwegian society: historical and political developments have made modern Norway a culturally homogenous and socially egalitarian society as compared with most other countries. The salary scale is more even and differences in prestige between various jobs and professions much less than in other industrialized countries. Evidence shows that in Norway there is very little difference between the salaries paid to those who have graduated from universities and to those who have not; the difference is only 5%, whereas in neighbouring Sweden and Denmark it is 10%. Furthermore, when salary differences are negligible, a two-year study is, naturally, very competitive compared to six- to seven-year university studies. This situation dates back to the Middle Ages, as feudal law was never established and the majority of Norwegian peasants were free men owning their farms. The absence of an aristocracy facilitated the introduction of universal suffrage and parliamentary rule 30 to 50 years earlier than in comparable countries.

ii) The lack of a classical tradition in schools is another reason which helps to explain why in Norway university and non-university institutions enjoy practically the same esteem. The first university started in 1811 and teacher training colleges started soon afterwards. There is a lack of classical tradition because the teaching of Latin and Greek was abolished in some 95% of the secondary schools, decades before this happened in other countries, and academic education has never had the same superior status as elsewhere. * The SCIs soon became closed institutions able to select their students from large numbers of applicants. Although data are insufficient, it is fair to assume that students at SCIs were on the same intellectual level as university students, if not higher. (This assumption is based upon the results of the matriculation examination, but it can of course be questioned whether this is a reliable indicator of intellectual capability). It is interesting to note that elementary school teachers are the most over-represented professional group in the history of the Norwegian Parliament. The traditional route to the teacher training colleges was not through the theoretical secondary school (gymnasia) but through the "folk high schools" which recruited directly from elementary schools.

iii) Norway has a higher recruitment of post-secondary students from lower social strata than most western countries, and a shorter education is an easier step to take for a "first in the family" student; even if the financing of studies does not constitute an obstacle, a shorter course is a less radical break with tradition in their particular milieu. On the other hand we have evidence that SCIs have avoided the bias of predominantly lower-class recruitment; middle and upper class youth also attend SCIs in large numbers. **

iv) As pointed out by Kjell Eide, there has in recent years been a growing distrust regarding the relevance of subject-oriented*** university education:

"This has been sharply brought out by the student revolution, which at this point became very significant because it confirmed suspicions widely held elsewhere in society. There had long been sufficient evidence of the inability of most lawyers to grasp the social dynamics underlying legal development, the incompetence of medical doctors in dealing with the increasing volume of psycho-somatic cases, the helplessness of engineers handling social and physical milieus,

* Universal elementary school (duration 7 years) was introduced in 1860.

** There is little precise knowledge about the factors that decide the choice of study route. The Ministry has engaged two sociologists to conduct a study on the student population in the Regional Colleges. This study will cover both the students' educational and social backgrounds, what were the first and second choices of study and several questions about the period at the Regional College. The survey will facilitate follow-ups on the future choices of Regional College graduates: which jobs, further study, etc. The first results will be available at the end of 1971.

*** Lacking pedagogical training.

the failure of subject-oriented teachers in dealing with children, the futility of economists' attempts to analyse essential societal problems within their narrow conceptional framework, etc."*

The cross-disciplinarity and vocational orientation of SCI studies are often considered by students, parents, employers and society more relevant than many of the traditional university studies. Political debate in recent years has shown an increasing awareness of the dangers of technocracy; the professional value of indoctrination in university education has become more visible and there are stern warnings against the experts' attempts to provide professional answers to political questions. The medical profession is an example. It is traditionally recruited from the isolated (and very selective) medical schools, and in the past was seldom subject to political criticism. In recent years critics (medical students being among the most articulate) have pointed out the need to introduce social sciences (especially sociology and psychology) into medical training, stressing the doctors' non-laboratory functions in dealing with human beings and their political responsibility to react against disease-producing situations in society (unhealthy working conditions, etc.).

v) Finally, it is significant that the four universities were situated in the largest urban centres, whereas the SCIs were dispersed throughout the country. On the large and sparsely populated territory of Norway, geographic proximity is an important factor. A criticism that seems well-founded is that the research activities in universities have been predominantly urban-oriented. Social research has shown very little interest in the serious problems of the small rural communities, where rapid decrease in the primary activities of the sector (due to technological change and other factors) is threatening the communities with emigration and eventually total collapse. Technological and economic research has shown little understanding of the social and human consequences of the development pattern now prevailing, the economic indicators and the GNP-growth ideology dominating the scene so far.

## 4. Other problems of the traditional post-secondary system

Although in 1969 total enrolment in Norway was relatively low (around 10% of the age group), it had more than trebled since 1955,

* Kjell Eide: Some Aspects of Post-Secondary Education in Norway. Proceedings of the Nuffield Canadian Seminar on the Costs of Post-Secondary Education in a Technological Society, June 1971.

when it was 3.1% of the age group. However, it was realized that there was still a large potential for growth due to comparatively low enrolment ratios, increasing generalization of secondary education and existing disparities in educational participation (although these were less obvious here than in other western countries). * The growth that had already taken place proved that profound reforms were needed both in the organisational pattern, admission rules, content/curriculum length of studies, location of institutions, etc. Some of the main conclusions of the debate on SCIs will be discussed in the following paragraphs together with plans for implementing them.

An evaluation of the results and experiences up to the present and a discussion of the hopes and risks for the future will conclude the paper.

A serious deficiency of the system of small, specialized and isolated SCIs was their lack of flexibility and capacity for innovation. There was too little internal stimulus because of the narrowness of the training provided (lack of interdisciplinarity). The composition of the teaching staff, the curriculum, the buildings and the organisational patterns all tended to repeat each year the activity of the previous year. Much the same can be said about the universities; the lack of creative initiatives in recurrent and part-time education, and the practical absence of interdisciplinary research and studies are both examples of this. The pedagogical aspect of university training was practically neglected, and, as mentioned above, the isolation from practical problems often resulted in increasing irrelevance.

The failure of the universities and the SCIs to provide personnel in important sectors such as the health service and for leadership posts at various levels in the economy added to the conviction that solutions to the problems in higher education could no longer be found along the "more-of-the-same" line. ** A special problem confronted the traditional SCIs: their small size made it difficult, if not impossible, to maintain and develop an inspiring milieu for the teaching staff. With one or two teachers in each subject, stagnation and resignation often became the inevitable result, and the shortage of libraries and other research facilities contributed to this. In short, they came under the "critical mass" mentioned in Chapter IV, Part I. In the long term, this would constitute a serious threat to the standard and prestige of the SCIs if it was not overcome by some profound reform.

* See OECD: "Towards New Structures of Post-Secondary Education: a Preliminary Statement of Issues", Part I, pp. 15-21. Paris, 1971.

** The lack of initiative on the part of existing institutions in adult and recurrent education was increasingly felt.

# III

## ARGUMENTS FOR THE CREATION OF REGIONAL COLLEGES AND STRATEGIES FOR LAUNCHING THEM

### 1. General points

Structural innovation seems necessary if the transformation from elitist to mass higher education is to be successful. To meet the challenge of new functions and goals for post-secondary institutions, there is an urgent need to develop institutions with a built-in capacity for innovation, diversification and change.

The main arguments behind the creation of Regional Colleges (RCs) are implicit in the criticism of the existing pattern given in the preceding paragraph. It was felt that the reforms necessary in higher education could only be brought about by structural innovation and organisational changes of a fairly radical nature.

The pressure of numbers was one of the vital factors. The fact that young people were refused admittance to the closed studies, both at universities and at SCIs, was becoming a political issue. Some 3,000 students (10% of total enrolment) were studying abroad. Further, was the drive towards decentralization that took place in general politics during these years: the wish to create institutions for higher education outside the largest urban centres played a decisive role in the political process which (extremely rapidly) implemented the proposal.

### 2. Goals of the RCs

The Royal Commission on Post-Secondary Education (1965 to 1970) formulated the following educational goals for the RCs:

i) To qualify matriculation candidates or others with an equivalent educational background for work in their chosen careers.

ii) To qualify matriculation candidates or others with an equivalent educational background for further studies at university/ college.

iii) To qualify students who have already taken more than the matriculation examination, e.g. part of a university course, for certain vocational tasks.

iv) To satisfy the need for insight into certain subjects, without necessarily aiming at qualifying for a career or further studies.

Goals of a more general political nature have also been assigned to the RCs:

- broadening educational opportunity, both socially and geographically;
- a more even distribution of the resources invested in higher education, which has been one of the fastest-growing sectors of national expenditure;
- broader interaction between higher education and society, the former engaging in new functions such as recurrent and part-time education, local development through research projects of a cross-disciplinary nature, directly relevant to the region, and through direct participation in planning and public debate. A build-up of scientific and professional knowledge in the regions is one of the central goals, as this is at present overwhelmingly centralized in universities and independent research institutes in the 3-4 largest towns.

The stress on relevance is both an educational and a general political goal of the RCs.

The same applies to the goals described as "quality of life", "individual development", "critical mind", etc. These indicate a shift from an investment-oriented to a more consumption-oriented perception of higher education, a trend which is followed by the RCs, both in their official documents and in the emerging practices.

## 3. Planning mechanisms for the development of the RCs

The main instrument for planning and launching the RCs was the Royal Commission for Higher Education. This was set up in 1965 with a very general mandate: to propose the overall structures and size of higher education establishments in Norway. The mandate included universities as well as the non-university sector and stressed the tasks of diversification, recurrent education and the creation of alternatives to existing studies. It is a point of interest that the majority of the members were not from higher education institutions: together with the professors and the student (one!) were people from the labour force and a couple of politicians (two of the members were elected to Parliament in 1969). The Chairman, Kr. Ottosen, is director of the student welfare organisation at Oslo University.

The Commission presented its first report for public debate in 1966. It contained general principles and a quantitative sketch of the total system. The second report in 1967 proposed the establishment of a new system of regional centres for higher study, called Regional Colleges, which were to integrate existing SCIs and develop new studies (new both in content and organisational pattern). The proposal immediately met with exceptionally strong political support. The Ministry at once asked the Commission to make a special report on the RCs, containing practical proposals. Following its presentation in April 1968, the Ministry established a working group to prepare a proposal to Parliament; this was submitted in March 1969. Parliament accepted the proposal on 20th June, 1969 and on 27th August of the same year the first courses started at three institutions. Three more institutions started work in 1970. All six Regional Colleges were established for a "trial period" until 1974. The Commission had initially suggested a network of twelve RCs, but recent political developments seem to indicate that there will finally be 14-15. The planning of RCs in those regions which were not included in the trial programme will probably start soon, but it is unlikely that the colleges will start functioning before 1974.

The Commission envisaged the need to treble the number of post-secondary students (30,000 to 100,000) in the next 20 years. It proposed that growth should be especially strong in the non-university sector (from 10,000 to 40/50,000), whereas the university sector should rise from 30,000 to 50/60,000. This would mean that the non-university sector would increase from 25% to 40-50% of total enrolment, and universities would be reduced from 75% to 50-60%. It described the RCs as multidisciplinary institutions with enrolment from 1,500 to 4,000 part-time students.

The Commission continued its work by presenting a report on recurrent education in 1969 and a report with the final conclusions in 1970. The Ministry of Education is currently working on the reports, and will submit a White Paper to Parliament at the end of 1971 with proposals concerning directives for the further development of higher education, with regard to both size and institutional patterns.

The fact that the RCs were "taken out" of the Commission's "package" for an early start indicates the political significance of the proposals, and the two years in action have no doubt produced experiences that will influence the solutions to be proposed to Parliament on the basis of the work of the Commission. It is important to note that the Commission strongly stressed the need to view the universities and the non-university sector as an integrated whole: the post-secondary sector. Some of the main implications of this policy will be discussed in Chapter IV.

4. Present planning (after establishment)

The study plans and the first organisational structure of the RCs were designed by the Ministry's working group on the basis of the Commission's report. When the proposal was submitted to Parliament - March 1969 - a central advisory board to the Ministry on RC matters was established. Its members were drawn from institutions and society at large, four of the eleven members were students (three from RCs, one from a university). The Ministry's section for RCs serves as secretariat to the advisory board.

Development work is conducted on two lines: the central advisory board appoints committees and working groups to prepare new plans of study in different disciplines (examples: technical education, training of social workers, EDP and systems engineering, general education, information, tourism, etc.). The individual RCs also conduct innovation work, seeking information from local experts, and the staff spend a considerable amount of time planning new projects. The central board sees much of its work as transitory; as staff numbers grow the development function will be gradually absorbed by the individual institutions. Although it is called "central", the advisory board actively encourages delegation of powers and decentralization. The exceptional speed of developments left open many questions to teachers, students and administration in the new institutions and this helped to create an atmosphere of initiative, responsibility and autonomy.

But the speed of this process also had bad effects - insufficient planning of libraries, lack of textbooks and teacher vacancies being the most important. Another point was that some of the more controversial questions were left unsolved; there was, for example, no clear political decision on whether, when and how the existing SCIs should be integrated into the RCs, and this has caused some unrest and uncertainty about their respective roles. It is hoped that this will be settled when the proposals are submitted to Parliament at the end of this year.

Another serious risk is lack of resources: if money is lacking, planning and development will suffer both in the institutions and centrally. The Commission emphasized strongly, in its final reports, the need for planning resources and argued that planning and development should be integrated into the day to day functioning of teachers and the institutions. It also emphasized that the percentage of the GNP should be more than doubled in order to reach the quantitative and qualitative goals of the total higher education system (from 0.75% today to 1.6-1.9 by the end of the 1980s). The risk of a financial squeeze is more serious for new institutions (some of them still in the planning stages) than for established ones with all the pressure that students and professors can bring to bear. Furthermore, there are other sectors wanting to increase their share of public expenditure: health, communications, environment, social welfare, etc. The total level of taxation (40% of the GNP) makes further growth more difficult. Curbing of inflation has high priority, and students fighting with policemen in the parliament buildings is bad publicity. Unless higher education can prove its societal relevance in new sectors, lack of money might prove the most serious obstacle to reaching the goals put before the RCs.

One area of hope lies in the integration of the RC into the regional community. Each RC has a board comprising mainly local representatives, and other forms of contact are also being tried. The balance between the regional board and the "internal government" of staff and students is under close investigation.

## 5. Regional Colleges as instruments for innovation in the post-secondary system

There are several aspects of the RCs which could serve as examples to be followed elsewhere in the system. New patterns of study allowing greater interdisciplinarity and the combination of subjects within or between institutions, can have greater societal relevance than probing deeply into isolated subjects. There is a growing awareness among staff at RCs that their future lies in developing a profile different from that of the universities. Instead of conforming to the subject orientation prevailing at the universities (and thus becoming poor replicas of these) there is a trend to develop integrated or inter-disciplinary studies by, for example, stressing pedagogical aspects, motivation, integration of practical work and case-studies. The development of post-work education, inversed sequences of theory/practice and general education/special education and part-time studies is, of course, an important part of these efforts. The reactions of students at the RCs seem positive so far. At the beginning, the RCs were criticized by radical university students who interpreted their practical orientation as a subordination to the capitalist system of society. This type of criticism has diminished, although it is difficult to say whether this is due to a change in the university students' perception of what the RCs are doing, or to other questions' being given priority. As to the RCs, it should be noted that combined groups of secondary school graduates and students with working experience have shown particularly good results. One reason for this could be the interaction of the students' pedagogical resources: graduates from the gymnasium have a good knowledge of theoretical disciplines, whereas the older students provide practical insight. The positive advantage of group work as compared to traditional lecturing has been shown in a recent survey. Various forms of learning by doing also have a great attraction. For example, the students of transportation in the town of Molde are now planning the traffic system in the town centre in co-operation with EDP students and town authorities. Political aspects of environmental questions, such as constraints on private cars, play an important role in the project, and the local press is showing much interest.

An obvious hazard is the fact that during their training the RC teachers have always been indoctrinated in the traditional university values of university disciplines. To counteract the danger that such values will be maintained, teachers with other backgrounds should be included on the staff of the RCs.

The prestige of the university must, of course, be reckoned with, but it is hoped that the disparity will be reduced by factors outside the educational system which provide for relative equality between universities and SCIs. This is sustained by the fact that the RCs have been able to recruit some very competent ex-university people who find the RCs better vehicles for some reforms which the universities have proved too inflexible to accept. Among these are some professional pedagogues engaged in the general task of making higher education more relevant and penetrated by conscious pedagogical thinking.

Another example of the new ideas introduced in the RCs is the development of "allmennfag", a term that might be translated as "general studies", "subject criticism", "societal, environmental and cultural studies", etc. The idea is to introduce in each study course some 15-25% of themes placing particular emphasis on the connections between study and society, profession and society, and broaden the student's perspective and perception of himself and his future job. For example: students of fisheries, aiming at jobs in fish production and the marketing of fish products, can take courses in organisational sociology, political science or economic geography, in order to understand better how various policies of organising the process affect the local communities, the freedom and incomes of fishermen and factory workers, and to realize how the profession and politics interact. The themes of "allmennfag" are closely integrated with the rest of the particular study course; for example, an engineer needs different elements than does the social worker or teacher. In the long term, it is hoped that the "allmennfag" will counteract too much specialization in the basic subject of each study course. Resistance from traditional groups must be expected as the attempts to broaden the students' perspective will be considered as encouraging "hybrids". It is only through experience that we will know whether interdisciplinarity can become fruitful. Committees are at present working on the development of the new concept of "allmennfag".

The idea of "allmennfag" fits in well with the general concept of the RC: a widely diversified, multidisciplinary study centre, allowing and encouraging cross-disciplinary fertilization among teachers and students. The milieu is also relevant here. If the teacher, the social worker, the engineer, the business manager and the journalist work together in an educational institution (particularly on the same courses), they may well come to know more about each others' functions and have a better relationship later in life. The philosophy of the RCs goes somewhat against the emphasis on professionalisation which is strongly rooted in the professional organisations (who oppose the RCs, as stated in Chapter V).

If advantage is to be taken of working in the same milieu, the institutions should not become too big. When a university department has some thousands of people, the chances of real interaction diminish. The search for an optimum size will have high priority in the development of the RCs. The work conducted in the RCs to find new internal structures, more democratic governing bodies, patterns that make for continuous change from within, with the stress on creativity and innovation, could "contaminate" existing institutions if it is successful. At present, one of the main ideas is to organise the staff along two lines:

1) in "competence groups", where people with the same and related subjects work together, aiming at the continuous development of the teaching staff. This continuous development is seen as absolutely vital for the future of the RCs: "a teacher is getting worse if he is not getting better";

2) in "planning groups" of an interdisciplinary nature, with responsibility for the various lines of study (teachers, engineers, business administration). The students will be strongly represented in the latter group, and teachers may, of course, be affiliated to various planning groups.

The outcome of this type of organisational reform might have important repercussions, even on so sacred an activity as research. The traditional authority of university research is based on disciplines. In the words of a critic, these are structured "so as to prevent research findings from getting too close to problems of essential relevance to the rest of society. Such relevance means interdisciplinarity which is still subject to severe sanctions by the academic reward system, being quite correctly conceived as a serious threat to established authority positions in the academic community". * The eventual disruption of such established balances would imply "more freedom for research institutions and individual researchers to provide informative criticism, but would leave no privileged positions to researchers to exert directive authority". ** Clearly this corresponds to the trend of breaking down the sharply defined barriers between the established professions.

The RCs may eventually become more competitive and challenge the universities' practice of training all students. This has not yet happened but the first signs of it can be seen. The RCs are accused of being superficial (not going deep enough into their academic subjects) and of being "hybrids". On the other hand, RC staff are becoming more aware of their position, and attacks on "university imperialism" can be heard.

The result of the competition depends to a large extent on how the rest of society reacts and some of these factors are discussed in the following paragraphs. Possibly, both university and SCI graduates will be considered as equals and there are strong political forces on the side of the RCs. However, tradition also has its pull.

In the debates in Norway - especially with regard to education - there seems to be growing agreement that the post-industrial society is not merely a society in which the instrumental thinking developed within manufacturing industries has penetrated all other areas. If our future societies are to be worth living in, they must increasingly be dominated by values traditionally confined to the services.

In education, this means that the present emphasis on output of institutions will have to yield to an emphasis on the educational process itself and the quality of the experiences involved for the students, who are the real clients of this service function. Education should not become a manufacturing industry, producing changes in students specified by society, industry, teachers or parents. ***

* Proceedings of the Nuffield Canadian Seminar on The Costs of Post-Secondary Education in a Technological Society, K. Eide, June, 1971.

** K. Eide, ibid.

*** See K. Eide, op. cit.

The development of "allmennfag" and of courses taken for their own sake without regard to a professional career can, if successful, become instruments of such changes within the educational system. Recurrent education is another aspect with possible consequences for the whole system. The traditional institutions have shown little will or ability to grapple with these problems. This has been a particular area of interest for the RCs, and Parliament has accepted a proposal that 25% of the total resources of the RCs be allocated to this task and part-time studies, these functions thus becoming integral parts of the institutions from the very beginning. The possible feed-back upon the institutions is mentioned above. This development widens the field for controversial projects such as the training of politicians, trade union leaders, etc., but it is too early to say much about this.

The growth of innovation depends upon several external factors: the reactions of society, of students, of universities, etc. Organisational links such as the exchange of teachers and students are important, and will be discussed in Chapter IV.

## 6. Pressure groups intervening in the process of establishing the RCs

Of the several pressure groups which have intervened during the establishment of the RCs, only a few will be mentioned here. University pressure will be dealt with later.

One important factor behind the exceptionally rapid acceptance of the RC was, as already mentioned, the decentralization - and even populist - trend in general politics. The idea of getting higher education out of the main urban centres was grasped with enthusiasm. A great part of the public debate about the RCs during the first months of the decision process centred on their location. The discussion in Parliament stressed the role of the RC in regional development, both through its direct economic consequences and on account of the knowledge and development potentials it would eventually present to the regions.

The idea of integrating existing SCIs met with immediate and organised resistance from some of the schools concerned and the affiliated professional organisations, which set out to defend "their" institutions (and the labour market monopoly established by a closed recruiting system to the professions). Partly as a result of this, the political decision to integrate was postponed (it was to be "considered at the end of the test period"). There are clear signs that the new Labour government - which came into office in March this year - will reconsider this postponement and propose a parliamentary decision in favour of integration (more mention is made of this in Chapter V).

Various pressure groups are taking an active interest in the question of priorities of studies; societal and professional groups which did not have study possibilities at the post-secondary level are mainly in favour of the RCs.

When dealing with pressure groups with negative views, RCs insist on their right to break educational monopolies, but this is of course a controversial question and might become a serious threat to the innovation functions mentioned above. The powers to deal with it may come from an alliance with social groups which suffer from shortage of personnel or from inadequate training in the "monopoly" institutions. When "professional" arguments are mobilized, it will be possible to bring the decisions up to the general political level.

# IV

## LINKAGES WITH THE UNIVERSITIES

### 1. Introduction

Many of the connections with universities resulting from the present strategy are discussed in the preceding paragraphs.

The problem is defined in Part I of this report as a search for diversification with a minimum of institutional hierarchy, a development of alternatives without these being regarded as (and eventually becoming) "less noble" than university education. In countries where such alternatives exist in institutions outside the universities, SCIs have the problem of achieving respectability without losing sight of the main functions for which they were created.

As is clear from the previous discussions, such respectability and equality can hardly be established within the educational sector alone. Attempts at achieving true equalization in education could certainly be frustrated by forces in the labour market: salary scales, for example, which differentiate between the various types of degrees and institutions. The questions involved are essentially political in nature. This does not make the role of the institutions a passive one, as they have to articulate their own policies, but one must be aware of their limited effect as compared with developments elsewhere in society.

### 2. General strategy: independent institutions with practical co-operation in several fields

Parts of the previous discussion may give too negative an impression of the RCs' attitudes towards the universities. The aim of the earlier discussion was to show that there is both room and need for initiative and diversification, and that some of these innovations might spread to the rest of the system.

They would be more likely to do so if there were organised links between the RCs and the universities. On the other hand, the RCs need such co-operation for several good reasons, the universities being undisputedly reservoirs of advanced knowledge in a number of fields.

The problem is to strike a balance between desired co-operation and undesired domination of values and even of direct control.

The desire for an independent profile and a programme for a rational division of labour should not hamper fruitful co-operation, and links are being developed with this in mind. There are clear signs that the attitudes of the universities are changing; the faculty of Humanities at Oslo University (the largest in the country) accepts RC courses as components of their degrees even when RC courses are different. Faculties and institutes of the universities are offering various types of co-operation.

## 3. Types and levels of courses

Several of the mechanisms in the struggle for independence have already been discussed. One major trend should be stressed: the priority given in the first stage of the development of RCs to courses different from those given in the existing institutions (priority to "alternatives"), because diversification is desirable both for its own sake and as an instrument for fostering values independent of the universities. Diversification is especially important in a small country with a tradition of centralization. Alternatives are found in fields where the universities have been unwilling or unable to take initiatives. Higher education in fisheries is an example that shows how regional and societal relevance carries weight, in spite of whether or not the universities will accept such studies as part of their degree courses.

The alternatives were established primarily with a vocational goal rather than as a first cycle of university studies, as has been the case with the affiliated universities in Sweden. One of the main arguments against the Swedish solution is that affiliated universities can only grow in one direction, namely towards the universities; that diversification would be less and that such a policy would strongly increase recruitment to the longer university studies. The size of Norway (less than 4 m. inhabitants) and its consequent lack of human and financial resources was an important factor in the decision to limit the number of universities to four.

Alternative courses of study already operating or in the planning stage are, for example, business administration, transportation, EDP and systems engineering, fisheries, social studies, technical fields, information and media, etc. But "alternatives" can also be developed by giving new content to traditional subjects or disciplines. An example: one of the RCs (at Lillehammer) offers a one-year course in pedagogics with the emphasis on the social consequences of various school patterns, as opposed to the individual/psychological stress in pedagogical courses at the universities.

The status of these "alternatives" will depend mainly upon their acceptance by students and society, especially employers in the public and private sectors. The first graduates after two years of study at RCs received well-paid jobs in fields where their qualifications were much in demand. A relatively small group of candidates (approximately 15-20% of graduates) wanted to continue studies in other institutions, and some also wanted to take extra courses at the RCs. The policy of universities towards RC graduates is not yet clear; with their autonomous status they have a wide range of options from awarding full credits to awarding none at all. They will probably settle for various "systems of equivalence", depending on the relation between the RC examination and the course the student wishes to enter.

The Rectors' Conference of the Norwegian Universities appointed a committee to submit proposals on mutual acceptance of credits between higher institutions. The RCs - who are not members of the Conference (the question of their membership will probably be settled after the first "test period", which expires in 1974) - were invited to send a representative to the committee, and it is believed that the proposals will be of a "liberal" character, allowing easy transfers. The committee's report is expected in July 1971, and the forthcoming decisions and their implementation will obviously be of strategic importance to further development. Progressive signs can also be seen in representative bodies within the faculties. This trend is no doubt connected with the increasing pressure of numbers which makes the universities interested in delegating basic courses to the RCs.

As seen from the stated goals of the RCs, basic university subjects are included, but they clearly have less priority. They will be taken up in fields where the pressure of numbers at the universities is especially heavy and where such courses fit into the plans of the RCs. For example: mathematics is an important part of economics/administrative studies at the RC, and a candidate from this line of study can, with a short additional course given at the RC, obtain the credit of the one-year basic maths. course in the science faculties. University courses are favoured when they come as "by-products" in this way.

The situation with regard to basic university courses is complicated by the activity of the so-called study organisations. These cover everything from hobby courses to basic university subjects, and in the latter field they operate with well-qualified teachers - mostly from secondary schools - who are accepted by the universities. The universities seem to be in favour of these activities being taken over by the RCs where these are established.

There is some pressure for more university courses, possibly influenced by the prestige of the university or promoted by the ambition of some of the RC centres to become universities. The sudden increase in applicants for entry in autumn 1971 indicates that students' confidence in the RC courses is growing rapidly (the present limited capacity of the RCs meant that only 50% of these applicants could be accepted). The increase was especially strong for the "alternatives", but the relative hesitancy of students to apply for the basic university courses may be explained by the fact that the credit question was not definitively solved. Another explanation of the preference for university courses inside RCs could be found in the ambitions of local politicians and institution leaders who would like to see their institutions grow faster - and the planning and realization of real innovations take more time and money than simply copying. There is a risk that universities may see the RCs as a place to send their drop-outs. In a situation where the RCs are closed, this fear is unfounded.

On the other hand, RCs are encouraged to provide studies that can also be useful to university graduates. University graduates in law and economics are already attending courses in maritime economy at the RCs, and in the autumn civil engineers and regional planners will take part in a course on environmental studies. This will no doubt contribute towards the two sectors achieving equal status.

## 4. The teaching staff

Strict rules govern the appointment of teachers in the RCs. To become an RC lecturer (assistant professor) the same qualifications are required as for a similar post in the universities. The procedure is that a commission of three members (usually two from the universities and one from the RC in question) evaluates the competence of the applicants for the post. On the basis of the commission's report, the board of the RC in question presents its proposal to the Ministry which then makes arrangements for the appointment of the successful candidate. The RC board is not bound by the ranking of the candidates prepared by the commission and the Ministry's participation is purely formal. It is expected that the RCs will eventually have the power to engage their own staff, and it is being discussed at the moment when they will be given full responsibility for this practice.

The reason behind the present rather complicated (and time-consuming) procedure is to ensure the competence of the personnel engaged, but it is clearly looked upon as a temporary arrangement.

If the university takes part in recruiting staff for the RCs there is a danger that the choice made will be influenced by traditional university values and be in favour of academic standards. It is interesting to note that one and a half years after the establishment of the RCs, the Ministry changed the job description for the teaching staff to give more credit for experience in teaching, administration and practical work in order that academic merits should not carry the only weight. Furthermore, the RC boards have, on several occasions, altered the ranking submitted by the commissions on the basis of considerations of this kind. On the other hand, it is clearly realized that university participation is important both for the establishment of flexible transfer and for information purposes.

Also important in this connection is the widespread and systematic use of part-time teachers, specialists from industry and services and guest lecturers from the universities. In the vocationally (professionally) oriented courses especially, this is considered of great importance to make the education relevant to the students.

University teachers participate as part-time lecturers both in the "alternatives" and in the basic university courses. The reverse is true, but more seldom - partly because the strong planning activities in the RCs set time limitations on the RC teaching staff.

RC teachers have the same salaries as university teachers at the same level. With regard to working conditions, the RCs have formulated a promising new system. The number of teachers is in proportion to student numbers. The only condition stipulated in the contract is that the teachers shall spend each full working day in the institution. There is no fixed number of teaching hours per week; whether the teachers use their time for lecturing, conducting seminars, individual tutorials, producing study materials, planning activities or other things is entirely up to the institutions, and the students are very active in evaluating which forms give the best results. (It is interesting to note that although we know that teachers work longer than the stipulated hours because of engagements in planning activities, etc. , these conditions are looked upon as "better" by, for instance, lecturers in the teacher training colleges who have a fixed number of teaching hours).

5. The students

Although the students show some confusion during the first weeks (the Norwegian secondary schools leave very little responsibility to the students in working methods), they soon realize the advantages of being able to experiment with different types of "learning situations".

RC students are entitled to exactly the same loans, travel grants, scholarships and other social benefits as university students. In some cases, this means that they are better off than students in the urban centres where housing and cost of living is considerably higher.

Students of RCs have been invited to join the national university students' union. They are considering this, but no decision has yet been made. Students of other SCIs are not members of this union, which has hitherto been a university students' union and a rather weak one.

## 6. Participation in planning

There are university people on the central advisory board, but these are individual appointments by the Ministry, not the institutions from which they come. University people are engaged in most of the curriculum planning committees established both under the Ministry (after recommendations by the central council) and by the particular RC. Such committees have, in several cases, been appointed initially by the Ministry, but it is expected that here, too, the initiative should pass to the RCs as they develop, and they are encouraged to take it.

A considerable number of committees are at work, some of which have already presented their reports. The following are examples: technical education (engineering level), training of social workers, education in fisheries, mass communication, tourism, transport, computers and system work, training of youth leaders, environment studies, training of administrative personnel for the municipalities, economic/administrative education, training of interpreters, accountancy. The considerable overlap between these various fields is one of the great advantages of the multipurpose, as compared with the specialized, model. The former allows, on the one hand, better use of scarce resources by making it possible to organise basic courses common to several fields of study (mathematics, statistics, foreign languages). On the other it increases the options for students and it has positive milieu consequences; journalists, engineers and social workers can meet each other in the classes and not merely with their professional colleagues as in a uni-disciplinary institution.

Governing boards of the RCs are mainly recruited locally: three members appointed by the regional authorities, one teacher elected by the staff, one student (and one deputy without right of vote) elected by the students, and the director (who is the secretary of the board and has no right of vote). Two other members are appointed by the Ministry of Education, one of whom is chosen from a university. He has no formal mandate from his institution, but this link proves to be very useful.

## 7. Participation at examinations

University staff also sit on the examining boards of RCs, which are given wide freedom in matters of examinations; they can decide the examination subjects and the forms the tests should take. They are encouraged to experiment with method and content of examination and evaluation, aiming to make evaluation an instrument for achieving the pedagogical and professional goals of the courses. This has resulted, for example, in the arrangement of group exams, where a group of students are given a task similar to those they will meet in practical life, with free access to the libraries and other working elements that would be available in normal circumstances. The examiners may be invited as counsellors to these experiments. They are appointed in the initial period by the central council of RCs, which has consultative status under the Ministry. The main point of bringing in examiners from outside is to establish contact with qualified people at the universities and elsewhere. The initiative for and administration of the examination is in the hands of the RCs. The examiners are called to the RCs to discuss with teachers and students the form the evaluation process will take. As was the case with staff recruitment, the RCs will also shortly take over the choice and appointment of the examiners, when the strength of the RC staff is fully established.

## 8. Financing

During the trial period the RCs are wholly State-financed, with the important exception of premises, which are the responsibility of the regions, though there is a strong expectation that this will be taken over by the State after the trial period. The main reasons for this are: universities, and their buildings, are 100% State-financed. The present system of regionally-paid premises was established in the hope that each region's desire for advancement would encourage the speedy development of the project, but this, of course, puts the richer regions in a better position than the poorer ones.

# V

# LINKAGES WITH THE NON-UNIVERSITY SECTOR

## 1. Integration undecided

As mentioned earlier, the important question of integrating existing SCIs into the RCs was postponed when Parliament launched the RCs. However, it is vital to obtain such integration because the multidisciplinarity and flexibility that is necessary for the RCs to reach their goals can only be obtained in a broader institution.

The two largest types of school in the Norwegian non-university sector are teacher training and technical schools (engineering). A working group in the Ministry is working on the question of teacher training college/RC relations. There has been some opposition to integration from teacher training colleges and teachers' organisations, but the Government (in a planned report to Parliament at the turn of the year 1971 concerning the five reports of the Royal Commission mentioned earlier) will most likely decide in favour of it. How and when this will be done will, of course, be as controversial as the whole question of it. The plans for integration with engineering schools have advanced more rapidly. The first integrated project will start in autumn 1971, and there are hopes that a more general solution will be reached in 1972. The integration is being prepared by a special committee set up by the Ministry.

There is also a committee discussing the eventual training of social workers at the Rcs; it also deals with relations with existing schools for social workers.

In the individual regions joint projects are being developed between teacher training colleges and RCs. Although the institution and central leaders are hesitant, if not directly opposed, the teaching staff show more willingness to co-operate and even integrate.

The examination question is no doubt very controversial where the existing non-university institutions, especially the teacher training colleges, are concerned. These have a fully centralized system of teacher recruitment and student enrolment, and decisions on content, examinations (testing and control) are all taken by a central board under the Ministry's Department for Primary and Secondary Schools. Teachers' organisations have considerable influence, and integration into the RCs would mean a lessening of central control as education became regionalised. It would also mean the abolition or weakening of that labour market considerations, which have always influenced access to the teacher training colleges.

## 2. Towards a Regional College system

The commission proposed that most of each RC should be concentrated in a study centre for each region, recruiting 1,500 to 4,000 students. However, the RCs as a regional system would also include existing schools located elsewhere in the same region. The main arguments for this were that a broader centre would have several advantages: the study centre could offer students a better choice of courses, a broader and more attractive milieu for the teaching staff allowing cross-disciplinary fertilization and thus a more flexible and innovative internal structure - a better utilization of such resources as buildings, libraries, welfare installations, etc. The commission stressed the need for institutions able to change and develop from within, pointing out that it is much easier to plan for total student capacity than foresee the distribution in the various fields of study. It mentioned that, historically, the small and specialized institutions have shown little ability for change and creativity, and concluded that in the world of tomorrow, it will be crucial to develop institutions that facilitate initiative and innovation.

# VI

## PERSONAL ASSESSMENT. SUMMARY

It is clearly much too early to draw conclusions after only two years of operation; there are risks ahead, but also some very positive signs. During the coming year it is expected that Parliament will be asked to decide whether the RCs should integrate all the SCIs outside the universities, and thus become a broad, comprehensive system. The decision will greatly influence the RCs' ability to fulfil their central tasks: to develop a broad and diversified range of studies, recruit a highly-qualified teaching staff, be continuously innovative with regard to curriculum, teaching methods and research, and to contribute to regional development. It is feared that the rigidities and inadequacies of the old specialized system may prevail if the opposition to integration is not overcome. There are, however, clear signs that integration will be favoured.

Important policy decisions which will also affect the RCs are now in preparation in the university sector. The most important concern the admission and credit systems. If the universities are restrictive on these matters, it could have serious effects on the RCs, which would then be forced to conform to university patterns to obtain transfer and credit. However there are clear indications that the universities are heading for an "open" system, preferring equality of levels to identity with regard to content.

### 1. Quantitative developments, applications for admission, employment

The establishment of the RCs began in 1969 on a very modest scale: 3 RCs with a total of 150 students. In 1970 there were 450 students in 4 RCs, and in 1971 there are 1,100 in 6 institutions. In 1972 there will be 6 RCs with a total of over 2,000 students. Although there has been a rapid increase in student places, the number of applicants has still exceeded the capacity of the RCs, with a resulting decrease in the acceptance rate from around 65% to below 50%. Admission policies did not bow to traditional criteria of accepting matriculation degrees only, so an increasing proportion of applicants succeeded in entering these colleges without secondary school certificates. This privileged position for the "second route" students was decided on both for the experimental value of having students with a varied background, and because students from a "second route" had performed very well in the first group.

The average length of an RC study course being 2 years, the first students finished their courses in the spring of 1971. They all found very satisfactory jobs, and a few have continued their studies.

## 2. The key factor: the teaching staff and policies for its development

The success of the RCs will depend very much on the development of the teaching staff. If they consider the RCs a second choice, much of the struggle for equality will be lost. There are, however, important factors that can help to avoid this. Parliament, in its decision to establish the RCs, stressed that the teaching staff must be given good opportunities for travel, free study terms, etc. With present-day communications, this is essentially a budget question. So, too, is the problem of bringing in experts from outside for planning, teaching, etc. Money is, of course, a necessary prerequisite for the general development of the RCs, but the acceptance of these institutions by politicians, regional authorities, the local press, etc., gives hope that the RCs can avoid financial frustration.

The most decisive factors in staff development are probably the professional milieu and the working conditions. There is the risk of isolation in the period of establishing the new institutions, but as staff numbers grow, this risk becomes less serious. The small size of each RC is also a positive factor: bureaucratisation comes with large institutions. At the RCs the results of initiative soon become apparent. The possibility for innovative work, the orientation towards studies with societal relevance and the contact with people from practical life in the regions taking part in teaching and planning activities are all to the advantage of the RCs.

There is a growing understanding among the staff that over-enthusiasm for recognition within the university system might spoil their liberty at the RCs. As mentioned at the beginning of this chapter, too much conformity with the universities can reduce the influence of the staff on the development of the RCs. Although experience so far is limited, it is possible to state that the policy of autonomy has a positive effect on the recruitment of teachers.

The organisational pattern and internal structure of the RCs are at present being considered, with the purpose of creating a milieu in which the qualifications of the staff members can be continuously developed. The RCs are not primarily research institutions; research is not a duty, but it is a natural consequence of the staffing policies that teachers can engage in research and development work. It is not realistic for the RCs to engage in activities requiring the most costly laboratory facilities, but it is certainly possible to undertake projects in fields such as social science and humanities. In planning adult education, the staff and the students engage in data collection to find out the needs of the population in the region. The idea is also pedagogical: students learn research methodology by doing, they come into contact with real life, and new knowledge is produced under the guidance of competent scientists.

Contacts with local and regional authorities as well as with people in the labour market, politicians, trade union leaders, etc., are encouraged. Such contacts allow a feed-back in the communications between colleges and the surrounding regions and help to pursue one of the main objectives, that of service to the community.

One important facility provided by the municipalities which is proving successful in the recruitment of staff is the provision of good housing at prices which are only 60-65% of the prices in the capital city, Oslo. The places where the RCs are located can offer better physical environment than the larger urban areas: less pollution, less over-crowding, shorter distance to work, better recreation possibilities, better surroundings for children, etc. We have evidence that these non-institutional factors have been decisive in a number of cases.

## 3. Summary: diversification/striking a balance

The Royal Commission which proposed the development of a system of twelve RCs covering the country (the population of Norway is 4 million), recommended that these institutions should take a relatively larger part of the increased number of post-secondary students than the universities. At the moment six institutions are operating and another 6-8 will most probably be established within the next few years. With the generalization of secondary school, the post-secondary system must be expanded and diversified. The tasks of the RCs at the moment can be summarized as follows:

- to develop new studies and a new content of existing studies;
- to integrate the new studies and existing institutions into a comprehensive system (following the hoped-for political decisions) stressing easy transfer and combination;
- to develop a structure that facilitates continuous innovation and the strengthening of the qualifications of staff, at the same time giving students possibilities for real participation in the life of the institution.

To fulfill these tasks, it seems necessary to strike a number of balances:

- between autonomy and contact with recognition by the universities;
- between vocational and general education;
- between basic and recurrent education;
- between service to society and criticism of it.

On the basis of what can be seen of the competence and enthusiasm of staff and students, it seems realistic to hope that the RCs will approach the stated goals, as well as participate in the articulation of new ones. The political backing of the RCs sustains this hope.

# II

## Community-Junior Colleges in the United States

by

S. V. Martorana
Vice-Chancellor for Two-Year Colleges
State University of New York
(United States)

## CONTENTS


I. Introduction .......................................... 87

II. Historical development .......................................... 93

III. Legal status .......................................... 99

IV. Forms of governance .......................................... 103

V. Methods of financing .......................................... 111

VI. Decisions about establishment and location .......................................... 117

VII. Inter-college and university relationships .......................................... 121

VIII. Relationship to common school systems .......................................... 127

IX. Curriculum content and structure of studies .......................................... 131

X. Relation to the community .......................................... 139

XI. Perspectives for 1970-1980 .......................................... 143

Concluding comment .......................................... 148

# I

## INTRODUCTION

### THE BROAD CHARACTER AND GOALS OF THE COMMUNITY AND JUNIOR COLLEGE

Since World War II, the two-year college has become the chief reliant in the United States for extending mass educational opportunities beyond the high school. There really is no national system of two-year colleges or standard nomenclature for these institutions. One thinks more properly of an aggregate of 50 different state systems. The two-year college in the United States, therefore, takes a number of forms and titles, exemplified as follows: Hudson Valley Community College, Troy, New York (a public community college); Los Angeles City College, Los Angeles, California (also a public community college); Miami-Dade Junior College, Miami, Florida (also a public community college); Wilbur Wright College, Chicago, Illinois (also a public community college); Cape Fear Technical Institute, Wilmington, North Carolina (a public technical institute); Vermont College, Montpelier, Vermont (a private junior college for women); Assumption College for Sisters, Mendham, New Jersey (a private junior college for Roman Catholic sisters); Xaverian College, Silver Spring, Maryland (a private junior college for Roman Catholic brothers). All these institutions, despite variations in title, mission, and support, offer two-year post-secondary programmes leading to the Associate in Arts, Associate in Science, or Associate in Applied Science degree as well as a wide array of shorter programmes leading to certificates or diplomas; are classified as junior colleges by the states in which they are located; and hold membership in the 813-member "American Association of Junior Colleges".

The public two-year college (increasingly coming to have the common designation "community-junior college") predominates in number and growth rate; hence it will receive major attention in this study. Table 1 illustrates the growth at irregular intervals of private and public junior colleges in the United States. It will be noted that over the past ten years public junior colleges have nearly doubled in number while private junior colleges decreased to a level below that which they had reached in 1929.

Table 1. NUMBER OF JUNIOR COLLEGES IN THE USA

(Irregular intervals, 1900-1970)

| | No. OF PRIVATE JUNIOR COLLEGES | No. OF PUBLIC JUNIOR COLLEGES |
|---|---|---|
| 1900 ................. | 8 | 0 |
| 1915 ................. | 55 | 19 |
| 1921 ................. | 137 | 70 |
| 1929 ................. | 258 | 178 |
| 1938 ................. | 317 | 258 |
| 1947 ................. | 323 | 328 |
| 1953 ................. | 260 | 338 |
| 1960 ................. | 273 | 405 |
| 1970 ................. | 244 | 794 |

SOURCE: Junior College Directory (1961 ed., 1962 ed., and 1970 ed.), passim. Washington, American Association of Junior Colleges, 1961, 1962, 1970.

The public two-year colleges, as well as predominating in number, serve the greater bulk of the enrolment. The table on page 89 shows comparative enrolments over the decade of the 1960s.

The public community-junior college, it is fairly generally agreed in the United States, has five major functions. The following definitions of these functions by the New York State Board of Regents in 1964 are typical of statements found repeatedly in the literature on the emergence of the community-junior college in the United States from the classical Commonwealth Study reported by Koos in 1922* to the most recent definitive comprehensive nationwide study by Medsker which appeared in 1960. **

* Leonard Vincent Koos, The Junior College, Research Publications of the University of Minnesota, Education Series, No. 5, Minneapolis, University of Minnesota, 1924.

** Leland L. Medsker, The Junior College: Progress and Prospect, New York, McGraw-Hill Book Company, 1960.

Table 2. TOTAL ENROLMENT IN JUNIOR COLLEGES IN THE USA, 1960-1969

| | ENROLMENT IN PRIVATE JUNIOR COLLEGES | ENROLMENT IN PUBLIC JUNIOR COLLEGES |
|---|---|---|
| 1960 ........... | 93,992 | 566,224 |
| 1961 ........... | 103,651 | 644,968 |
| 1962 ........... | 105,535 | 713,334 |
| 1963 ........... | 113,290 | 814,244 |
| 1964 ........... | 122,870 | 912,093 |
| 1965 ........... | 140,667 | 1,152,086 |
| 1966 ........... | 147,119 | 1,316,980 |
| 1967 ........... | 143,220 | 1,528,220 |
| 1968 ........... | 143,152 | 1,810,964 |
| 1969 ........... | 134,779 | 2,051,493 |

SOURCE: Junior College Directory 1970, pp. 8f, Washington, American Association of Junior Colleges, 1970.

"A. General Education. To provide post-secondary-school general background and experience for all students in conjunction with study in their major academic fields.

"B. College or University Transfer Education. To provide the requisite courses for 2 years of collegiate study for students who are interested and competent to carry their studies to the bachelor's degree.

"C. Occupational or Terminal Education. To provide programs of education and training beyond the high school, but below the professional level, for students seeking, for whatever reason, immediate entry into the productive labor force in business, industry, or government organisations in need of employees with higher level abilities; and for persons already employed but seeking to improve or learn new skills required in our changing economic and cultural environment.

"D. Adult or Continuing Education. To provide programs of continuing education appropriate to and consistent with the level immediately above the high school in the educational system to assist adults of all ages to meet changing educational, cultural, and economic conditions and to implement changes in their personal objectives.

"E. Guidance and Counseling. To provide for all students the necessary testing, guidance and counseling to enable each one to know and accept his strengths and limitations and to choose the program most suited to him in the light of objective information and his personal situation at the time". *

That these objectives prevail quite generally throughout the nation and continue to be accepted is illustrated in action by the Oklahoma State Regents for Higher Education, which in recent 1970 guidelines for the role and scope of Oklahoma higher education, identified four functions for the two-year colleges in that state: "1) provide general education for all students, 2) provide education in several basic fields of study for the freshman and sophomore years for students who plan to transfer to senior college and complete requirements for the bachelor's degree, 3) provide terminal education in several fields of vocational and technical study, and 4) provide both formal and informal programs of study especially designed for adults and out-of-school youth in order to serve the community generally with a continuing education opportunity". **

Although there appears to be very strong consensus from all sides on the proper objectives to be achieved by two-year community-junior colleges, there is considerable controversy over the degree of success that has been attained in reaching these goals. Moreover, great differences of opinion exist on the best ways and means to effect desired improvements in community-junior college education. The nature of the debates and related research on the major issues of concern are described in the sections which follow in this paper.

## Analysis and Prospects

The community-junior college is a people-serving institution. These colleges have more than doubled in number since the end of World War II. Their enrolments have nearly quadrupled in the past ten years. There are many indicators for continued growth, both in number of colleges and enrolment. Some of these indicators are: increased college-going rate (predictions of 80% of the college-age group in the United States pursuing some form of post-secondary education are not uncommon); increased retention rates or holding power of the high schools, yielding larger number of high school graduates;

* The Regents Statewide Plan for the Expansion and Development of Higher Education, 1964, p. 124. Albany, The University of the State of New York, The State Education Department, 1965.

** The Role and Scope of Oklahoma Higher Education, p. 47. Oklahoma City, Oklahoma State Regents for Higher Education, 1970.

another rise in the birth rate (despite increasing growing programmes of birth control, use of the "pill", and relaxed abortion restrictions) as the large World War II crop of babies reaches child-bearing age; increased attention to the educational needs of minority groups and the disadvantaged illustrated by the growth in number of colleges with open-door admissions and "full-opportunity" programmes; increased emphasis on the development of vocational and technical programmes in the community-junior colleges; and increasing recognition of the community service and continuing education roles of the community-junior colleges.

The Carnegie Commission on Higher Education, chaired by Clark Kerr, former president of the University of California, has proposed that from the perspective of its pervasive analysis of current conditions and likely future development, there is a need for anything from 230 to 280 new community-junior colleges in the United States by 1980. There would then be a community college within commuting distance of 95% of all Americans, according to the Commission's estimates. This growth in numbers of institutions as well as the large expansion in enrolment of existing institutions will undoubtedly result in a very large increase in the number of associate degrees granted in higher education in the next decade. In 1967, 15. 5% of all higher education degrees were associates. *

* A Factbook on Higher Education, Washington, American Council on Education, 1969, pp. 9190 and 9285.

another rise in the birth rate, despite increasing growing programmes of birth control, use of the "pill", and relaxed abortion restrictions, as the large World War II crop of babies reaches childbearing age; increased attention to the educational needs of minority groups and the disadvantaged, illustrated by the growth in number of colleges with open-door admissions and "full-opportunity" programmes; increased emphasis on the development of vocational and technical programmes in the community-junior colleges; and increasing recognition of the community service and continuing education roles of the community-junior colleges.

The Carnegie Commission on Higher Education, chaired by Clark Kerr, former president of the University of California, has projected from its comprehensive and intensive analyses of current conditions and likely future [illegible] a need for something from 230 to 280 new community-junior colleges in the United States by 1980. These would then be community colleges within commuting [illegible] of [illegible] Commission's estimates [illegible] as well as the large expansion in enrolment of existing [illegible] will undoubtedly result in a very large increase in the number of [illegible] degrees granted in higher education in the next decade. In [illegible] of all [illegible] degrees were associates.

# II

## HISTORICAL DEVELOPMENT

The American two-year or junior college is essentially a twentieth-century phenomenon, as the growth shown in Table 1 has indicated. Its place in the American educational "ladder" has gained increasing recognition since World War II. Again, it should be emphasized that there is no uniform national system or ladder of education in the United States. Any state taken as a sample of one would show variations from the ladder sketched below. The sketch, however, represents the general pattern of educational progression through the formal common school and higher educational institutions in the nation. As periodic residence and migration studies indicate growing mobility among American families one can fairly expect that interstate differences in educational patterns will become fewer and less accentuated.

This is not to say that the future success and growth of these institutions is fully assured or if effected will come about easily and without serious crises. Their future success is not guaranteed automatically by success to date. Indeed, there are serious difficulties in the path of fulfilment of the Carnegie Commission's recommendations and forecast cited above. Among the obstacles are: the onset of a new rigidity and resistance to change which will take from the community-junior colleges much of their current advantage of flexibility and freedom of action, the challenges inherent in the emergence of new post-high-school educational institutions claiming to be "open-door" in their programmes and in some baccalaureate degree-granting colleges and universities moving to the "open access" concept, the incessant battle for status and identity in the face of competition from longer established colleges and universities, difficulties in keeping programmes "student centered", and the ever present hardships in acquiring the fiscal resources needed. These difficulties will be pointed out again and elaborated on more fully in later statements of analysis and prospectus which concludes each major section of this paper.

Figure 1. THE AMERICAN EDUCATIONAL LADDER

| ELEMENTARY JUNIOR HIGH (OR MIDDLE), AND SENIOR HIGH SCHOOL | JUNIOR COLLEGE | COLLEGE OR UNIVERSITY | UPPER DIV. COLLEGE OR UNIVERSITY | UNIVERSITY |
|---|---|---|---|---|
| | | | | 8-Ph. D., M. D. |
| | | | | 7-J. D. |
| | | | | 6 |
| | | | 5-Mas. Degree | 5-Mas. Degree |
| | | 4-Bach. Degree | 4-Bach. Degree | |
| | | 3 | 3 | |
| | 2-Assoc. | 2 | | |
| | 1 Degree | 1 | | |
| High School - 12 | | | | |
| Diploma 11 | | | | |
| 10 | | | | |
| 9 | | | | |
| 8 | | | | |
| 7 | | | | |
| 6 | | | | |
| 5 | | | | |
| 4 | | | | |
| 3 | | | | |
| 2 | | | | |
| 1 | | | | |
| Kindergarten | | | | |

Grade or Year

The earliest American educational pattern was derived quite naturally from an English model. The rudiments of learning were gained in the home or from private instruction, or, at a later period, in the "district school". Direct preparation for college was secured under private instruction or in a Latin grammar school. The college offered a four-year classical curriculum leading to the bachelor of arts degree, although Harvard College, following the Cambridge model from England, initially offered a three-year curriculum.

The key element which led to the evolution of the junior college was the introduction of the academy by Benjamin Franklin in the mid-18th century, at Philadelphia.

Franklin, a man of civic affairs, sought for more than the traditional élitist and narrowly classical type of education, characteristic of the four then-existing American colleges - Harvard, William and Mary, Yale, and Princeton. Hence his borrowing the English Dissenters' academy as a model and the offering in this new academy (foundation of the University of Pennsylvania) of both the classical curriculum and the "English" curriculum. The Dissenters' (Nonconformist) academies, in turn modelled on John Calvin's Geneva Academy, sought to provide a complete university education for the children of the English Dissenters, who had been effectively denied admission to Oxford and Cambridge by renewal of the Uniformity Act in 1662. The American academy with its eventual two-track curriculum, the classical and the more "practical" English, supplanted the Latin grammar school as the chief type of college-preparatory institution in the American colonies, later states. The fact that the academy's classical curriculum so greatly overlapped that of the American four-year college, however, is the prime cause of the evolution of the American junior college - and of some of its major problems on the modern scene, to which reference will be made later in this paper.

So overlapping were the academy and college in New York State, for example, in 1787, that Ezra L'Hommedieu of the Board of Regents argued against fellow-Regent Alexander Hamilton that academies should have the right to award bachelor's degrees to such of their graduates as would have covered the full collegiate span of studies in the academy. * Hamilton and his Columbia College colleagues were too strong politically, however, so as a compromise academy graduates were permitted to gain advanced standing, by examination, to the second, third, or even fourth years of the college while the academies were given the legal capability of escalation to college status upon reaching stated financial and curricular levels. The second, third, and fourth colleges created in New York State - Union, Hamilton, and Hobart - all proceeded through this academy-to-college development.

As the frontier moved westward in the 19th century, this pattern of academies overlapping colleges in curriculum moved with it. After the War of 1812, however, young scholars began to return from university studies on the Continent, particularly the German states, and to draw invidious comparisons between the American hodge-podge of secondary-higher education and the neatly articulated systems observed abroad. Ticknor, Sparks and Bancroft of Harvard and Henry E. Dwight of Yale were among the earliest to suggest supplanting the academy-

* Sidney Sherwood, "University of the State of New York: Origin, History and Present Organisation", Regents' Bulletin No. 11, January, 1893, p. 243. Albany, University of the State of New York.

college pattern by a German gymnasium-university pattern. * Their two bellwether institutions, Harvard and Yale, however, never seriously considered the abolition of the freshman and sophomore years - later called the lower division - and no major university has even taken this step even to the modern era.

Henry P. Tappan, first president of the University of Michigan, and William W. Folwell, first president of the University of Minnesota, both advocated that their frontier state universities foster the development of strong academies and high schools which would complete a student's general education near his home, leaving the universities free to develop the upper-division, professional and graduate studies as did the universities of France and Germany. Both Tappan and Folwell saw their hopes of abolishing the lower division fail but did establish the idea that a formal cleavage between the general-education lower division and the professional-education upper division was viable. ** President William Rainey Harper adopted such a pattern for the reconstituted University of Chicago in 1892, aiming at the eventual abolition of the lower division or "junior college" (first use of the term) as he named it in 1896. Like Tappan and Folwell before him and David Starr Jordan and Ray Lyman Wilbur at Stanford after him, Harper was never able to achieve the abolition of the lower division. It was when Harper at the turn of the century gave the name junior college to the two-year (13th and 14th grade) extensions of the public high school and to free-standing colleges of only two years' duration that the institution began its slow growth to the importance which it has gained in the modern scene.

## Analysis and Prospects

The American two-year college emerged partly as a historical accident and partly in response to new educational needs of a politically democratic and an economically technological new and developing society. The Calvinists in Europe had set up the academy as a surrogate for the traditional university. When the lineal descendants of these two types of institution had to co-exist on the 18th century American scene, they overlapped. The four-year college was the older model and it prevailed as the standard of "higher" education. The academy was relegated to secondary education status, but the better academies

* Kenneth T. Doran, "New York, New Yorkers, and the Two-Year-College Movement: A History of the Debate over Structure in Higher Education", pp. 18-24 (Unpublished dissertation). Syracuse University, 1961. University Microfilms No. 62-1098, Ann Arbor, Michigan.

** Kenneth T. Doran, op. cit.

throughout most of the 19th century continued to offer work which paralleled that of the first two years of the four-year college. Some influential university presidents attempted to capitalize on this overlapping in an attempt to rid their institutions of the lower-division, general-education programme and thus to become the "university proper" of the German type. To date such proponents have failed, but from their struggle has emerged a viable, free-standing two-year post-secondary institution - the American community-junior college.

This community-junior college promises yet to free the university to become the "Citadel of Learning", as James Bryant Conant has termed it, free of obligation to provide for the needs of mass education and to specialize in advanced scholarship, professional preparation and research. * While the future could still hold development of the "university proper", there seems at this moment little likelihood that the dreams of the original theorists will soon be realized - that the four-year colleges and universities will abolish their first two-year programmes and rely on the two-year community-junior colleges alone as feeder institutions. Indeed there is evidence that colleges and universities offering bachelor's and higher degrees have in recent years been claiming willingness to be as "open door" as the community-junior colleges. The state-supported and controlled colleges and universities especially are under great pressure to show their open access to all types of students and particularly those from disadvantaged educational and socio-economic background. As a result, confusion is growing about the educational mission to be accomplished by these institutions in relation to the purposes established for the community-junior colleges.

Neither does it appear likely that large numbers of the two-year colleges will become four-year colleges. Such conversion occurs only rarely among publicly supported and controlled two-year colleges. ** This is especially in states which have a strong approach to statewide planning to meet all higher educational needs and which therefore can identify localities which need the programmes of four-year colleges and can support the establishment of such institutions. Where such statewide planning takes place, as in California, Florida, and New York, there has never yet been a conversion of a public community-junior college to one offering baccalaureate or higher degrees. Only when a vacuum occurs in needed educational services at the upper-divisions' advanced collegiate levels do pressures for such conversion of community-junior colleges to four-year status develop.

* James B. Conant, The Citadel of Learning, New Haven, Yale University Press, 1966.

** W.C. Eells and S.V. Martorana "Do Junior Colleges Become Four-Year Colleges?", Higher Education, 13, 110-115, Feb. 1957.

It has been said that "the American public is now so conscious of the need for the community college that if a given state transformed its two-year colleges en masse to four-year colleges it would eventually have to create a new system of community-junior colleges". With one significant exceptional indicator, the two-year and the four-year members of the American higher education family appear increasingly to be reconciled to the need to live harmoniously together.

The significant exceptional indicator is the concept of the "upper-division college" to build on the "open-door community-junior college". As Figure 1 indicates, the upper-division institution has no freshman or sophomore students. It accepts students from two-year (or four-year) colleges who are ready to take up work of the junior year. In his report of his in-depth study of this new type of college, Altman reports that there are seven such upper-division institutions now operational and eight others have reached various stages of legislative or state board of higher education approval. Six other states have started to consider establishing upper division colleges. * With respect to the dynamics of development of these upper-division colleges in relationship to that of the two-year community-junior colleges he writes: "predicated upon assumptions of societal need - whether demonstrated or assumed by power groups which can affect public policy - upper division institutions are a logical response for a public system facing enrolment pressures at the junior year or a need for additional baccalaureate education. If junior colleges did not exist, if they were not predominantly public, or if the hesitancy to convert or expand them did not exist, upper division colleges would not develop in increasing numbers and locations. Yet, public junior colleges are the fastest-growing segment of American higher education; there is every indication that public upper division institutions will be developed apace". **

* Robert A. Altman. The Upper Division College, San Francisco, Jossey-Bass Inc., 1970.

** Robert A. Altman. The Upper Division College, pp. 171 f., San Francisco, Jossey-Bass, Inc., 1970.

# III

## LEGAL STATUS

The variability of legal bases for community-junior colleges reflects the US Constitution's recognition of education as a function of the individual states. Members of the National Council of State Directors of Community-junior colleges rarely fail to comment at their annual meetings on the observable differences among their states as regards the legal status of the public community-junior colleges. Only one state constitution - that of California - specifically mentions junior college education.

All states except one - South Dakota - however, now include among their laws general enabling statutes for community-junior college establishment. These statutes provide for the foundation of two-year colleges either under some form of local governing board or as state-controlled colleges. The two predominant patterns of local institutional organisation in current general enabling legislation are the unified district and the junior college district. In a unified junior-college district the same board of trustees is responsible for the junior college and lower public schools whereas local boards of junior-college districts are responsible only for this level of educational program. There are many variations in laws authorizing local junior colleges districts. All in one way or another create a local or regional area to be served by the junior college, to contribute to its support, and to have local representation on its controlling board. These board members are usually elected to office by the people residing in the district served, although in some states, like Maryland and New York, they are appointed by a local governmental body such as a city council or county board of supervisors.

State two-year colleges, in contrast, are governed by a board of control which represents the state in the legal sense and not a given sub-section or region of the state. Board members in these cases are normally appointed by the governor. Examples of state junior colleges are to be found in Virginia, Massachusetts, Minnesota and Oklahoma, among others.

Another variation of legal basis of authorization gives rise in some states to two-year branches of colleges and universities which grant bachelor's and higher degrees. These are commonly termed branch campuses or centers. They derive their legal authority from the statutes pertaining to the parent college or university and are governed by the same board of control.

Although the unified district type of legal structure for community-junior college operations prevailed during the early years of the movement, the trend has definitely shifted to placing these colleges under either the separate local district form or state-level control. During recent years a number of states have revamped their basic community-junior college general enabling laws to permit former unified districts to separate the two-year college programs into new community-junior college districts under their own boards of trustees. This is true, for example, of Illinois, Michigan and Iowa. For many years, California has gradually shifted its legal authorization so that now a large majority of its 93 junior colleges are operating under boards separate from elementary and high schools. Among the growing list of states which have set up state-level boards of control during the past ten years without any local governing institutional boards are Connecticut, Minnesota and Virginia. During this period no state has authorized only unified districts in its general legislative enactments.

## Analysis and Prospects

Most states are now categorizing public junior colleges as comprehensive, two-year educational institutions at the level immediately above the high school and are incorporating these institutions into the state structure of post high-school education. The evidence is strong that this will be the direction of prevailing practice as additional states move to expand and improve their programs of post high-school education. All but one state now has general enabling laws approving junior colleges. Although a majority approves an administrative structure which places the junior college in a unified school district, almost as many approve separate junior college districts of one type or another. Whether or not the college's legal board of control is local or state in its legal representation, the principle of local voice in control is generally and strongly evident in the laws, attempts towards this being present even in states where no legal controlling local board is created in the law. For example, the state boards responsible for the public two-year colleges in Colorado, Massachusetts, and Virginia have all created local area advisory councils to each operating college president, administration and faculty. This practice seems to be consistent with the educational purposes and modus operandi of community-junior colleges and is likely to be adopted by future state boards and parent authorities of branch institutions.

Although the number of states with general enabling legislation for establishing and operating junior colleges is increasing, so is the number with special laws pertaining to these institutions. If these tendencies continue, there will probably come a time when all 50 states will have both general enabling laws and special statutory provisions. Such developments would not be surprising in that specific legislation may round out details not included in the general statutes and be made necessary to resolve strictly local matters. The maxim guiding state and Federal lawmakers in phrasing general enabling legislation is to avoid undue detail in the law. As experience with the law develops, however, the usual history, so well typified by California, Texas, and Illinois, states with the oldest records of junior colleges, is that more and more specifics of operation become matters of legal attention and action. Accordingly, the expectation can well be that new state laws in the next decade will move from procedures for establishing and locating new colleges and for their general operation to more direct treatment of matters relating to specific administration, programs, and student and faculty affairs.

A number of questions may be raised about theoretical conceptions of the public junior colleges and their characteristics as opposed to their actual forms as defined in state laws. Relatively few states have general statutory enactments that describe or establish institutions with all the characteristics, scope of function, and method of operation theoretically considered by specialists to be best in the field of junior college education. Indeed, the existing diversity of patterns and the tendency toward even greater diversity shown in recent state enactments challenge the possible conclusion that the general development of the legal status of public junior colleges is progressing toward such a hypothetical ideal. This is a matter to which scholars and researchers in junior college education, as well as advocates of the comprehensive, locally controlled and state- and locally-supported community-junior college (or those who would propose any other single scheme of junior college organisation and administration) should give more study and attention.

created local area advisory councils to advise [illegible] tutor colleges on administration and [illegible] is generally seems [illegible] the educational purposes [illegible] collectors and is likely to be adopted by [illegible] authorities of [illegible] institutions.

Although the number of [illegible] with [illegible] establishing and supporting [illegible] is increasing [illegible] [illegible]

[illegible] development [illegible] specific [illegible] [illegible] in [illegible] however [illegible] [illegible] relating to [illegible] and [illegible] matters.

[illegible] of [illegible] of the public tutor colleges and their characteristics [illegible] [illegible] concluding to the possible conclusion that the general development of the legal status of public tutor colleges is progressive [illegible] [illegible] [illegible] who would [illegible] further [illegible] compensation [illegible] and attention.

# IV

## FORMS OF GOVERNANCE

In a strict legalistic sense most community-junior colleges are governed at two levels, one local and institutional and the other state and inter-institutional. At the local, institutional level there is generally a board of trustees of lay citizens residing in the district served by the college and elected to office by the general public. Such elected boards of trustees are by far most characteristic, being found in California, Illinois, Michigan, Texas, Washington, and most other states with well-developed public two-year college systems. In a few states, the board of control membership is appointed by the local sponsoring government as in the case of the New Jersey County Colleges, and, as in New York State, the boards are in part made up of appointees of the local sponsoring body and in part of appointees of the governor.

These local governing boards derive their powers and duties from the enabling state statues. Typically they are the centers of legal authority and responsibility for all aspects of local institutional operations within broad statewide and inter-institutional coordinating policies and procedures set by the state-level supervisory controlling board which is also established by law. The local board of control hires personnel, holds title and is responsible for care of property; it identifies and approves curriculum offerings, and develops and administers institutional operating and capital development budgets.

All these local administrative operations, as just indicated, however, must conform to the general statewide plans and policies of the state-level controlling agency. Such agencies can be identified in all states with public two-year colleges, but they vary greatly from one state to another. The two most commonly designated agencies with responsibility of this type are the State Board of Education, which also gives state-level surveillance to public elementary and secondary schools, or a separate State Board of Community Colleges. Florida and Iowa illustrate the former while California, Illinois, and Texas illustrate the latter. In recent years several states have put all public two-year colleges under a single statewide board with no local institutional boards. This is true of Colorado, Massachusetts, Minnesota, and Virginia. In a very few states, including New York State, the governing board of the State University is also the statewide coordinating board of the public two-year colleges.

Governance of a community-junior college, however, like that of other complex educational institutions, involves more than the board of trustees or official controlling body which holds final legal authority over it and subsequent approval by an official state agency. Basic policies and broad operating procedures take shape not only from the statutes and chartering actions of state legislatures and controlling educational agencies but also from the day-to-day deliberations, analyses of local conditions bearing on the college, studies and recommendations for change advanced by the president, members of the administration, the faculty, and students. All these groups in addition to boards and councils representing the general public find a voice in the governance of the college by means of participation in the organised structure for student, faculty, and administration involvement in institutional decision making. By this machinery, which is always an item of close scrutiny by the education team when a two-year college is up for membership in a higher education accrediting association, new policies, programs, and institutional adaptations are initiated, examined, and acted upon as necessary from the lowest to the highest levels of operation.

Both the complexity and the manner of functioning of this decision-making machinery at work in a state's system of public community-junior colleges may be illustrated by a hypothetical case of a Community College X in State Y and its introduction of a new curriculum.

The college has an existing curriculum in Electrical Technology and another in Mechanical Technology, both leading to the associate in applied science degree and both preparing graduates to take entry-level positions as technicians in the respective fields. For each curriculum the college has an industrial advisory committee composed chiefly of representatives of industrial firms in the area.

On the occasion of the semi-annual meeting of the Mechanical Technology advisory committee, a committee member suggests that a joint meeting be held with the Electrical Technology advisory committee, to explore the desirability of proposing a new curriculum representing a wedding of the two technologies into one - electro-mechanical technology. It is pointed out that in the computer industry, a computer maintenance technician is no longer adequately prepared if he possesses only the skills and knowledge characteristic of either the electrical technician or the mechanical technician.

After the joint meeting of the two advisory committees, a recommendation is advanced to the president of the college. He refers the assignment of an exploratory study to the standing college committee of faculty and students on Curriculum and Instruction, which uses as a guide the following state outline of specifications for a new curriculum proposal:

## OUTLINE OF A NEW CURRICULUM AND/OR OPTION PROPOSAL

### 1. PURPOSE OF THE CURRICULUM

State whether or not this is a curriculum designed primarily to 1) prepare for further education at an upper-division college or 2) prepare for employment. List occupational titles, if any, for which the graduates will be prepared. Mention specific industries, if any, that will be served. Is it to be offered during the day or evening?

### 2. NEED FOR THE CURRICULUM

A complete justification is required, including, if applicable, the results of a survey and copies of letters of request from business, industry, or labor.

### 3. POTENTIAL ENROLMENT

Conduct a study to determine the student need and the eventual placement possibilities. Project the anticipated enrolment as far as possible, but at least five years.

### 4. POSSIBLE CONFLICTS WITH EXISTING CURRICULA

List and describe similar curricula being offered within commuting radius of your college. Explain why the existing curricula do not meet all present and anticipated needs.

### 5. ABILITY TO PROVIDE FOR THE CURRICULUM

a) Show that the proposed curriculum is within the scope of the two-year college program and that it is within the ability of the faculty and administrative staff to conduct such a curriculum.

Provide as an addendum a one-page vitae on each available faculty member you anticipate will instruct in the new curriculum.

b) State whether or not the proposed curriculum can be offered without increase in classrooms and laboratories.

Describe in an addendum the physical facilities, classrooms, laboratories and shops, necessary to implement the program. Special attention should be devoted to clinical facilities for health-related curricula. Indicate in the addendum whether or not each of these facilities is currently available or will need to be added or increased to support the proposed curriculum.

6. NECESSARY ADDITIONS TO FACULTY

How many additional faculty members will be required for this new curriculum? Give their titles and indicate the work load for each position. Provide as an addendum a description of the qualifications sought in prospective additional faculty members to implement the program.

7. NECESSARY ADDITIONAL INSTRUCTIONAL MATERIALS

List the additional items of equipment and other instructional materials that will be required in order to implement the curriculum.

a) Describe in an addendum the additional equipment needed. Provide estimates of its cost, including installation.

b) Describe in an addendum library holdings available or to be acquired in support of the proposed curriculum. For example, numbers of journals, books, films, etc. , listing a few of the major journals and books by title.

8. NECESSARY ADDITIONAL BUILDING SPACE

If space is required in addition to that already available to the College, describe the needed space in detail. Can the space be rented? If so, give the annual rental, location, amount of space and tentative conditions of rental contract. If additional buildings are to be erected, indicate where, the amount of space required, and the estimated cost.

9. ANALYSIS OF COSTS AND INCOME

Make a complete projection of estimated costs and a corresponding budget for this new curriculum. Be sure to include administrative overhead, clerical and maintenance costs, supplies -

as is normally done in preparing the college budget. Prepare a summary analysis of anticipated income from tuition, from the local sponsor, and the State. Include amounts from gifts, income from the operation of part-time classes, etc.

10. CURRICULUM OUTLINE (TENTATIVE)

Prepare a curriculum outline, listing the subjects, laboratory hours, and classroom hours, by term. Be sure to total each column.

11. LOCAL RESOLUTIONS

Transmit local resolutions by the college board of trustees, council, local civic bodies, advisory committees, professional organisations, and others.

Upon eventual passage by the faculty as a whole, the curriculum proposal is placed by the college president on the agenca of the next monthly meeting of the college board of trustees. Once adopted by the community college board of trustees, the curriculum proposal is forwarded for the approval of the state board for community-junior colleges. After review of the proposal in the office of the state director of community-junior colleges, recommendation is advanced to the state board. Upon approval of the state board of trustees at its monthly meeting, the curriculum is legally established. Then, since the laws of the state call for coordination of all higher education programs in a statewide plan overseen by a state board of regents, the curriculum proposal is advanced to the regents for validation of consistency with the statewide plan. When cleared in this respect, the college is free to announce and start instruction in the new program.

Thus, there is interaction among levels of government as illustrated in the flow chart on page 108.

## Analysis and Prospects

The interaction of institutional, local community, and state levels of interest in the governance of community-junior colleges is a natural consequence of the purposes, programs, and history of these colleges as described earlier. Although clearly the voice of state agencies is becoming stronger in the governance of community-junior colleges, laws and regulations assure that there is not a heavy-handed imposition of the state will on the colleges. The initiative, typically, is the

Figure 2. FLOW CHART OF CURRICULUM APPROVAL

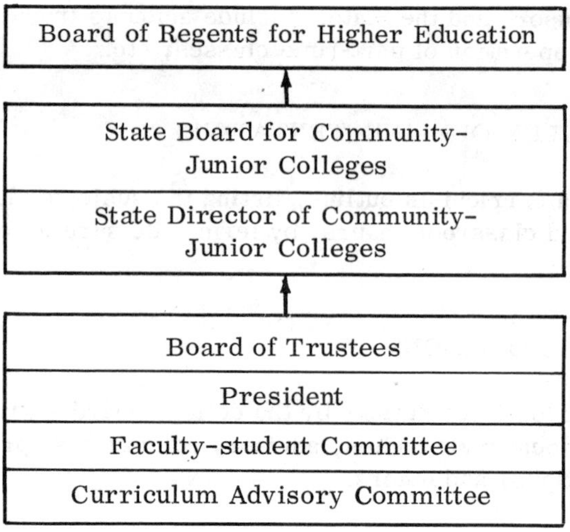


college's to take, subject to reasoned approval at each succeeding higher level.

A community-junior college may experience more difficulty in achieving local resolution and adoption of an institutional decision than it does afterwards at the higher levels. Trustees and administrators may chafe at an emerging stronger role for the faculty in institutional governance as collective employee bargaining laws are adopted by state legislatures, as they have been recently, for example, in California, Hawaii, Michigan, New York and Pennsylvania. Students, too, have been seeking an even stronger role in institutional governance, some having asked for a seat on the board of trustees. However, legal restrictions to a legal minor holding such a public position as a community-junior college trusteeship now exist in many states. If 18-year olds are ultimately given the voting franchise on a widespread basis among the 50 states, however, perhaps this bar to trusteeship may also be removed.

There is also to be noted among the several groups of personnel associated with two-year colleges a herding phenomenon among the various interest groups in the community-junior colleges. The presidents in a state generally have a statewide Association of Presidents of Public Community-Junior Colleges. There is usually, also, a Faculty Council of the Community-Junior Colleges, an Association of Academic Vice-Presidents and Deans, the Business Officers Associations, the Association of Marketing Educators, Two-year College Physics Instructors, etc. All these organisations seek to wield influence in the development of laws, policies, rules and regulations favourable to their group interests and sometimes to their colleges as a class of institution. From all indications, this splintering of interests and simultaneous seeking by each to have a recognized and stronger voice in institutional and statewide decision making will increase rather than decrease in the foreseeable future.

Of particular importance to the question of what changes in operational governing procedures will occur during the next decade is the rapidly growing trend toward formal organisation of faculties for purposes of collective action in negotiating contracts of employment. As already indicated, several states have already passed laws requiring governing boards to hold such negotiations. Others are moving to do so. As a result, all professional faculty associations display a new interest in contracts on working conditions which deal often not only with questions of salary and fringe benefits but also with such more basic academic issues as teaching loads, availability of faculty for counseling students, and faculty participation in college committee work. This growing interest is true of the American Association of University Professors and the Junior College Faculty Association, affiliate of the National Education Association, as well as the more clearly union-related American Federation of Teachers. Already the faculty's role in governing institutions is moving from traditional structures stressing an integrated "college community" where students, faculty and administrators are viewed as colleagues in a common venture to new arrangements which emphasize "management versus worker" roles in college operations. How far-reaching the already noticeable divisive effects will ultimately be remain to be seen.

to [illegible] in the development of [illegible] and [illegible] to their group interests and [illegible] as a [illegible] of [illegible] interests and [illegible] to have a recognized and stronger [illegible] and [illegible] will [illegible] rather than decrease in the [illegible] future.

[illegible] importance to [illegible] in [illegible] Others are [illegible] As [illegible] of contracts of work [illegible] with [illegible] of salary and fringe benefits but also with such more [illegible] as [illegible] of [illegible] in [illegible]

[illegible]

# V

## METHODS OF FINANCING

Varying by states as to legal status and governance, the community-junior colleges naturally vary among the states also as to modes of financing. Having their origins in the earliest instances as 13th and 14th grade extensions of the public school systems, the community-junior colleges have tended to receive more support from local tax funds than have other types of colleges and universities. Likewise, the typically lower tuition rates and student fees in the community-junior colleges have stemmed from their historic relationship with the free elementary and secondary school systems.

As the trend to regard the community-junior colleges as higher education institutions rather than extended secondary schools has increased, however, the financing pattern has changed, away from the public school financing pattern. Nearly all community-junior colleges now require some degree of tuition and general fee charges, although the California community-junior colleges, largest number among the states, continue to be tuition-free. The community-junior colleges generally receive more support from gifts and grants than do the high schools. The proportion of support they receive from state funds is comparable to that of the bachelor-degree colleges rather than that of the secondary schools. On the other hand, the distribution of state aid to community-junior colleges is often by formula, as with the public schools, rather than by direct appropriation from the state legislature as is typical of funding for the four-year colleges and universities.

Comparative examinations of operating revenue sources in the mid-1950s, and again in the mid-1960s, will illustrate some shifts making an appearance in recent years.

It will be noted:

1. The community-junior colleges are holding firmly to a principle that tax revenues and student revenues should

Table 3. OPERATIONAL REVENUES OF PUBLIC TWO-YEAR COLLEGES BY SOURCE[1]

Percentages

| | TUITION AND FEES | STATE GOVERN-MENT | LOCAL GOVERN-MENT | FEDERAL GOVERN-MENT | OTHER |
|---|---|---|---|---|---|
| 1955-56 ........ | 13.8 | 34.2 | 36.6 | 1.1 | 14.3 |
| 1965-66 ........ | 14.5 | 37.7 | 37.6 | 4.4 | 5.8 |

1. Median percentages, the states taken collectively.

NOTE: Data for 1955-56 adapted from S.V. Martorana and D.G. Morrison, Patterns of Organization and Support of Public Two-Year Colleges, Washington, Government Printing Office, 1959, p. 5.
Data for 1965-66 adapted from Paul F. Mertins, Financial Statistics of Higher Education, Washington, Government Printing Office, 1969.

constitute their major sources of operating funds. These sources made up about 90% of the current operating income in both 1955-56 and 1965-66.

2. The tendency is for the state government to move towards providing more funds than the local government. In 1970, New York State, as a very recent example, has increased its state share from 33 1/3% to 40% for community colleges offering an approvable "full-opportunity program" (open-admissions) plan to the State University Board of Trustees.

3. The Federal government is increasing its participation. Even though the proportion is still modest, an aggregate of nearly $30 million was given to two-year colleges by the Federal government in 1965-66, and most of this to the public community-junior colleges.

As to capital revenues, the author surveyed 18 of the leading states for 1967-68 fiscal year data, and it was found that the median percentage of revenue from the state was 49%, from the locality 40%, and from the Federal government 9%.

An earlier investigation (1960-61) had shown that over half the funding plans for various types of two-year colleges throughout the United States required total capital financing by the locality while another large proportion required total capital financing by the state. * It is clear, then, that a shift is now occurring and that the current practice among the states is to expect both state and local funds for capital financing.

The Federal government, commencing with the enactment of the Higher Education Facilities Act of 1963 during the Johnson administration, became an increasingly significant source of capital construction funds for community-junior colleges. This new breakthrough, Federal legislation in support of community-junior colleges, specifically identified in the statute, provided 398.6 million dollars in the period 1963-1970 for all types of facilities needed by these colleges to keep pace with enrolment increases. **

The principal functions of current fund expenditure were found in 1965-66 to be, approximately, 60% Instruction and Departmental Research; 15% General Administration; and 10% Maintenance and Operation of Plants; with no other function exceeding 4% (Libraries). Precision in such percentage studies is difficult to achieve because of differences in accounting practices and definitions of terms among the states and even among colleges within a state. Standardization is increasingly needed as the trend grows to make inter-institutional and interstate comparison - by state-level higher education bodies, by state budget offices, and by national organisations and agencies. The growth of PPBS (Planning, Programming, Budgeting System), nationally, should be of some help in the direction of standardization. In PPBS, requests for funding are made in terms of the college's program objectives, such as, for example, a thrust towards more comprehensive curricular programming or an increased emphasis on student personnel services. The fiscal impacts which each of the programs will have on the various budget categories (instruction and departmental research, general administration, library, extension and public service, etc.) is then analysed and fiscal resources budgeted.

## Analysis and Prospects

Although past practice has been to rely on state and local tax funds and on student tuition and fees as the principal sources of operating revenues for community-junior colleges, the role of the Federal

* Data adapted from D.G. Morrison and S.V. Martorana, State Formulas for the Support of Public Two-year Colleges, Washington, Government Printing Office, 1962.

** Telephone report to author from Bureau of Higher Education, U.S. Office of Education, Washington, D.C.

government is now becoming increasingly significant. This trend is even more evident in regard to the funding of construction costs.

The financing of community-junior colleges requires more research, and, certainly, more refined fiscal procedures must be devised. Two notable efforts in these directions are now under way.

First, the new Management Information Systems Program of the Western Interstate Compact in Higher Education is studying the refinement of terminology, better forms for gathering data, and improved accounting and financial reporting procedures. Second, the National Educational Finance Project financed by the U. S. Office of Education, with a Satellite Study of Community-Junior Colleges, is under way at the University of Florida. The focus of attention here is on the determination of community-junior college instructional unit costs and related analyses of revenues and expenditures. These two efforts will go far towards regularizing current vagaries in community-junior college financing.

As the number of community-junior colleges grows and enrolments increase, the attention and concern of the supporting public on the costs of operation, productivity, and efficiency of these institutions will surely rise. Accordingly, the call for more precise data on instructional costs will grow and demands will increase for more penetrating analyses of use of resources provided. Heretofore, the non-comparability of fiscal data and information from one state to another was accepted because of the aforementioned state responsibility for education and the variations in practice and historical structure from state to state. Already this acceptance is breaking down and the public is now beginning to insist on educational accountability. The primary impetus to the initiation of the WICHE Management Information Systems Project was the steadily increasing pressure by the 13 states of the region on the colleges and universities in the region to be accountable for use of fiscal resources provided them by the states. The three primary objectives stated in the WICHE project proposal for funds from the U. S. Office of Education to carry it on are indicative of the motivating pressures as well as of some future implications that can be expected to flow from the use of the project's findings. The three purposes were stated to be those of 1) promoting the development of various aids to more knowledgeable resource allocations within institutions and agencies of higher education, 2) enhancing the ability of institutions and agencies to exchange and report comparable information, and 3) provide training resources for personnel to make the systems operational. With added Federal Office of Education support the WICHE program has now become nationwide, reaching over 500 participating institutions and agencies, including community-junior colleges, in all 50 states. Already it has identified among its several "sub-project" developments one designed to formulate "Higher Education Cost Indicators" which indexes would serve to assess needs for new national higher educational policy much as currently accepted "national economic indicators" are used to guide formulation of necessary new economic policies in the nation. *

Clearly the decade of the seventies will bring the community-junior colleges more and more into these kinds of studies. In the process questions of whether cost/benefits to the supporting public are greater when post-secondary education is provided by these institutions rather than by others like single purpose vocational-technical institutes or colleges and universities offering bachelors and higher degrees as well as programs of two-year, associate-degree or shorter duration, will come more sharply into focus.

* Report by Ben Lawrence, Project Director, Management Information Systems Project, Western Interstate Commission on Higher Education, at annual conference of National Council of State Directors of Community-Junior Colleges, Denver, Colorado, November 9, 1970.

# VI

## DECISIONS ABOUT ESTABLISHMENT AND LOCATION

Late in the fifties a nationwide survey of factors used to judge the need for a community college and to approve its establishment determined that the primary considerations were 1) size of enrolment likely to be attracted to the institution, 2) ability of the locality to contribute to the costs of operating and housing the new programs, and 3) the proximity and accessibility of other post high-school educational institutions which could be affected by the starting of a new college. * With one exception these factors continue today to be paramount. The exception is that of accommodation to statewide planning for higher education. During the past two decades the United States has experienced a great advance in statewide and regional planning of higher education. This is evident in the creation of state-level boards of higher education with official responsibility to plan for and to coordinate the development of post high-school education on a statewide basis. Since World War II there has been a rapid acceleration of such state-coordinating boards. Between 1945-57 seven states established coordinating boards; between 1959-65, fifteen additional states did so. ** As a result of the emergence of these boards, which plan for all types of higher educational developments, local and state-level boards responsible only for community-junior college programs need to project for the future in a manner that is acceptable to and fits validly into the larger design. In the process both helps and hindrances to the community-junior college projections occur.

Decisions about location of community-junior colleges may be illustrated, again, by a description of the practices in a hypothetical situation in State X.

* D.G. Morrison and S.V. Martorana, Criteria for the Establishment of 2-Year Colleges, pp. 61-67, Washington, Government Printing Office, 1960.

** E.G. Palola, T. Lehmann, and W.R. Blischke, Higher Education by Design: The Sociology of Planning, pp. 56f, Berkeley, University of California, 1970.

The State Board for Community-Junior Colleges has had a master planning responsibility for the establishment of community colleges ever since its inception just after World War II. The law creating the Board included among its "planning functions": "Formulate a long-range master plan and make recommendations for the establishment of community colleges in areas most suitable for and most in need of such institutions". Similarly, the State Board of Regents for Higher Education has legal authority and responsibility for development of a statewide Master Plan for all post high-school education.

The first Master Plan accepted by State Board of Community-Junior Colleges contained conclusions based on careful area-by-area surveys, that: "Each of the 11 economic areas in State X requires one or more two-year institutions". Succeeding revisions of the Master Plan, at four-year intervals, have specified a number of counties where in the Board's judgment new community colleges should be established. The actual responsibility, however, for determining the need for and initiating the establishment of a community college rests with the community itself. The State Board for Community-Junior Colleges offers its staff resources to a prospective local sponsor throughout the process of establishment.

Following is a condensed version of the first nine steps for the establishment of a community college in State X as contained in a booklet, Realizing a Community College, which is made available in quantity to local citizens' committees:

1. Consult the State Board for Community-Junior Colleges.

2. The local community forms a community college committee.

3. The committee prepares an educational needs study.

   - This study should analyse such factors as present and potential student population, interest of parents, student desires for higher education, personnel needs of local employers and the financial ability to support a community college. The local supporting area shall have a true valuation of at least $150 million and an assessed valuation of at least $75 million. Superintendents, principals and guidance counselors of local schools, and others intimately acquainted with local educational problems are sources of advice and information. The proposed college shall have a potential enrolment of at least 500 full-time equivalent students within four years of its opening. Local business and industry should be able to provide appropriate and continued opportunities for graduates of the college.

4. The local committee presents the study with recommendations to the State Director of Community-Junior Colleges.

IF APPROVED,

5. The State Director requests formal application from the local committee in the form of a resolution for consideration by the State Board for Community-Junior Colleges.

IF APPROVED,

6. The State Board requests approval by the Board of Regents for Higher Education, the statewide higher education coordinating agency for validation in relation to the State Board's Master Plan.

IF APPROVED,

7. The question of establishment of the new two-year college district is put before the electorate of the district for formal vote.

IF APPROVED,

8. The State Board calls for election of the Board of trustees and the community college is established.

Analysis and Prospects

The location of community-junior colleges in a state's system of post-high school education is not a random process. A statewide master plan defines the gross regional needs. Citizen committee actions based on educational needs studies are the prelude to the assumption of responsibility by a specific local initiating agency and ultimate approval at the state level. Factors of proximity to pre-existing institutions and avoidance of undue competition are considered. Again, the process of decision recognizes the need to balance judiciously and equitably the interests of the local community to be served, and of the state.

Indeed, evidence is growing that the process of planning for establishment and location of new community-junior colleges will involve the national level of interest. This is not to say that the Federal government will become a part of the approval decision-making mechanism, but to recognize that national-level agencies and, indeed, Federal governmental agencies seem to be moving toward greater participation in identifying needs and criteria for locating new community-junior colleges. The best evidence of this emerging involvement of national-level agencies is the impact already produced on public opinion and attitudes toward the community-junior college movement and a new thrust for its rapid growth made by the Carnegie Commission on Higher Education. This Commission suggests that criteria of population density and measures of accessibility of post-high school programs drawn from the states which have made exemplary progress in community-junior college education should be goals to be attained throughout the nation.* The likelihood is strong that this will become a widely accepted national objective supported generally by both the powerful national-level educational associations like the American Council of Education and the Education Commission of the States and by the Federal governmental agencies which help mould new legislative proposals in the Congress and the White House. As already noted in Chapter I of this paper, were the proposals of the Carnegie Commission to be translated to programs of joint local, state, federal action there would be a community college within commuting distance of virtually the entire population of the nation.

* Carnegie Commission on Higher Education, The Open-Door Colleges, New York, McGraw-Hill Book Company, 1970.

# VII

## INTER-COLLEGE AND UNIVERSITY RELATIONSHIPS

Overlapping the first two years of the bachelor's degree-granting college or university from the beginning, the community-junior college has been regarded with suspicion by many of its institutional brethren: suspicion that it harbors overweening ambitions to escalate to baccalaureate degree-granting status, and thus eventual rivalry; suspicion that its "open door" admissions policy, its non-requirement of the Ph. D. degree of its faculty, its non-emphasis on faculty research and publication, and the inclusion in its comprehensive curriculum offerings of vocational studies - all may combine to downgrade and dishonour higher education, to which the community-junior college legally claims to belong. Attitudinal biases sometimes die slowly among academic brethren, but progress toward their eradication is being made. One scarcely hears any more the muttered "glorified high school" or "if you call that a college ...". The biases linger covertly, however, and do most of their damage when articulation is to be forged between the two-year college programs and those of the upper division in the four-year colleges.

The regional accrediting association accords to the faculty of every member college autonomy in setting its own degree requirements. As a result, department chairmen in colleges and universities of advanced levels are inclined to assess the courses of the junior colleges from which students seek transfer in these terms: "How do their faculty ... their catalogue descriptions of courses ... their course syllabi ... their textbooks ... their laboratory facilities ... compare with ours?" The stickler for precise parallelism in the past has refused admission altogether or required that courses be repeated. Increasingly, however, as the baccalaureate degree-granting colleges have gained experimental evidence that community-junior college graduates can perform creditably in the upper-division studies of their institutions, even the most cautious of the advanced colleges are becoming more liberal in their appraisal of transfer relationships. And, of course, smooth articulation is a sine qua non in a mass education scheme where heaviest reliance is placed on the two-year college as the first higher education experience for most high school graduates.

The question of acceptability of performance of "junior college transfers" in the upper-division (junior and senior) years of baccalaureate colleges and universities is one of the most researched in American higher education. * The results of the research consistently establish the fact that students of comparable ability do equally well in study at the advanced levels regardless of whether the students go through the immediate post high-school level in a two-year college or as freshmen and sophomores in four-year or larger colleges and universities. Yet this type of research will surely continue to attract attention because of the growing numbers of students who will pass through community-junior colleges on their paths to bachelors' and higher degrees. According to latest statistics available from the U. S. Office of Education there were in the fall of 1968, 7,571,636 students in higher education in the United States of which total 23.7% were enrolled in two-year colleges. The growth in proportion of first-time students in college is particularly significant. In 1967, the two-year colleges enrolled 38.1% of all such students; a year later the percentage rose to 41.5%, clearly indicating the relative increase in two-year over four-year college enrolments. **

Articulation between occupational*** programs of the community-junior colleges and upper-division programs of the four-year colleges is an especially sticky problem. The occupational curriculum by design includes one-half to two-thirds of its content in knowledge and experiences calculated to make the graduate immediately employable at the entry level of a technical or middle management cluster of positions (the remainder of the content being liberal arts and sciences, or general education). The student who follows such a curriculum but then has a change of mind near or after graduation and seeks transfer rather than employment will usually find himself penalized by loss of credits. It may take him as long as three additional years to complete the requirements for the conventional baccalaureate degree. For this reason, there is now increasing pressure for the four-year colleges to create a new bachelor's degree, the Bachelor of Technology or the Bachelor of Science in Technology, especially for the would-be transfer from an associate in applied science degree curriculum.

* For example, D.M. Knoell and L.L. Medsker, From Junior to Senior College: A National Study of the Transfer Student, Washington, American Council on Education, 1965.

** Data for 1967 from Marjorie Chandler and Mabel Rice, Opening Fall Enrolment in Higher Education, 1967, p. 7; Washington, Government Printing Office, 1968. Data for 1968 from M. Chandler, Opening Fall Enrolment in Higher Education, Part A: Summary Data 1968, pp. 6, 26. Washington, Government Printing Office, 1969.

*** "Terminal" is rarely used now.

A complicating factor in the transfer of A. A. S. graduates has been the differing theories of placement of subject matter held by the four-year and the two-year colleges. The latter may, for example, concentrate a full range of Accounting courses within the two-year span of the A. A. S. degree curriculum in Accounting. The four-year college says: "We will not honor credits for a course in Cost Accounting taken in your second year. With us, it is a fourth-year course. We simply do not believe that a student has the proper foundation of general and related courses, or the maturity, to attack Cost Accounting until he is a fourth-year student". The two-year college counters by saying: "Ah, yes, but we have had students go on to complete success in other colleges with this arrangement. Furthermore, we have had students return informally to us, having been required to repeat Cost Accounting in your fourth-year, and they report it as a waste of time - needless and costly duplication". This problem, quite frankly, remains to be solved.

A concluding problem must be mentioned - the paucity of student financial aid available to the transfer student. National studies have shown that transfer students from two-year colleges, although on the average from less affluent backgrounds than "native" four-year college students, tend to receive financial aid with only about one-half the frequency of entering freshmen in the four-year colleges. * A 1970 survey of a sample of seven four-year campuses of State University of New York confirms this finding - 15% of their freshmen but only 7% of their transfer students received Federal financial aid. In addition, it was found that one-half of the transfers who were eligible for federal awards and who applied for them did not receive any aid because funds were not available.

Financial-aid officers mention four primary factors relating to this discrepancy:

1. Limited financial aid funds.

2. Admissions practices, which result in transfer students being admitted after most aid funds have been committed.

3. Failure of the transferring student's previous institution to forward the necessary information on aid formerly received by the student.

4. Tendency of a few institutions to give freshmen priority over transfers when awarding aid.

* Warren Willingham and Nurhan Findikyan, "Transfer Students: Who's Moving from Where to Where and What Determines Who's Admitted?", College Board Review, Summer, 1969.

It seems clear that Master Plan promises of an "assured opportunity" for qualified graduates of two-year colleges to transfer into other State University of New York institutions would be more realizable if financial aid were available to more potential transfers in need of it. Exploratory investigations are now under way as to the feasibility of appropriating special state funds for financial aid to transfers from two-year colleges.

## Analysis and Prospects

Although it has been a half-century since the junior colleges became numerous enough in the United States to warrant forming their own association, The American Association of Junior Colleges, articulation with senior colleges continues to be one of their major problems. A community college president recently wrote in an ironic vein to a state official responsible for fostering articulation in substance as follows: "I really enjoyed our recent seventeenth annual conference on articulation at which we cited the same problems and received the same inconclusive answers as at the sixteenth, the fifteenth, the fourteenth ... " Regrettably, even in a state with one of the longest histories of public junior college development, California, there remain articulation problems in the 1970s.

The late William Fels, then associate provost, Columbia University, at a 1957 conference on articulation in New York State, cited the four-year colleges' "narcissism of small differences" as a major etiological factor, and prophesied that articulation as a systemic problem would yield only to the "Chinese water-torture method ... drip common sense and goodwill drop by drop upon these problems until they vanish". *

There is little reason to expect that the problems of articulation of two-year to four-year programs of study will be resolved during the years immediately ahead. Rather there are good reasons to believe the problems will accentuate before they ease. There can be little question of the fact that currently the major state universities and the faculty in these institutions like the University of California, Illinois State University, and the University of Wisconsin, and the State University of New York hold the key to success in resolving positively the continuing issue of effective transfer of students from community-junior colleges to advanced studies in programs of higher education culminating in bachelors' and higher degrees. How they will finally react

* 2 + 2=?, Proceedings of the Conference on Two-Year and Four-Year College Relationships in the State of New York, p. 45; Albany, The University of the State of New York, The State Education Department, 1957.

to the growing pressure on them to accommodate the increasing numbers of transfer students will bear watching. The rising proportion of students enrolling in community-junior colleges for their first post high-school educational experience, the growing strength of community-junior college faculty in professional academic associations and agencies, the expanding number of occupationally directed programs the graduates of whom seek a free choice between entering the labor force immediately after graduation or continuing in programs leading to the bachelor's degree - all these factors which complicate the articulation question can be predicted to grow in magnitude and intensity during the foreseeable future. Where the end lies at this point cannot be seen.

# VIII

## RELATIONSHIP TO COMMON SCHOOL SYSTEMS

Articulation with the high schools is not as severe a problem as articulation with upper-division programs. The academy-high-school roots of the junior-college idea have been referred to in earlier chapters. The junior colleges in the Midwest and West represented simply an added 13th and 14th grade program in the local high school building. Many of the same faculty members served both high school and junior college. The same principal or superintendent served as chief executive officer for the two institutions. Articulation, therefore, presented little if any problem in these circumstances.

In due time, however, the advantages of the students continuing within the same physical plant for both levels of program began to be questioned. Would it not be better psychologically for high school graduates to have a sense of "going to college" by leaving the building in which they had done four years of school work and progressing to a discrete junior college? The history to date has substantiated an affirmative answer to this question. There are few public junior colleges housed under the same roof with a high school any more, and in the few cases where this situation does prevail it is usually temporary while a new junior college makes plans for its own buildings elsewhere.

Separation of physical plants, however, does not generally mean a deterioration of close articulation and effective academic co-operation. The college admissions requirements are kept in fairly close relationship to the high school graduation requirements for academic diplomas. High school faculty and counselors typically maintain considerable understanding of the programs and nature of instruction offered in the two-year colleges' programs of liberal arts and sciences. In the fields of vocational and technical studies, however, the degree of understandings that exist and the smooth articulation of academic experience of students proceeding from high-school business, industrial, or health services programs to further study in similar fields in two-year colleges is much less. As a consequence, two educational efforts of apparently divergent types are now operative. On the one hand, some common school system-community college joint curriculum development programs have emerged, like the Richmond Plan in California. These seek to develop new joint faculty and program connecting links to improve the sequence of studies from high-school through community-college levels. On the other hand, a new type of institution is developing, the "area vocational-technical school", which disclaims both the comprehensive high school and the comprehensive community-junior college. Aided considerably by the increased Federal funds for vocational education provided by the Vocational Education Act of 1965 and 1968 amendments, the area vocational-technical schools provide only this kind of instruction and in many states encompass programs from 9th grade high-school level through 14th year community-junior college level. Interestingly, different states are reacting differently to these divergent approaches to high-school and community-junior college relationships, such states as California, Washington, Illinois, Michigan, and New York holding to the comprehensive community-junior college to articulate with high-school level programs of all types, and others, like Minnesota, Oklahoma, and Kentucky, moving to strengthen the 13th and 14th year vocational and technical programs in the area vocational schools.

A measure adopted in most of the states for the benefit of returning World War II veterans is the High School Equivalency Examination. Persons who have failed to complete high school for any reason will usually find pass marks on this general-education examination acceptable for admission to most junior colleges. The "brush-up" course which prepares one for the examination is usually offered in the high schools as an evening, adult education course.

## Analysis and Prospects

Articulation between junior colleges and high schools is considered by this author to be less of a problem than articulation between junior and senior colleges. This is not to say it is well done nor that it does not merit attention. Quite the contrary, as more and more two-year colleges develop, more attention to high-school and community-junior college relationships is needed. The problems, however, are more manageable by virtue of the common local interests in the high schools and community-junior colleges. The author is mindful, however, that not all his professional colleagues so view the relative magnitudes of the two problems. Indeed, there is good reason to be concerned lest the community-junior colleges in their drive for full acceptance as institutions of higher learning, often prompted by an academic status conscious faculty and pressures of local civic pride to have a "real college" in the locality, will break from a close, sound articulation with a lower high-school level with negative results on the commitment of the community-junior colleges to retain "open admissions" policies and programs which serve the students' individual educational interest and needs". Dr. Edmund J. Gleazer, Jr. , executive director of the American Association of Junior Colleges, has publicly decried the community-junior college which in its desire to avoid the label of "glorified high school" would spend inordinate time and effort in identifying itself with higher education, thus, perhaps, permitting "a wide chasm" to develop between itself and the high schools in its service area. Articulation both ways must be a continuing concern of the community-junior college which is to fulfill its functions optimally.

facility, will begin from a [illegible] sound orientation with respect to high-school level with negative results on the commitment of the community junior college to [illegible] [illegible] and programs which serve the students' individual and community interests and needs." Dr. Edmund J. Gleazer, Jr., executive director of the American Association of Junior Colleges, has stated that "the community college [illegible] a desire to [illegible] the label of [illegible] school [illegible] and [illegible] [illegible] [illegible] [illegible] [illegible] [illegible] [illegible] [illegible] [illegible] [illegible] [illegible] [illegible] [illegible] [illegible] [illegible] [illegible] [illegible] [illegible] [illegible] [illegible] [illegible] [illegible] [illegible] [illegible] [illegible] [illegible] [illegible] [illegible] [illegible] [illegible] [illegible] [illegible] [illegible] [illegible] [illegible] [illegible] is to facilitate function effectually.

# IX

## CURRICULUM CONTENT AND STRUCTURE OF STUDIES

Consistent with the broad and pervasive educational objectives usually set for them, the comprehensive community-junior colleges offer a wide array of instructional programs. They range in length from a full two-year academic program (approximately 60 semester hours of credit), leading to the associate degree, through one-year or six-month diploma courses, to programs of only a few weeks for purposes of adult education and community services. A state with a well-developed system of community-junior colleges will find over 200 different occupational programs (vocational and technical curricula) geared to direct employment of students after attendance and completion of the program at the two-year college. Such programs include offerings in four broad areas of curriculum classification: business - data processing, accounting, etc.; industry - civil technology, electrical technology, drafting, etc.; health - nursing, x-ray technology, etc.; and community/public service - police science, fire science, social counselor aide, teacher auxiliary, etc. The colleges need this broad range of curriculum comprehensiveness in order to make good their claims to being open-admissions or "full-opportunity" colleges and not to have the claimed "open door" to the college become a "revolving door".

It will be noted that the curricula of the two-year colleges fall into two main types, the university- (or college-) parallel and the occupational. As the names imply, the university-parallel curriculum is comparable to the studies of the first two years of the baccalaureate curriculum, while the occupational, a blend of general and specialized courses, prepares for immediate employment at the technician or middle-management level of business and industry or at the artisan or skilled labor level of employment. Variants from the main types include General Studies and Individual Studies. The General Studies is much like the university-parallel Liberal Arts and Sciences curriculum, except that the courses are usually less rigorous and less further-study oriented, since it is postulated that the General Studies curriculum will represent the non-transfer-bound student's final exposure to formal full-time education before assuming the responsibilities of citizenship. The Individual Studies is not so much a discrete curriculum as a flexible plan of studies whereby the student, under competent advisement, makes eclectic choices of courses from the full array of curricula offered by the college.

Enrolment proportions in the two main types of program differ by states. In California, for instance, it is said that two-thirds of the public two-year college students imply a wish to prepare for transfer by enrolling in university-parallel programs, but that only half of these students (or one-third of the total students) actually do transfer. In New York on the other hand, 55-60% of the students enroll in occupational programs but of these it has been noted that there is a rising trend to seek transfer (as high as 40% of the graduates of some "terminal" curricula in recent years have sought further study rather than immediate entry into employment). The difficulty of satisfactory articulation in these circumstances was mentioned in Chapter VII.

A variety of national and state agencies provides helpful guidance in the construction of curricula for the two-year colleges. Two examples of national agencies are the American Society for Engineering Education, with its publication Characteristics of Excellence in Engineering Technology Education, and the American Association of Junior Colleges Curriculum Commission which fostered a project report, Technical Education in the Junior College/New Programs for New Jobs by Professor Norman C. Harris, University of Michigan.

Two examples of state agencies, both from New York, are the New York State Community College Health Careers Project, which produced curriculum materials for 10 paraprofessional health careers, and the New York State Education Department which since 1950 has maintained Administrative Policies for the Associate Degrees. The initial issue of these policies was quite specific as to subject matter distribution, for example:

"ASSOCIATE IN ARTS (A. A.)

Total program, 60 semester hours or more, but less than 120.

The course of study leading to this degree should be an organised curriculum, composed essentially of courses in the liberal arts. To be specific, at least 80% of the program in terms of credit hours should comprise work in the following fields:

1. Communication Skills (written and spoken English) and Literature in English - a minimum of 12 semester hours.

2. Social Studies (human relations, government, history, economics, sociology, psychology, etc.) - a minimum of 12 semester hours.

3. Mathematics and Science - a minimum of 9 semester hours.

4. Selections from the following group (frequently known as the humanities): foreign language and literature, drama, philosophy, fine arts, etc. - a minimum of 6 semester hours.

It is to be understood that, instead of separate courses in the above subjects, an institution may integrate them into other courses or programs, but such courses or programs all together should devote to these subjects amounts of time equivalent at least to the minimum hours indicated above.

"ASSOCIATE IN APPLIED SCIENCE (A. A. S.)

Total program, 60 semester hours or more but less than 120, to include content in both Areas I and II, as specified below:

I. 1. General education - a minimum of 20 semester hours, including 1 Communication Skills (written and spoken English) - a minimum of 6 semester hours.

2. Social Studies (human relations, government and citizenship, history, economics, sociology, psychology, etc.) - a minimum of 6 semester hours.

3. Mathematics and Science - a minimum of 6 semester hours.

It is to be understood that, instead of separate courses in the above subjects, an institution may integrate them into other courses or programs, but such courses or programs all together should devote to these subjects amounts of time equivalent at least to the minimum hours indicated above.

II. Major concentration and electives

This part of the program should be designed to prepare a student for a career in industry, business, agriculture, homemaking and other fields by providing training that in most instances is directed at an intermediate occupational level between the trades and professions. In general, the major concentration and related courses will consist of 20 to 30 semester hours of work.

The current revision (1965) of these policies is considerably less restrictive, leaving much to institutional discretion.

"ASSOCIATE IN ARTS (A. A.)

The course of study leading to this degree should be an organised curriculum composed primarily of courses in the pure liberal arts and sciences. At a minimum there should be 48 semester credit hours of work taken in the humanities, the natural sciences and mathematics, and the social sciences. The exact balance within the 48 semester hours among these three major fields is at the institution's discretion, but there should be a reasonable distribution of work in these three categories as well as depth in some.

"ASSOCIATE IN SCIENCE (A. S.)

The course of study leading to this degree should be an organised curriculum composed of courses in the liberal arts and sciences. At least 30 semester hours of credit should be offered in the humanities, the natural sciences and mathematics, and the social sciences. The exact balance within the 30 semester hours among these three major fields is at the institution's discretion but there should be a reasonable distribution of work in these three categories as well as appropriate depth in one.

"ASSOCIATE IN APPLIED SCIENCE (A. A. S.)

The course of study leading to this degree should be an organised curriculum with a minimum of 20 semester hours of credit drawn from the liberal arts and science areas comprising work distributed in the humanities, the natural sciences and mathematics, and the social sciences. In general, the 20 semester hours should be distributed with balance among the three major areas".

## Analysis and Prospects

Issues related to the program of studies, the content and structure of the curricula offered in community-junior colleges lie at the very heart of the institution. Though serious and clearly demanding of critical analysis, such issues are not unexpected. The community-junior college is, and since its inception in American education has been, a highly flexible educational institution, resisting as much as possible and as a matter of policy those rigidities and stereotyped notions of educational programming at post-secondary levels which worked to the detriment of a comprehensive service to youth and adult students in the community.

Early in the sixties decade, however, a challenge to the flexibility of the community-junior colleges emerged in America which grew and continues to demand a response from these institutions. It was a challenge of a new and expanded fiscal support to institutions offering vocational-technical specialties of less than four collegiate years, that is, bachelor's degree level. Since the 1963 amendment to the Federal Vocational Education Act, many states have established new, post-secondary "area vocational schools", many offering post high-school specialties in engineering, health, business and other career fields. This is true, for example, in Massachusetts, Minnesota, and Oklahoma. These new post-secondary institutions differ from community-junior colleges in their institutional philosophy, scope of program, and breadth of purpose. Caught between on the one hand these specialized vocational schools and on the other the entrenched powerful four-year colleges and universities which exercise strong influence over the more traditional arts and sciences institutions preparatory to advanced specialization and higher education, the future of the community-junior college can be very insecure for many years to come.

Fundamental questions about community-junior college curricula can be raised in nearly all facets. Those believed to be of highest importance currently and for the foreseeable future can be described by four key words - length, depth, balance and relevance.

As long as the American formal educational program continues to be structured in a manner that has within it definite and sharp breaking points, for example, high school graduation at the completion of Grade 12 and the award of a bachelor's degree on completion of about 120 semester hours of study after high school graduation, questions about the validity of courses of study fitted rigidly into such time spans will be raised. Proponents of a greater degree of flexibility and a closer validation of study programs against performance or achievement objectives set for the student to accomplish, regardless of the time needed for him to reach them, point to the fact that the compartmentalized American educational system encourages an artificial fixing of study duration. Defenders of the structured system point to the fact that a completely unstructured educational program can be achieved only in a theoretical sense and, moreover, raises other questions as to methods of evaluation of student achievement. The debate and research that has centered around the adoption of an "ungraded program" at the elementary school level will quite possibly be repeated with reference to the immediate post-secondary school level. While it is going on, there will continue to be the trouble currently found in getting an acceptance of programs of less than two years' duration in many community-junior colleges, even though such offerings can be shown to be quite effective in producing qualified workers at the artisan and skilled labor level, and the economy needs such personnel in the work force. Simultaneously, there will be the equally vexing question of where in the sequence of two-year and four-year college offerings should be located the programs that really need two and one-half, three, or three and one-half years of study to complete. American educators recognize the truth of the contention that they seem to be caught in a rigid notion of structure and institutional systems; they seem destined to wrestle with the consequent problems for some time.

The proper depth of the subject matter covered in the different curricula offered in a community-junior college is another persistent and continuing issue. Here the different views center on whether it is the obligation of the college to produce personnel prepared at the "job entry" level with the expectation that further study and educational growth will occur as job experience is acquired, or whether the initial preparatory program should include in-depth preparation especially in the foundation arts, sciences, and mathematics courses from which flow the theories and principles used in a given field of work. Here again, the energy of scholars in the research and development of community-junior college curricula will be needed indefinitely.

The constant concern about balance that should prevail in a given program of study between courses of a general or liberal education content and those of specialized vocation and technical application was indicated in the material presented earlier about associate-degree requirements. This issue arises from the fact that the community-junior college generally accepts the obligation to achieve in its program growth of students toward a higher level of performance as citizens, family members, and individual personalities, as well as toward an improved competence and status as workers. Actually no definitive methods for determining a proper balance in the students' learning experience that contribute to these two objectives has been found, despite inquiries into the matter dating back to the earliest junior-college research. Nonetheless, objective methods for handling and resolving the question are sorely needed and the research efforts will be pursued.

In recent years a new evaluative word has appeared and taken on a technical meaning in the language of American education. The word is "relevance". Put simply, it is a demand that the learning content and experiences students undertake during their college careers be made to show in concrete terms a relationship to the real life problems students are likely to be facing when they leave. The demand represents a revolt on the part of students and some faculty and representatives of the supporting public against the "ivory tower" approach to programming higher education and the resultant detachment of the college community that develops. The demand for relevance is the primary force that has given rise in recent years to a greater participation of students in the governance of colleges and universities than ever was permitted before.

It should be noted that the question of relevance of the programs offered by the community-junior colleges has not been pressed by students nor by the supporting public as forcefully as it has with regard to colleges and universities offering bachelor's and higher degrees. This undoubtedly is a reflection on the fact that community-junior colleges by definition of their basic educational policies and program objectives have placed a positive premium on close association with the local community. This positive observation, however, does not imply capability of the community-junior colleges to rest on their past achievement. Indeed, as will be mentioned in the last chapter of this paper, Dr. Edmund J. Gleazer, Jr. , Executive Secretary of the American Association of Junior Colleges, presents a strong position that these institutions more than ever before will need to show their relevance to positive community improvement now that their place in the American educational structure seems to be assured.

The persistence, complexity and very fundamental nature of the four aspects of the issues indicated suggest that these should be the targets of new research and development energies in the community-junior college field. From the start of the junior college development in America through the present, the primary effort of leadership has been to clarify the educational purposes, the organisation, administration and the place of the community-junior college in the overall formal educational pattern. While scholarly work was also being devoted to some extent to the problems of curriculum development, evaluation, and improvement, they attracted a secondary notice to those of institutional organisational development. A reversal of these emphases in research and development in the seventies and eighties appears to be a strong possibility.

# X

## RELATION TO THE COMMUNITY

Several types of evidence can be presented to document the close relationships that community-junior colleges typically maintain with the general community that they serve.

From the side of administrative management can be drawn the fact that these colleges more than any others operate under the direct control of citizens drawn from and responsive to the locality served. A study by Walter Crosby Eells* reported that in 1960 only about 7% of the public baccalaureate degree-granting colleges or universities in the United States were governed by a board of control whose members were elected by the general public; a count of the public two-year colleges listed in the American Council on Education's directory of the same year shows that the boards of trustees of over 50% of the public two-year colleges were elected to office by the general constituency served. If boards whose members are appointed by local governments are added, over 60% are directly responsible to the local community. This is not a surprising finding in view of the fact that most public community-junior colleges are financed in part by local tax funds. It does indicate, however, the considerably greater pressure that develops on the institution by virtue of the method of financing and control as well as by virtue of basic educational philosophy and purpose for it to be sensitive and responsive to local community educational needs.

Responsiveness to local community requirements also shows up in the curriculum offerings of community-junior colleges in the form of courses in vocational and technical fields and short courses and special institutes for out-of-school youth and adults. Every community-junior college operates under expectation and critical review of both local and state-level officials that it provide as many such special programs as

* Walter Crosby Eells, "Board of Control of Universities and Colleges", The Educational Record, XLII (Oct., 1961), page 338.

are needed in the locality between the high-school and the upper-division collegiate levels of educational specialization. As a result, even small colleges in relatively small centers of population such as Mesa Community College in Arizona and Northern Idaho Junior College offer some courses of occupational emphasis and some short programs for adults.

State agencies responsible for reviewing and supporting institutional plans for program development, budgets for operating and capital construction, and plans for acquisition and development of campuses and physical plant consistently examine these plans against criteria of sensitivity and responsiveness to local community needs. The college, therefore, in presenting its plans and requests for approval and support must present evidence about the demand for the services envisioned, document the fact that these propositions were developed with full participation of local citizens advisory councils and related interest groups, and report the level of support such co-operating groups express for the proposals advanced.

Advisory citizens councils, therefore, are organised and requested to assist community junior college administrators, faculty, and students in all sorts of institutional developmental projects - new curricula, new building programs, campaigns to help assure favorable popular votes on special bond or operating levy elections, organisation of placement and follow-up of graduates, and many others. It is not unusual for a college to be working with a sizeable number of such local advisory councils at one time. At this writing, for example, Alfred Agricultural and Technical College in New York State reports that it has 20 active local citizens advisory committees covering projects in curriculum development and evaluation alone, and Cuyahoga Community College is utilizing 40 local citizen advisory groups in developing its multiple-campus programs in Cleveland, Ohio.

Finally, community-junior college identification and close co-operation with local community interests shows up in enrolment statistics. These colleges show a larger percentage of out-of-school youth and adults among their student bodies than any other types of higher educational institution in America. The U. S. Office of Education reports that in the fall of 1969, 47% of the part time and adult students in public higher education was enrolled in community-junior colleges and in the fall of 1968 the proportion was 48%. States with well developed programs of community-junior colleges* such as California, Illinois, and New York reflect this fact also in their positions of leadership in enrolment and scope of services for adult students.

* Telephone report from U. S. Office of Education to author.

"The community college is fast becoming a dynamic force which affects the thought process, habits, economic status, and social interaction of people from every walk of life, in every part of the country. More and more, it is becoming the most important element of this nation's educational structure".

"While the full potential of the program of community services has not yet been realized by all institutions, there is reason to believe that the next great thrust of the community college development will be in the direction of community services".

These are concluding statements made in the final report of a large scale and definitive study of community services in the public community-junior colleges reported recently to the American Association of Junior Colleges. * The study report goes on to identify seven directions which this major emphasis on the community-service dimension will take and which flow from the findings of the study. This writer believes that the predictions are sound and defensible not only from the data obtained in the study but also from close observation of current day-to-day happenings in the community-junior colleges. The seven directions of predicted development and the ways they are likely to be implemented are abstracted as follows:

1. The community college will develop aggressive multi-service outreach programs designed to truly extend its campus throughout the entire college district. This outcome is expected to result from the greater use of extension centers whereby the community-junior college offers short courses, forums, and lectures in a multiplicity of locations scattered throughout the district. In addition, programs of industrial in-plant training would be increased to bring instruction directly into the places where workers can use it. Also mobile and portable units are envisioned in greater use for counseling and public information purposes as well as for instruction.

2. There will be an increased emphasis on community education for all age levels and all age groups. The primary mechanisms foreseen for enhanced delivery of educational services to more out-of-school youth and adults are short courses, special in-service training programs for personnel in business, industry, local governments, and the human service professions.

* E.L. Harlacher, "New Directions in Community Services", Junior College Journal, Vol. 38, No. 6, March 1968, pp. 12-17.

3. The community college will utilize a greater diversification of media in meeting community needs and interests. Among the listing of such new and diversified instructional media are telecommunications, seminars and symposia, performing groups, self-instructional packages, educational and cultural tours, workshops and conferences, counseling and consultative services, recreational activities, science experiments and exhibits, multi-purpose facility usage, public lectures, and fine arts events. Increasingly, the classroom will be only one of a plethora of media utilized for community services and instruction.

4. The college will steadily provide greater use of its catalytic capabilities to assist its community in the solution of basic educational, economic, political, and social problems. This is already evident in the increasing number of special programs for educationally disadvantaged and poverty-ridden groups in the community and in the formulation of community leadership training and development programs in community action programs aimed at many different kinds of community problems - pollution, city planning, public welfare and the like.

5. There will be increasing concern over the cultural growth of its community and state. In this connection, both the physical facilities and the programs of the colleges will see greater direct utilization and relationship to the programs of music, fine and performing arts, literature, and other creative activity of the community. Community arts councils and similar action and reporting groups will become general college-based activities.

6. The community college will place greater emphasis on interaction with its community. Stimulation of "institutional synergism", defined as "simultaneous action of separate agencies which together have a greater total effect than the sum of their individual efforts", is to be a larger responsibility of the college. This will generate even greater use of advisory committees and community councils in college-sponsored and supported community-development programs.

7. The college will increasingly recognize the need for co-operation with other community and regional agencies. This inter-institutional and inter-agency co-operation will include both educational and non-educational but social service groups. It is necessary to avoid unnecessary duplication of services and waste of local area human and material resources. The community college is seen more and more as the central coordinating mechanism for co-operation between and among educational institutions (common schools, community-junior college, advanced colleges and universities, public and private), and a wide array of community agencies, again both public and private, such as the Community Chest, Public Library, Conservation and Fish and Wild Life Clubs, and the like.

# XI

## PERSPECTIVES FOR 1970-1980

Throughout this paper the reader's attention was called to particularly pressing emerging or continuing problems which confront community-junior colleges. The way these problems are tackled and the types of solutions that are found to them will shape the promose of the foreseeable future for these institutions. Grouped into a few major classifications for purposes of recapitulation and special summarization in this concluding section, the future-determining issues and problems are four: 1) the more precise and sharp identification and definition of the place and status of the community-junior college level of education in the American formal school-college-university system of education for the masses; 2) the retention of focus on local community and individual student services when basic state and institutional policies on financing, curriculum offerings, and administration are formulated; 3) the determination of the proper and most effective balance of student-faculty-administrator participation with lay members of boards of control and with official state-wide coordinating agencies in governing structures and procedures; and 4) the development of valid and reliable methods of assessing the educational output or productivity of the programs of educational services and instruction offered in service to the local community, state, and nation.

It will be noted that these are quite similar to and encompass in broader form the major topics of "concern and caution" for the future which Gleazer states at the conclusion of his volume on the community college: rapid development, local control, diversification of curricula, tuition policies, administrative policies, and leadership and future direction. *

* Edmund J. Gleazer Jr., This is the Community College, New York, Houghton Mifflin Company, 1968, pp. 128-136.

While differences of viewpoint and educational philosophy are being debated, decisions are also being made. Legislators at the local, state, and Federal levels of government influence the mould of American education by their decisions on many different aspects of school and college operation, especially those that relate to financing. Educational agencies, again at all levels of government, similarly are shaping the nation's formal educational structure and program by their current decisions. Educational programming and structuring is an on-going process and must necessarily be examined, evaluated, and restructured as it is carried on.

There seems to be little reason now to doubt that during the seventies there will occur a greater recognition and reliance on the community-junior college as a full-fledged step in the formal American school-to-university program. But within this positive and broad statement many points of refinement remain. The focus of chief responsibility for initiative and accountability for effective articulation of learning experiences from one education level to another, for example, is as yet very unclear. Is it the high-school authorities who must bend their programs to fit what the community-junior college faculties and administrations demand, or vice versa? Should community-junior colleges be made accountable for the adjustment of students to upper-division colleges or should the latter be held responsible for developing programs and using methods of instruction that take up where community-junior colleges leave off? These and other related questions are as yet without answers in the United States, even in those states with well developed and long histories of dealing with the community-junior college.

Much of the direction taken to find answers to such questions, thereby influencing profoundly the direction of development community-junior colleges will follow, lies in the structure and procedure for advanced planning in higher education in a state. In states with strong methods for maintaining a statewide perspective of educational requirements and educational resources, sounder answers to the questions can be expected. Without it, educational vacuums develop, like the lack of sufficient programs of baccalaureate and higher levels and consequent pressures on two-year colleges to add upper-division and graduate programs of study. With this, states can keep in balance the need to provide the necessary manpower for the economy, to assure full opportunity for continued educational opportunity after high school for all the high school graduates who can profit from it, and to assure that the educational systems of schools, colleges, and universities is both as complete and yet as economical as financial and other resources permit. In these cases, there is much less chance of there being either gaps or wasteful duplication in educational programming. Such advanced planning is most evident in states like California, Florida, Illinois, Oklahoma, and New York. In such states, there has been thus far a steady growth in recognition and support given to the place of comprehensive-two year post-secondary community-junior colleges as a definite part of the total educational system.

That this will continue to be the main posture and statewide planning of post-high school education, however, is by no means an assured proposition. So far, advanced planning in higher education on a statewide basis has helped community-junior colleges to keep their focus on being "open admission" colleges, on flexible programming to meet individual student needs, and their role of service between the high school and upper-division levels of educational specialization. It has also helped community-junior colleges to get needed fiscal support. But this could change in the decade of the seventies. The emergence of the area vocational schools, often planned on a statewide basis and in direct duplication of community-junior college programs in vocational-technical fields, was noted earlier. The leadership in these schools will certainly have a stronger voice in statewide decision-making in the foreseeable future. Such planning, too, is greatly influenced by the powerful interest and wishes of established baccalaureate degree-granting colleges and universities. What final results will be reported from these influences after another ten years remains to be seen.

Student-Faculty-Administrator Participation in Governance

Both students and faculty activist groups are striving to gain a greater voice in the governance of their institutions. This is true at both the local institutional level and at the state level of policy formation and administrative decision making. During the next decade, therefore, there may well be a dramatic departure from the traditional practice in America of keeping the fundamental control of education in the hands of lay citizens and keeping students, faculty, and administrators strictly to roles of recommending and advisory aides.

Such a development would pose new questions, especially about the future of the community-junior colleges. Research results reveal that faculties in these institutions display strong ambivalences and sense of role conflicts in accepting and supporting the concepts of institutional purpose and program generally set by lay boards for the community colleges. * Students also are inclined to favor certain

* Roger H. Garrison, Junior College Faculty: Issues and Problems, Washington, American Association of Junior Colleges, 1967, pp. 85-90.

aspects of programming of these colleges as opposed to support of a balanced comprehensive service at the immediate post high-school level. Given a stronger place in decision-making procedures at both institutional and state levels, what will the impact of student and faculty participation be? Data helping to provide insight to the answer to this question will surely be interesting objects of community-junior college research in the seventies.

Retention of Focus on Local Community- and Student-Centered Services

There are several threats to the central focus of community-junior colleges on local community and individual student services which have traditionally characterized these colleges. Among the most powerful of these is the clear trend toward relocating the primary source of fiscal resources for operating and capital expenses from the local area served to the state and Federal governments. This trend will be further strengthened in the seventies as proposals now before the Federal congress and several state legislatures would indicate. With this, the expectation would be that state- and Federal-level agencies would gain more powerful voices in the affairs of the institutions.

This would abet further the development and influence of such agencies, already evident in a growing number of states, which have been created even under existing patterns of financing. The needs of states to coordinate institutional development and program offerings in statewide systems of education; to project long-range plans on a coherent, objective basis; and to suggest allocation of resources in the form of consolidated budget requests strengthen the state board of community-junior colleges and state boards for coordinating all higher education.

In the consequent adoption of practices and procedures for decision making that stress wider governmental and geographic coverages, such as the recent widespread interest in the WICHE project, the balance of local versus state control will most probably shift toward the latter. The question to be resolved in that event is: What mechanisms can be invented and adopted that under the new procedures for policy and decision making will retain the emphasis on local community situations and on the needs of each student as an individual?

Evaluation and Improvement of Programs and Services

The pattern of public reaction in America to each historical phase of upward extension of mass education, elementary education in the days of Horace Mann, nearly two hundred years ago, through the practical universalization of this century, has been two-phased. The first phase presents large-scale public debate and discussion as to the wisdom, the need, and the feasibility of the new developments. The second, when the successive moves in educational expansion at a given level make debate over its justification only an academic exercise, presents strong and pervasive demands for evaluation of the new programs and its results.

The community-junior college level of education in America seems at the point of change in educational historical attention from debate over its feasibility to demand that it be productive and efficient. The community-junior colleges during the next decade will need more than ever to show how, in fact, their claims to being "open door" institutions are being fulfilled; how really comprehensive their provision of vocational, technical, and community service program is; what telling results flow from their counseling and guidance services to students; and overall how much benefit the supporting public is getting for the costs it incurs by maintaining these institutions.

As a result of this the seventies will probably see a new emphasis in the operations of the community-junior colleges on institutional, self-evaluative research. This will be good both for the colleges and those whom they serve.

## CONCLUDING COMMENT

This paper attempted within a brief number of pages to describe the nature of the newest and most dramatic 20th century development in American education - the rise and consolidation of the community-junior college - and to point to its shape in the foreseeable future. The first part of the undertaking was difficult only in the need to include or exclude in the narrative. The second part was much harder. Forecasting is a practice fraught with danger. In this case, the risk is believed to be not in predicting that community-junior colleges will grow in numbers, enrolment, and importance in American education, but in predicting the specific form future changes will take. The place of community-junior colleges is no longer a speculative matter. The risk, rather, is in the attempt to foresee its shape and form its priorities in emphasis, its major as opposed to minor problems. The community-junior college is by definition, record of action, and philosophic commitment an institution which adapts to the societal conditions in which it functions. In the final analysis, therefore, the perspectives of the community-junior college in the seventies will be shaped by the technological, cultural, social, and economic changes that occur in the United States during that decade.

# III

## Development of Two-Year Post-Secondary Schools in Yugoslavia

by

the Department for Research in Higher Education
Institute for Social Research
University of Zagreb
(Yugoslavia)

## CONTENTS

I. Introduction .......................................... 153

II. Objectives and functions of first-level higher education and its development .......................... 159

A. Development and problems of first-level faculty education .................................. 160

B. Introduction and development of two-year post-secondary schools .............................. 164

III. Status of two-year post-secondary schools ............. 173

- Legal status .......................................... 173
- Financing ............................................ 175

IV. Need for better integration into the system of higher education ............................................ 177

V. Teachers ............................................... 181

VI. Admission and status of students ..................... 187

VII. Part-time study ....................................... 191

VIII. Relations between post-secondary schools and society .. 195

- Employment of post-secondary school graduates.... 195

- Types of co-operation between two-year post-secondary schools and the economy ............... 202
  1. Results of the survey in schools ............... 202
  2. Results of the survey in business organisations ................................ 207
  3. Summary ................................ 208

IX. Conclusion ................................ 209

# I

## INTRODUCTION

A characteristic feature of the post-war period in Yugoslavia is a rapid expansion of education at all levels.

While the dramatic increase in enrolments at the elementary level can be ascribed to the implementation of the law on compulsory education (9 years) resulting subsequently in increased enrolments at other levels, the growing number of university and post-secondary students has been mainly due to social and economic factors.

Among these factors, the following deserve to be mentioned:

- free instruction;
- scholarships and student loans, which enable students from less wealthy families to seek higher education;
- the status of a university graduate, which is higher than the status that a person can achieve by taking a job at the end of secondary school and then proceeding normally by promotion on the basis of seniority;
- the second-level university degree opens the door to post-graduate studies, thus further increasing the student's prestige and social standing.

Table 1 shows how enrolments have increased - by type of institution - compared with the pre-war period.

Apart from the increase in the number of institutions of higher learning, enrolments, and teachers, the post-war development of higher education in Yugoslavia has also been characterized by considerable qualitative changes.

Table 1. TOTAL ENROLMENTS, BY TYPE OF INSTITUTION

| YEAR | FACULTIES | COLLEGES | TWO-YEAR POST-SECONDARY SCHOOLS | ART ACADEMIES | TOTAL |
|---|---|---|---|---|---|
| 1938/39 | 16,491 | 986 | 259 | 288 | 17,964 |
| 1959/60 | 82,927 | 1,161 | 19,286 | 1,412 | 104,786 |
| 1961/62 | 112,005 | 3,461 | 40,898 | 1,646 | 158,010 |
| 1962/63 | 106,225 | 4,268 | 47,782 | 1,817 | 160,092 |
| 1963/64 | 99,056 | 6,177 | 53,381 | 1,981 | 160,595 |
| 1964/65 | 98,631 | 6,815 | 63,073 | 1,980 | 170,499 |
| 1965/66 | 107,329 | 6,930 | 68,650 | 2,014 | 184,923 |
| 1966/67 | 111,232 | 6,848 | 75,344 | 2,030 | 195,454 |
| 1967/68 | 111,045 | 7,142 | 82,570 | 2,053 | 210,810 |
| 1968/69 | 140,647 | 4,745 | 83,947 | 2,105 | 231,444 |
| 1969/70 | 152,519 | 7,011 | 77,901 | 2,180 | 239,611 |

SOURCE: Statistical Yearbook of Yugoslavia 1963, p. 301; 1965, p. 324; 1966, p. 308; 1967, p. 288; 1968, p. 293; 1970, p. 282.

Table 2. DISTRIBUTION OF ENROLMENTS BY TYPE OF INSTITUTION

(percentages)

| YEAR | FACULTIES | COLLEGES | TWO-YEAR POST-SECONDARY SCHOOLS | ART ACADEMIES | TOTAL |
|---|---|---|---|---|---|
| 1938/39 | 91.7 | 5.4 | 1.7 | 1.2 | 100 |
| 1961/62 | 70.9 | 2.2 | 25.9 | 1.0 | 100 |
| 1962/63 | 66.4 | 2.7 | 29.8 | 1.1 | 100 |
| 1963/64 | 61.7 | 3.8 | 33.2 | 1.3 | 100 |
| 1964/65 | 57.8 | 4.0 | 37.0 | 1.2 | 100 |
| 1965/66 | 58.0 | 3.7 | 37.2 | 1.1 | 100 |
| 1966/67 | 56.9 | 3.5 | 38.5 | 1.1 | 100 |
| 1967/68 | 56.5 | 3.4 | 39.2 | 0.9 | 100 |
| 1968/69 | 63.7 | 2.9 | 32.5 | 0.9 | 100 |
| 1969/70 | 63.7 | 2.9 | 32.5 | 0.9 | 100 |

SOURCE: Calculated on the basis of the data in the preceding table.

Table 3. TEACHERS AND AUXILIARY TEACHING STAFF IN HIGHER EDUCATION INSTITUTIONS IN YUGOSLAVIA

| YEAR | TEACHERS | | | | | | | | AUXILIARY TEACHING STAFF | | | | | | | |
|---|---|---|---|---|---|---|---|---|---|---|---|---|---|---|---|---|
| | FACULTIES | | COLLEGES | | ART ACADEMIES | | TWO-YEAR POST-SECOND. SCHOOLS | | FACULTIES | | COLLEGES | | ART ACADEMIES | | TWO-YEAR POST-SECOND. SCHOOLS | |
| | TOTAL | FULL-TIME | TOTAL | FULL-TIME | TOTAL | FULL-TIME | TOTAL | FULL-TIME | TOTAL | FULL-TIME | TOTAL | FULL-TIME | TOTAL | FULL-TIME | TOTAL | FULL-TIME |
| 1938/39. | 555 | 361 | - | - | 40 | 24 | 89 | 21 | 507 | - | - | - | 10 | - | 3 | - |
| 1956/57. | 2,191 | 1,467 | 16 | 2 | 269 | 192 | 765 | 410 | 3,024 | 2,165 | 16 | 7 | 76 | 47 | 61 | 29 |
| 1961/62. | 3,666 | 2,620 | 273 | 124 | 314 | 205 | 2,421 | 1,038 | 5,052 | 3,507 | 159 | 86 | 95 | 58 | 495 | 127 |
| 1965/66. | 5,077 | 3,552 | 515 | 263 | 401 | 264 | 3,140 | 1,388 | 5,462 | 4,092 | 322 | 174 | 99 | 71 | 744 | 290 |
| 1968/69. | 5,447 | 3,975 | 371 | 186 | 303 | 270 | 3,288 | 1,507 | 5,477 | 4,211 | 186 | 93 | 100 | 76 | 698 | 282 |

One of the important qualitative innovations in the system of higher education has been the fact that all forms and levels of education have been brought closer to the social forces and factors which have the greatest interest in them - namely, the economy and social service organisations. The changes that have taken place in practice have also been regulated by law, so that business firms and various social organisations, as well as territorial and political communities, can now apply for the opening of their own institutions of higher learning.

The expansion of higher education has been marked not only by an increase in the number of institutions but also by the growing number of towns and cities in which such institutions operate. In 1961/62, there were 63 towns and cities in Yugoslavia with one or more such institutions (faculties, art academies, colleges, two-year post-secondary schools) as against only five such cities in 1938/39. The extension of the network of higher education institutions into the provinces has resulted in a more balanced regional representation of the student body, and particularly in greater numbers of students from the less developed parts of the country.

This has had a considerable effect on the qualification structure of the labour force and on the regional distribution of technical personnel with post-secondary and university qualifications. The greater and more even participation of young people from all social strata and all geographic regions in higher education has created the conditions for faster progress and development of the whole country.

# II

## OBJECTIVES AND FUNCTIONS OF FIRST-LEVEL HIGHER EDUCATION AND ITS DEVELOPMENT

With its per capita income of about 600 dollars, Yugoslavia has joined the ranks of the economically medium-developed countries. The higher level of economic development has also entailed a change in the mode of business operation towards more intensive methods of production, requiring changes in the qualification structure of the country's labour force.

With the higher rate of economic growth an increased need was felt for highly qualified manpower - which traditionally was trained by secondary technical and vocational schools and by Faculties.

However, neither secondary technical schools nor Faculties, with their traditional concepts of education, were able to supply the specialists needed in the new situation. Thus a need for new forms of higher education developed and the solution offered was the so-called first level of higher education.

First-level higher education must therefore be seen as an expression and direct consequence of the level of economic and social development already achieved. The system began to develop on an extensive scale following the adoption, in the Federal Assembly, of the Resolution on Technical Personnel Training and Education. The Resolution defined the principles of a long-term policy for technical education and described the tasks of the system of higher education. It spoke of the need to differentiate between first-level/post-secondary/ and second level/ university graduates and suggested that two-year post-secondary courses of study would be needed in addition to the traditional four-year university courses. The latter alone could not meet all the needs of modern society and a modern economy for specialists with different profiles and qualifications. The reason, as described by the Resolution, was that the gap between secondary school graduates on the one hand

and Faculty and College graduates on the other was too wide: the former could meet the needs at the level of a skilled worker (or a person entrusted with the execution of certain actions or operations in the process of production), while the latter had the function of creating new development in science and technology. In other words, there was a "vacuum" between those performing specific operations and those working on the design of new solutions. It was suggested that this gap could be filled by first-level higher education graduates, who would become direct organisers of technological and production processes and who would apply their knowledge of science and technology to industrial production and the running of social services. It was further suggested that such specialists could not be trained through traditional four-year courses of study at Faculties and that different, self-contained courses of study, lasting two to three years, were needed in many disciplines. Such courses could either be offered as the first level of university study at Faculties or at the new type of Two-Year Post-Secondary Schools.

Such were the main lines of argument in the Resolution, serving subsequently as a basis for new higher education legislation which provided for the introduction of first-level courses of study at Faculties and for the creation of a large number of Two-Year Post-Secondary Schools (Viša Škola).

## A. DEVELOPMENT AND PROBLEMS OF FIRST-LEVEL FACULTY EDUCATION

The Federal Law on Faculties and Universities and the laws of different Republics deriving from it did not impose on Faculties the introduction of first-level education. It left the Faculties free to organise their four-year courses of study either as two self-contained and inter-related levels (the first level during the first two years) or as an undivided continuous four-year sequence. The advocates of the separate first-level study pointed to the need for specialists at different levels of qualification and to the fact that there were many jobs in which post-secondary qualifications were required but in which the employment of university graduates was neither necessary nor socially justified. This was particularly true of some jobs in production, and sometimes even in research laboratories, which did not require the kind or amount of knowledge possessed by university graduates. Since their education and training was very expensive, it was uneconomical to entrust them with jobs in which their knowledge and skill could not be fully utilized.

The introduction of first-level higher education was accompanied by heated debates and disagreements; it also resulted in organisational difficulties at many Faculties and Colleges.

The spread of first-level study was fairly rapid but rather uneven: some Faculties introduced it while others working in the same field refused to do so; some Faculties first introduced it and then dropped it; still others retained the four-year system and merely added extra two-year streams. There was considerable variation among the Universities too: thus the Universities of Belgrade and Ljubljana introduced first-level study in most of their Faculties, while the University of Zagreb introduced it in very few.

Despite careful preparations and a great deal of effort put into the organisation of first-level study by teachers and whole Faculties, practical solutions in adjusting programmes and methods of instruction to this new type of education have not always been satisfactory. There have also been cases of first-level study being introduced in disciplines where no need existed for this type of qualified manpower.

In the academic year 1963/64, first-level courses of study were offered by 55 Faculties, 7 Colleges and 10 Art Academies in Yugoslavia; by now, 38 Faculties, 9 Colleges and 4 Art Academies have retained the four-year system.

First-level graduates began to come out in 1962 from the Faculties, Colleges and Art Academies in Serbia and Slovenia; in the following years such graduates also appeared in other Yugoslav Republics, as seen from the table on page 162.

The figures clearly show that Faculties are gradually abandoning first-level study. The table on page 163, expressing the above figures in index numbers, makes this trend even clearer.

In the last few years, starting with the academic year 1966/67, most Faculties with first-level courses reverted to the traditional four-year scheme. In 1968/69, first-level study was offered by no more than 25 Faculties, 4 Colleges and 6 Art Academies. Even those Faculties whose statutes still provide for first-level study now stipulate that such study can only be organised in addition to (and apart from) a normal four-year course, provided extra funds are obtained for this activity and provided there are enough applicants for this type of study. It appears that in practice, such a stipulation is equivalent to the suppression of this level of study.

The following reasons have been given by Faculties to justify the elimination of the first-level study:

i) the majority of first-level graduates proceed to the second level; very few go straight into employment, partly because of temporary stagnation in employment in the years when first-level

Table 4. FIRST-LEVEL GRADUATES FROM FACULTIES, COLLEGES AND ART ACADEMIES

(Breakdown by Republics)

| YEAR | YUGOSLAVIA | BOSNIA AND HERZEGOVINA | MONTENEGRO | CROATIA | MACEDONIA | SLOVENIA | SERBIA |
|---|---|---|---|---|---|---|---|
| 1961 .................... | - | - | - | - | - | - | - |
| 1962 .................... | 3,175 | - | - | - | - | 631 | 2,544 |
| 1963 .................... | 4,673 | 104 | - | 589 | - | 923 | 3,057 |
| 1964 .................... | 5,579 | 276 | - | 541 | - | 837 | 3,925 |
| 1965 .................... | 5,661 | 335 | - | 504 | 77 | 919 | 3,826 |
| 1966 .................... | 5,382 | 598 | - | 576 | 105 | 844 | 3,259 |
| 1967 .................... | 4,986 | 455 | - | 458 | 116 | 671 | 3,286 |
| 1968 .................... | 3,389 | 363 | - | 407 | 166 | 308 | 2,145 |
| 1969 .................... | 2,185 | 294 | - | 406 | 151 | 330 | 1,004 |

SOURCE: Statistical Yearbook of Yugoslavia 1963, p. 480; 1964, p. 509; 1965, p. 527; 1966, p. 500; 1967, p. 479; 1970, p. 481.

Table 5. FIRST-LEVEL GRADUATES FROM FACULTIES, COLLEGES AND ART ACADEMIES (1963=100)

| YEAR | 1963 | 1964 | 1966 | 1968 | 1969 |
|---|---|---|---|---|---|
| Yugoslavia .... | 100 | 119.4 | 115.2 | 72.5 | 46.8 |
| Bosnia and Herzegovina .... | 100 | 265.4 | 575.0 | 349.0 | 282.7 |
| Montenegro .... | - | - | - | - | - |
| Croatia ....... | 100 | 91.8 | 97.8 | 69.1 | 68.9 |
| | (1965) | | | | |
| Macedonia ...... | 100 | - | 136.4 | 215.6 | 196.1 |
| Slovenia ....... | 100 | 90.7 | 91.4 | 33.4 | 35.8 |
| Serbia ........ | 100 | 128.4 | 106.6 | 70.2 | 32.8 |

SOURCE: Calculated on the basis of data given in the Statistical Yearbook of Yugoslavia (see references cited at the bottom of the Table 4).

graduates began to appear on the labour market and partly also because the economy does not seem to be sufficiently interested in personnel of this type. Another reason that facilitates transfer of first-level graduates to the second level is the lack of barriers preventing them from doing so, contrary to the principles proclaimed when the first level was introduced; in the first place it had been intended that the transfer should be made more difficult:

- by differential examinations in some theoretical subjects,
- by allowing the transfer only to the students graduating from the first level with excellent grades.

But the unpreparedness of industry to receive the graduates from the first level and to give them appropriate jobs was one of the reasons for not placing any barriers to the transfer of students to the second level. Also students were not asked when they entered the first year whether they wanted to do the two-year course or not. All of them were obliged to enter the first level, and it was not known in advance who would graduate from the first level only and who would proceed to the second level;

ii) more teachers and greater resources would be needed for a proper organisation of first-level teaching;

iii) most teachers believe that the introduction of the first level lowers Faculty teaching standards; the introduction of these courses called for the inversion of the curricula because the stress at first level had been on the practical aspects preparing the students for the actual work while the theoretical aspects were accorded minor importance. This lack of a theoretical basis was one of the reasons why teachers had a low esteem of the teaching standards at first-level study. As opposed to this the four-year course demands a considerable theoretical basis which, to be effective, has to precede all the practical activity;

iv) there are enough Two-Year Post-Secondary Schools in the country offering the same kind of education as the first-level Faculty courses.

However, more detailed analyses and evaluation of the first-level study in Faculties and of the reasons for its failure are still lacking.

## B. INTRODUCTION AND DEVELOPMENT OF TWO-YEAR POST-SECONDARY SCHOOLS

Parallel to the introduction of first-level study at Faculties, Colleges and Art Academies, Two-Year Post-Secondary Schools were introduced in many parts of the country. The post-secondary schools which opened after the Resolution on Technical Personnel were designed in the first place to train the qualified manpower needed by the economy and social service organisations.

The Resolution urged all social groups to seek new approaches to technical education and training in order to satisfy the economic and social needs of the country. The authority to establish higher education institutions was transferred from the Federal level to the Republics and Provinces, and even to smaller territorial and political units, communes, business firms, social organisations, and other interested bodies.

The development of Two-Year Post-Secondary Schools can best be understood by an examination of how such schools were established in different parts of the country over a given period of time.

An example of this is the establishment of post-secondary schools of engineering and technology designed to meet a real need for technical personnel at an intermediate level, between technicians with secondary school qualifications and graduate engineers with university qualifications.

The need for a different structure of technical personnel was brought about by changes in technology, and methods and techniques of production. A particularly acute need was felt for a type of person who would possess sufficient knowledge to take direct control of technological and production processes and who would thus be able to replace graduate engineers working in production. The two-year post-secondary technical schools were meant to train precisely such people and it was thought appropriate that their graduates should be given the title of "Production Engineer".

Similar considerations prompted the formation of other types of post-secondary schools - those training personnel for social work, public administration, textile and clothing industry, leather and footwear industry, printing industry, maritime navigation, foreign trade, building materials industry, personnel services, industrial organisation, computer application, public health and hygiene, physical therapy, etc.

Personnel of this type was not being trained in Faculties and it was understandable that the organisations which needed such personnel should use their legal rights and their funds to establish educational institutions which would cater for their needs.

In this situation, Two-Year Post-Secondary Schools multiplied rapidly. Between 1960 and 1962, their numbers more than doubled. Such schools were established not only in traditional centres of higher education but also in many other places. An important consequence was that a great variety of people became involved in higher education, providing fresh blood for all social and economic processes in the country.

The establishment of Two-Year Post-Secondary Schools helped to make higher education more democratic because a large proportion of young people and adults already in employment were given an opportunity to pursue higher studies.

The new schools also stimulated a healthy change in the students' preference for different fields of study: more and more students began to study technical subjects and economics and those disciplines previously neglected by the educational system.

The fact that post-secondary schools were scattered throughout the country was very beneficial in that it enabled them to develop close ties with local industrial firms and social service organisations and thus direct their educational effort to areas most useful to the community. At the same time this made for a more balanced distribution of graduates over different regions of the country, different branches of industry, different localities and different business firms.

The status of Two-Year Post-Secondary Schools was strengthened between 1962 and 1964, when they were formally brought into the scope of the higher education system and thus given a good opportunity for further systematic development.

Although the number of this type of school subsequently declined (some closed and others merged), we can still speak of their continuous growth and development - but this time on the basis of new criteria and of a different approach. *

An important, though often neglected, feature of these schools is the high proportion of their part-time enrolments; this also indicates their special role in the system of higher education.

Table 6 shows the proportion of part-time students in Faculties and in Two-Year Post-Secondary Schools:

Table 6. PROPORTION OF PART-TIME STUDENTS IN TOTAL ENROLMENTS

| YEAR | FACULTIES | TWO-YEAR POST-SECONDARY SCHOOLS |
|---|---|---|
| 1938/39 ........... | - | - |
| 1961/62 ........... | 27.4 | 56.3 |
| 1963/64 ........... | 23.0 | 53.5 |
| 1965/66 ........... | 21.0 | 54.1 |
| 1967/68 ........... | 17.8 | 52.2 |
| 1969/70 ........... | 17.1 | 50.3 |

SOURCE: Statistical Yearbook of Yugoslavia.

* In the course of their rapid development, many Two-Year Post-Secondary Schools, opened in the same region and offered similar teaching content. Later, it was necessary therefore to merge some of them as each had only a small number of students. Also many opened without sufficient material support and had to close because of lack of financial resources.

Table 7. PART-TIME ENROLMENTS IN DIFFERENT TYPES OF INSTITUTIONS OF HIGHER EDUCATION

| YEAR | FACULTIES | COLLEGES | TWO-YEAR POST-SECONDARY SCHOOLS | ART ACADEMIES | TOTAL |
|---|---|---|---|---|---|
| 1938/39 | - | - | - | - | - |
| 1961/62 | 30,684 | 1,005 | 23,026 | 34 | 54,749 |
| 1962/63 | 25,461 | 1,721 | 26,408 | 62 | 53,652 |
| 1963/64 | 22,764 | 2,592 | 28,573 | 40 | 53,969 |
| 1964/65 | 22,978 | 3,263 | 37,228 | 71 | 63,540 |
| 1965/66 | 22,438 | 3,470 | 37,087 | 104 | 63,099 |
| 1966/67 | 20,557 | 2,834 | 39,228 | 156 | 62,775 |
| 1967/68 | 21,231 | 2,855 | 43,114 | 180 | 67,380 |
| 1968/69 | 22,868 | 1,465 | 43,133 | 164 | 67,630 |
| 1969/70 | 26,113 | 3,061 | 39,156 | 164 | 68,494 |

SOURCE: Statistical Yearbook of Yugoslavia 1965, p. 324; 1966, p. 308; 1967, p. 288; 1968, p. 293; 1969, p. 291; 1970, p. 282.

Table 8. DISTRIBUTION OF PART-TIME STUDENTS IN DIFFERENT TYPES OF INSTITUTIONS OF HIGHER EDUCATION

(percentages)

| YEAR | FACULTIES | COLLEGES | TWO-YEAR POST-SEC. SCHOOLS | ART ACADEMIES | TOTAL |
|---|---|---|---|---|---|
| 1968/69 ......... | - | - | - | - | - |
| 1961/62 ......... | 56. 0 | 1. 8 | 42. 0 | - | 100 |
| 1962/63 ......... | 47. 5 | 3. 2 | 49. 2 | - | 100 |
| 1963/64 ......... | 42. 2 | 4. 8 | 52. 9 | - | 100 |
| 1964/65 ......... | 36. 2 | 5. 1 | 58. 6 | - | 100 |
| 1965/66 ......... | 35. 5 | 5. 5 | 58. 8 | - | 100 |
| 1966/67 ......... | 32. 7 | 4. 5 | 62. 5 | - | 100 |
| 1967/68 ......... | 31. 5 | 4. 2 | 64. 0 | - | 100 |
| 1968/69 ......... | | | | - | 100 |
| 1969/70 ......... | 38. 1 | 4. 5 | 57. 2 | - | 100 |

SOURCE: Calculated on the basis of absolute figures in Table 7.

From Table 8 it is clear that most part-time students have been enrolled in Two-Year Post-Secondary Schools. This, in a way, reflects one of the objectives of the reform of higher education in Yugoslavia: to relate higher education to the needs of the economy. It can be assumed that part-time students have usually taken up their studies in response to such needs, for it was industry and the economy which directly financed their education, and this too has brought higher education within the reach of an increasing number of people in different parts of the country.

In general, the growing importance of Two-Year Post-Secondary Schools can be appreciated from Tables 9, 10 and 11.

In the period 1962-69 the number of graduates at Two-Year Post-Secondary Schools rose steadily (by almost 2. 5 times), while at the same time the number of graduates at Faculties remained unchanged.

Table 9. NUMBER OF GRADUATES AT TWO-YEAR POST-SECONDARY SCHOOLS IN YUGOSLAVIA, BY TYPES OF SCHOOL, 1950-69

| TYPE OF SCHOOL | | 1950 | 1955 | 1960 | 1965 | 1968 | 1969 |
|---|---|---|---|---|---|---|---|
| Teacher training | Total | 5,008 | 8,761 | 13,037 | 19,850 | 6,749 | 7,871 |
| | Women | 2,342 | 3,783 | 6,135 | 9,446 | 3,414 | 4,234 |
| Engineering | Total | - | - | 2,995 | 5,756 | 1,651 | 1,704 |
| | Women | - | - | 150 | 472 | 157 | 255 |
| Agriculture | Total | - | - | 917 | 1,553 | 399 | 403 |
| | Women | - | - | 46 | 103 | 35 | 27 |
| Transport | Total | 48 | 213 | 1,335 | 1,344 | 408 | 456 |
| | Women | - | 4 | 30 | 73 | 40 | 30 |
| Business management | Total | 124 | 397 | 5,650 | 8,716 | 2,491 | 2,211 |
| | Women | 27 | 23 | 1,090 | 2,655 | 893 | 828 |
| Statistics | Total | - | - | 409 | 364 | 100 | 94 |
| | Women | - | - | 107 | 153 | 40 | 52 |
| Law and administration | Total | - | 1,564 | 4,943 | 3,811 | 1,190 | 1,530 |
| | Women | - | 77 | 464 | 687 | 248 | 351 |
| Medical auxiliaries | Total | 298 | 615 | 1,434 | 1,726 | 559 | 599 |
| | Women | 119 | 533 | 1,074 | 1,174 | 403 | 435 |
| Social work | Total | - | 223 | 1,250 | 1,476 | 387 | 388 |
| | Women | - | 95 | 580 | 891 | 247 | 258 |
| Political science | Total | 25 | - | 421 | 622 | 37 | - |
| | Women | 9 | - | 24 | 51 | 5 | - |
| Social insurance | Total | - | - | 433 | 307 | 21 | 185 |
| | Women | - | - | 85 | 78 | 5 | 74 |
| Personnel management | Total | - | - | 46 | 485 | 94 | - |
| | Women | - | - | 6 | 64 | 12 | - |
| Production organisation | Total | - | - | - | 284 | 284 | 605 |
| | Women | - | - | - | 21 | 21 | 55 |
| Total - all schools | Total | 5,503 | 11,773 | 32,870 | 46,294 | 14,370 | 16,046 |
| | Women | 2,497 | 4,515 | 9,791 | 15,868 | 5,520 | 6,599 |

Table 10. DISTRIBUTION OF HIGHER EDUCATION GRADUATES BY REPUBLIC AND TYPE OF INSTITUTION (1969)

| REPUBLIC | TYPE OF INSTITUTION | | | | | | | |
|---|---|---|---|---|---|---|---|---|
| | FACULTIES | | COLLEGES | | TWO-YEAR POST-SECONDARY SCHOOLS | | TOTAL | |
| | | % | | % | | % | 1) | % |
| Bosnia and Herzegovina | 1,151 | 9.5 | 74 | 10.6 | 1,802 | 11.2 | 3,339 | 10.7 |
| % | 34.5 | | 2.2 | | 54.0 | | 100 | |
| Montenegro | 82 | 0.7 | - | - | 256 | 1.6 | 338 | 1.1 |
| % | 24.3 | | - | | 75.7 | | 100 | |
| Croatia | 3,324 | 26.7 | 611 | 87.7 | 4,341 | 27.1 | 8,649 | 27.7 |
| % | 37.3 | | 7.1 | | 50.2 | | 100 | |
| Macedonia | 1,609 | 8.9 | - | - | 1,032 | 6.4 | 2,252 | 7.2 |
| % | 47.5 | | - | | 45.8 | | 100 | |
| Slovenia | 973 | 8.1 | 12 | 1.7 | 1,217 | 7.6 | 2,548 | 8.1 |
| % | 38.2 | | 4.7 | | 47.8 | | 100 | |
| Serbia | 5,566 | 46.1 | - | - | 7,398 | 46.1 | 14,110 | 45.2 |
| % | 39.4 | | - | | 52.4 | | 100 | |
| Yugoslavia | 12,065 | 100 | 697 | 100 | 16,046 | 100 | 31,236 | 100 |
| % | 38.6 | | 2.2 | | 51.4 | | 100 | |

1. Including Art Academies.

Table 11. INCREASE IN THE NUMBERS OF GRADUATES OF HIGHER EDUCATION 1962-1969

| | 1962 | 1969 |
|---|---|---|
| Faculties | 12,023 | 12,065 |
| Index | 100 | 100 |
| Two-Year Post-Secondary Schools | 6,809 | 16,064 |
| Index | 100 | 100 |

SOURCE: Statistical Yearbook of Yugoslavia 1963, p. 479; 1970, p. 481.

# III

## STATUS OF TWO-YEAR POST-SECONDARY SCHOOLS

### Legal status

From a legal point of view, two-year post-secondary schools are recognized institutions of higher learning at the first level of a three-tier system of higher education. From the social point of view, these schools have an important role in preparing the qualified personnel needed by the economy and social service organisations.

Article 2, paragraph 1, of the Higher Education Law states:

> "Higher education institutions shall educate three levels of personnel for different fields of the economy and for social service organisations: personnel with post-secondary qualifications, personnel with university qualifications, and personnel with specialist, post-graduate qualifications."

The law thus specifies that higher education should depend in the first place on social needs. In defining the social tasks of two-year post-secondary schools, the law makes it clear (Article 3) that the primary duty of these schools is to train qualified people for certain branches of the economy while the scientific tasks - if any - of such schools will be confined to the areas in which they specialize.

The fact that the two-year post-secondary schools are regarded as an integral part of the system of higher education follows clearly from Article 5, which states that the Yugoslav education system represents a comprehensive structure embracing pre-school institutions, elementary schools, different types of secondary schools, then post-secondary schools and colleges, art academies and faculties, and other educational and training institutions.

As for the relative position of two-year post-secondary schools in the system of higher education itself, Article 41 stipulates that the first level of higher education obtained at such schools or through first-level Faculty courses shall be a recognized basis for further, second-level study in accordance with the law and Faculty statutes.

The draft Croatian Higher Education Bill* is even more specific in defining the role and place of two-year post-secondary schools in the system of higher education. The Bill** speaks of Faculties, Colleges and Art Academies as scientific institutions engaged in scientific research activities and training of personnel at a high academic level; two-year post-secondary schools are defined primarily as teaching institutions:

> "Two-year post-secondary schools are institutions of higher education engaged in the teaching of personnel at the post-secondary level of education." (Article 14, paragraph 1).

The Bill also specifies different procedures for the establishment of Faculties, Colleges, and Art Academies on the one hand, and of the two-year post-secondary schools on the other. It lays down that the two-year post-secondary schools can also be created by "social and political communities, working and other organisations and associations".

Actually, the Bill does nothing more than regulate an already established practice. The only new element is that the post-secondary schools are now more clearly distinguished from Faculties and Colleges by their basic educational tasks and orientation. In the past, the distinction was not very clear, which was one of the sources of misunderstanding in the relations between two groups of institutions in the higher education system. The Bill, unlike the present Law, uses the term "study" in reference to the process of learning at two-year post-secondary schools:

> "Post-secondary study shall be organised for training of personnel for jobs in which less theoretical knowledge is sufficient but which require a sound mastery of the specific technology and of skills necessary to performance of operations characteristic of those jobs.
>
> Teaching at the post-secondary level shall last for two years." (Article 23 of the Bill).

* Similar provisions, with minor modifications, are contained in the legislation of the other Yugoslav Republics.

** The Bill modifies the law in the sense that it clearly stresses that the two-year post-secondary schools are part of the system of higher education, a fact that was not recognized by earlier laws. The Bill also points out the difference in teaching functions between faculties and two-year post-secondary schools, these latter being exclusively teaching institutions as opposed to the faculties, whose function is to prepare the scientific research staff.

Defined in this way, the two-year post-secondary school is an institution of higher education specifically designed to train personnel for specific segments of the economy. But it is important to note that this also implies fundamentally different relations with the users of its services from those involved in the case of Faculties, Colleges and Art Academies. A clear orientation of post-secondary schools to the needs of the users of their services (e.g. the economy and public services) cannot leave their organisation and curricula unaffected. These schools must be forever responsive to changes on the labour market: on the one hand, they must react to them and offer what the market demands; on the other, they must try to influence changes and stimulate new organisational and technological solutions. This, of course, requires a highly flexible teaching organisation, flexible curricula, adaptation to changing needs, and a determined effort to push through programmes whose usefulness can be predicted.

## FINANCING

Until 1960/61, all higher education was financed through the budget. When budgetary financing stopped, a special fund was created to finance higher education, but the amount of money that accumulated in this fund proved to be insufficient and contributions from the budget continued to be needed. In fact, the budget remained the main source of funds. However, the new situation meant that higher education institutions were allowed to earn their own income from independent sources and to spend this income as they saw fit. One of the sources of income, for instance, was post-graduate study for which payment was made by students themselves or by organisations interested in their further education.

The financing of the two-year post-secondary schools followed the pattern of other institutions of higher education, but each Republic was allowed to organise, and also to finance, these schools according to its own needs.

In Croatia, such schools were founded by business organisations, social service organisations, and the smaller socio-political communities (local authorities, Communes and Districts) which also provided all funds for their operation. The only exceptions to this rule were the post-secondary schools of public administration, social work and statistics, which had been founded before the passage of the Resolution and which therefore continued to be financed from the Croatian Republic budget.

In the other Republics, two-year post-secondary schools were instituted in a different way: they were founded mostly by Republic government decrees or acts of parliament and were therefore financed through Republic budgets or special educational funds. Business and social service organisations appeared only exceptionally as founders of such schools in these Republics. That is why changes in post-secondary school networks (merging, liquidation, etc.) were more easily made in the other Republics than in Croatia.

New schemes for educational financing were adopted in all Republics in the course of 1968/69. They involved the formation of Associations for Educational Financing as new, independent bodies that accumulate all funds intended for education and then distribute them among educational institutions. However, also under the new scheme, the pattern of relations between the education system and its users is different in Croatia from that in the other Yugoslav Republics.

In addition to the Association for the Financing of Compulsory Education (9 years), Croatia also has the Association for theFinancing of Post-Compulsory Education for all secondary and post-secondary schools, Colleges and Faculties. The funds that the Association accumulates derive from taxes on wages and salaries (3%, taxed at source) and are then distributed on the basis of contracts concluded between the Association and individual educational institutions. Ideally, the funds should be allocated to institutions in accordance with their educational programmes, but in practice they are still allocated according to their earlier spending patterns. The method of educational financing in Croatia at present is regarded as temporary, because it is expected that the Association will in the future establish direct relations with those interested in the financing of education (i. e. business and public service organisations) and determine with them, in the spirit of self-government, what the policies of education should be and how much should be spent on it.

The Associations for Educational Financing in the other Republics are nothing but a new type of budgetary body formed with the express purpose of serving as channels for educational funds. In these Republics, too, representatives of the economy and social service organisations influence the policies and distribution of funds in the sphere of education, but Croatia remains the only Yugoslav Republic to envisage a direct link between schools and those who pay for their operation or use their "products". Only time will show which of the two approaches is more effective.

In addition to the funds received from the Association, the two-year post-secondary schools may supplement their income by selling their services (in the form of special courses, consultantships, etc.) directly to business and social service organisations.

# IV

## NEED FOR BETTER INTEGRATION INTO THE SYSTEM OF HIGHER EDUCATION

It will be recalled that according to the existing legislation, the two-year post-secondary schools are essentially teaching institutions of post-secondary level whose main aim is to train personnel for jobs requiring limited theoretical knowledge and sound mastery of a given technology, together with certain operational skills. Faculties and Colleges, on the other hand, are engaged in scientific activities and in training and educating personnel for jobs requiring broader scientific and theoretical foundations and prepared to follow the development of their scientific disciplines and develop new technologies in their fields of study. In addition, the existing legislation authorizes Faculties and Colleges to organise two-year post-secondary courses as a self-contained whole, with the awarding of corresponding degrees, or as a part of a four-year course.

However, a new Higher Education Bill is now in preparation (reference is made to the Croatian Bill, but the situation is not much different in the other Republics) which represents a radical departure from the existing Higher Education Act in one important respect: while, until now, faculties and colleges have as a rule organised first-level study as a separate, self-contained unit, and only exceptionally, and where the division was impossible, as an integral part of the total two-level education, the new legislation - when adopted - will on the contrary make integrated first- and second-level study a rule while a separate first level will be considered an exception.

The following conditions govern admission of students from the first to the second cycle:

- Faculty or College Statutes and Faculty or College Boards (assemblies of teachers) determine the types of two-year post-secondary schools whose graduates can be admitted to the second level;

- if the curricula of particular post-secondary schools do not allow their graduates to pursue further studies at the second level, faculty boards may establish for these graduates special examinations (which can be passed before or during study at the second level);
- the post-secondary schools affected by Faculty or College Board's decisions may - if dissatisfied with these decisions - appeal to Faculty or College Councils and ask that unfavourable and what they consider to be unfair decisions be reconsidered.

According to the present legislation, two-year post-secondary schools can, theoretically, become part of the university. Universities themselves have made provisions for this in their statutes. Thus, for instance, the statutes of the University of Zagreb provide for the membership of those post-secondary schools which satisfy certain general requirements (that their foundation and operation is in accordance with the Higher Education Act and that they accept the Zagreb University statutes), and on the condition that this membership will contribute to the school's operation and also reflect creditably on all the Faculties and Colleges already included in the university. In practice, however, not a single two-year post-secondary school has been admitted into any Yugoslav university. This situation is very interesting in view of the fact that, first, there are Faculties which still run first-level courses of study corresponding closely in all essential respects (such as duration and curricula) to similar courses run by post-secondary schools, and, second, that a number of post-secondary schools train graduates with qualification profiles that no university institution offers at present. In short, it can be said that co-operation between two-year post-secondary schools and universities is still only sporadic, despite quite real possibilities for such co-operation. The only examples of closer co-operation can be found between some faculties and post-secondary schools working in the same fields of study.

As already mentioned, according to the new Higher Education Bills, some Yugoslav Republics have chosen to include two-year schools in an integrated system of higher education, but that does not imply that they are an integrated part of the university set-up.

Representatives of two-year post-secondary schools want them to be part of the universities: they claim that this would improve the status of such schools and have a very favourable effect on their educational standards; as part of the university, these schools would be more ready to accept standards of work and behaviour characteristics of Faculties and Colleges.

Representatives of universities, on the other hand, claim that the fundamental difference between Faculties and post-secondary schools is that Faculty teachers must engage in research, while post-secondary schools - being essentially teaching institutions - have teachers for whom scientific research is only optional. Furthermore, they claim that the inclusion of post-secondary schools would make universities too large. However, the problem of size plagues universities even now when post-secondary schools remain outside: it could be resolved by forming independent organisational units within the university - either on a territorial basis or by fields of study.

In a conference on the training of economists held in Zadar recently a model of education was presented which proposed to organise University, College and post-secondary school training under a "single roof". All institutions training personnel in a given field would form a community and co-ordinate their efforts. This proposal deserves our full attention as a serious attempt to approach the problem of personnel training at all levels in a new light and also as a potential solution to the problem of relations between post-secondary schools on the one hand and Faculties and Colleges on the other.

In conclusion, we feel that existing legislation does not yet define adequately the role and place of first-level education; the draft new legislation would even abolish it altogether at Faculties and Colleges, merging it with the second level into an integrated whole.

There can be no doubt that the need for personnel with first-level qualifications is very great and will not be easily satisfied in the foreseeable future. The fact that the draft Higher Education Bill does not even provide for separate first-level study at faculties and colleges suggests that these institutions are too busy to engage in separate first-level training. Also, since faculties will have to pay increasing attention to research (as stipulated in Article 34 of the Bill), the best solution would seem to be to take first-level study from the universities altogether wherever feasible and to leave it to special two-year post-secondary schools. Faculties and Colleges would then have more time to concentrate on second- and third-level study, where the tasks are different from those on the first level.

# V

## TEACHERS

There are two types of teachers at two-year post-secondary schools: a) professors and b) lecturers. According to existing legislation and statutes of different schools, a post-secondary school professor's post can be held by a person who has a doctor's degree, or who is a second-level (university) graduate with a number of professional publications. In addition, he should have several years of teaching experience or experience in leadership positions in his profession and should show ability for independent teaching.

The post of lecturer can be held by university graduates showing complete mastery of their discipline, as well as experience and ability in independent teaching.

The auxiliary teaching staff at two-year post-secondary schools includes Assistant Lecturers, Foreign Language Teachers, Practical Exercise Supervisors, Skill Instructors, Technical Assistants, Laboratory Teachers, etc. Their teaching tasks, as well as the manner in which they are appointed, are regulated by the statutes of individual schools.

Appointment to all teaching positions is by public competition. Appointments are made on the basis of the report of a specially nominated commission, consisting of three to five members, two of whom must be experts in the discipline for which the appointment is being made and all of whom must already hold similar or higher positions. The commission reports to the Board of Teachers, which then appoints the candidate. But before the appointment becomes effective, it must be confirmed by the School Council.

Professors are subject to re-appointment every five years, and lecturers and the auxiliary teaching staff every three years. The procedure for re-appointment is the same as that for initial appointment.

When two-year post-secondary schools were first established, a great deal of attention was paid to the recruitment of teachers and the auxiliary teaching staff. A certain number of teachers came from Faculties, while the rest came from various scientific and research institutions and business firms.

In view of the general shortage of teachers at all levels of education, only some of the teaching posts could be filled by full-time teachers; the majority were filled by part-time teachers from Faculties, Colleges and other post-secondary schools, as well as from different institutions and business firms. Part-time teachers for theoretical subjects came mainly from Faculties, while teachers of practical skills were prominent specialists from industry and social service organisations.

Wherever possible, the policy has been to fill all teaching posts by full-time staff, but the fact remains that many posts, especially for some critical subjects, are still filled by part-time teachers.

However, this solution offers certain advantages as well. First, it is sometimes desirable to have a part-time teacher for a particular subject - for instance, when the required amount of teaching, tutorials, examinations, etc. does not justify the employment of a person full-time. Second, and more important, there are subjects for which it is vital for the teacher to remain in constant touch with practical developments. The teacher who spends part of his time on an important job in industry, business or in a social service organisation is best qualified to teach students how to combine theory with practice and how to apply new discoveries in science and technology most rationally in everyday practical work. In addition, he is the person most willing to introduce innovations in teaching.

Another development worth noting is that many post-secondary school teachers leave their jobs to become teachers at Faculties. Often they do this because Faculties offer better opportunities for research; sometimes they do it for reasons of prestige, or because salary scales are higher at Faculties. A typical example of this development is the situation in Niš (Serbia) where a two-year post-secondary school of Commerce and Economics was opened in 1956. In 1959 the Faculty of Law and Economics was opened in the same city and during the first five years of its life seven teachers left the post-secondary school and joined the Faculty. Similar examples can be found in other parts of the country.

Since the number of teachers, compared to the number of students, is still inadequate, further efforts are being made to increase the number of teachers and the auxiliary teaching staff and create conditions for their faster professional, pedagogic and scientific upgrading.

Table 12. TEACHING STAFF IN TWO-YEAR POST-SECONDARY SCHOOLS IN YUGOSLAVIA, 1967/68

| TYPES OF TWO-YEAR POST-SECONDARY SCHOOLS | TEACHERS | | | | | | AUXILIARY TEACHING STAFF | | | | |
|---|---|---|---|---|---|---|---|---|---|---|---|
| | GRAND TOTAL | FULL-TIME | | | | PART-TIME | GRAND TOTAL | FULL-TIME | | | PART-TIME |
| | | TOTAL | PROFESSORS | LECTURERS | OTHER | | | TOTAL | ASSISTANT LECTURERS | OTHER | |
| Total - All schools .......... | 3,288 | 1,507 | 1,044 | 431 | 32 | 1,781 | 698 | 282 | 118 | 164 | 416 |
| Teacher training ........... | 1,217 | 817 | 555 | 239 | 23 | 400 | 195 | 106 | 24 | 82 | 89 |
| Technical and Engineering .... | 736 | 234 | 155 | 79 | 1 | 501 | 250 | 77 | 49 | 28 | 173 |
| Agriculture ................. | 185 | 91 | 56 | 28 | 7 | 94 | 18 | 10 | 9 | 1 | 8 |
| Transport ................... | 158 | 60 | 48 | 12 | - | 98 | 21 | 4 | - | 4 | 17 |
| Economics and Business Administration ........... | 383 | 164 | 133 | 31 | - | 219 | 59 | 13 | 11 | 2 | 46 |
| Statistical .................. | 33 | 3 | 3 | - | - | 30 | 9 | 1 | - | 1 | 8 |
| Law and Public Administration. | 150 | 43 | 34 | 8 | 1 | 107 | 6 | 5 | 4 | 1 | 1 |
| Medical .................... | 155 | 24 | 15 | 9 | - | 131 | 106 | 49 | 18 | 31 | 37 |
| For social workers ......... | 82 | 26 | 23 | 3 | - | 56 | 17 | 4 | 1 | 3 | 13 |
| Production organisation ...... | 154 | 36 | 14 | 22 | - | 118 | 17 | 13 | 2 | 11 | 4 |
| For Social Insurance personnel. | 28 | 2 | 2 | - | - | 26 | - | - | - | - | - |
| Social and political sciences .. | 7 | 6 | 6 | - | - | 1 | - | - | - | - | - |

Table 13. SALARY GRADES FOR TEACHERS AND THE AUXILIARY TEACHING STAFF AT FACULTIES AND TWO-YEAR POST-SECONDARY SCHOOLS IN CROATIA

| TEACHER GRADES AT FACULTIES | TEACHER GRADES AT TWO-YEAR POST-SECONDARY SCHOOLS | ESTIMATED MONTHLY SALARY, IN NEW DINARS | |
|---|---|---|---|
| Full professor ................. | | 3,200 | |
| Associate professor ............ | | 2,800 | Supplementary payment: |
| Senior lecturer ............... | | 2,500 | (a) for Doctor's degree, 300 |
| Assistant professor ........... | Professor | 2,400 | (b) for M. A. degree, 200 |
| Lecturer ..................... | Lecturer | 2,000 | |
| Foreign language teacher ......... | | 1,900 | |
| Assistant lecturer .............. | | 1,800 | |

Table 12 shows the number of teachers and the auxiliary teaching staff in Yugoslav two-year post-secondary schools in 1967/68.

Remuneration schemes for teachers in two-year post-secondary schools are still rather uneven. Teacher salaries have so far depended on the financial resources of the founding organisation: in schools founded by rich industries or business organisations, salaries have been much higher than in those where founders were various social or public bodies or less well-to-do business organisations.

Many schools have introduced tuition fees to supplement their income. Since their students were mainly people already employed and whose employers were willing to pay their tuition fees, such schools generally managed to secure enough money to pay reasonably high salaries to their teachers. Thus, in a number of cases, teachers at two-year post-secondary schools have had considerably higher salaries than their colleagues in comparable grades at Faculties.

The situation changed to a certain extent when the Association for the Financing of Post-Compulsory Education began to operate as a body collecting funds from all industrial and business organisations and distributing them to educational institutions on the basis of contracts which stipulate the kind of educational programme to be offered by each particular institution. The qualifications of the institution's teaching staff is one of the criteria that determine the amount of money that it can get from the Association.

However, post-secondary schools still find it easier than Faculties to obtain additional funds from other sources and to use them to improve the salaries of their teaching staff. These additional funds are mainly the result of special arrangements that schools make with certain business (and non-business) organisations - usually for courses specially prepared for groups of employees in these organisations.

Table 13 gives the monthly salaries of teachers that the Croatian Association for the Financing of Post-Compulsory Education used for guidance when signing contracts with Faculties and two-year post-secondary schools for 1970. *

* Bulletin of the Croation Association for the Financing of Post-Compulsory Education, No. 3, Zagreb, May 1970.

# VI

## ADMISSION AND STATUS OF STUDENTS

### Admission requirements

According to existing Yugoslav legislation, all institutions of higher education (including two-year post-secondary schools) admit graduates of "adequate" or "corresponding" secondary schools, and the statutes of each institution of higher learning specify which types of secondary schools are to be regarded as "adequate" for enrolment in that particular institution. In practice, however, two-year post-secondary schools and all other institutions of higher learning also accept those candidates who come from secondary schools which are not "corresponding", but who can pass the institution's entrance examination and satisfy the admission board that they have the necessary knowledge to follow the chosen course of study in that institution. Criteria are also set for candidates without any formal secondary qualifications: they should be over eighteen, have completed at least the eight-year elementary school, have a certain amount of working experience, and pass the prescribed entrance examination for the chosen course of study.

Such admission regulations were designed to take account of the situation in Yugoslav society: a considerable number of people who had no opportunity of completing regular secondary education, but who had accumulated valuable practical experience and possessed both the inclination and ability for higher education, were thus given a chance to complete their academic education.

The draft of the new Higher Education Bill assumes that the situation has now changed, that everyone who so wishes can complete secondary education, and that only holders of secondary school-leaving certificates may be admitted to institutions of higher education. However, since the Bill is still in its public discussion stage, it is difficult to say whether all interested forces in the country (for instance, the Trade Unions) will accept this provision.

The present legislation, in providing for the enrolment of persons without the necessary secondary school qualifications, stipulates that such persons must have worked at least four years in jobs related to the candidate's future course of study at a Faculty, College or two-year post-secondary school.

Enrolment in the first year of study is by competitive examination which must be publicly announced at least three months before it is due to be held (six months in cases where enrolment is limited by numbers of places available).

Grammar schools (Gymnasia) are generally regarded as "corresponding" or "adequate" for enrolment in all types of institutions of higher education. The general rule is that secondary schools are "adequate" when they correspond to the same field of study as the institution of higher education to which the candidate applies. Thus, for instance, the secondary technical school of mechanical engineering will be considered "adequate" for enrolment at the Faculty of Mechanical Engineering or the two-year post-secondary school of Mechanical Engineering. Similar relationships exist in other disciplines; for example, the secondary school of business administration is "adequate" for enrolment at the Faculty of Economics, College of Business Administration, or the two-year post-secondary school of Business Administration.

The entrance examination for candidates without the necessary secondary school qualifications covers the subject matter taught in the secondary school in the following subjects: the mother tongue and literature of the Yugoslav peoples, mathematics, history, geography, physics, chemistry and a foreign language. The contents of the examination vary with different institutions of higher education. In most cases, the candidate must demonstrate his ability to express himself in writing in his mother tongue (this is tested by a composition paper he writes), while the scope of coverage in the other subjects listed here depends on their relevance to the course of study chosen by the applicant. Thus, for instance, Engineering Faculties, Colleges and two-year post-secondary schools stress the knowledge of mathematics, physics and chemistry.

Differential examinations are set for those candidates who come from secondary schools not regarded as "adequate".

When the number of applicants exceeds the number of places in a particular higher education institution, all applicants must take a selective examination. Applicants with top secondary school grades and recipients of awards for outstanding results in secondary education are exempt from qualifying examinations at many Faculties and two-year post-secondary schools.

The breakdown of students attending two-year post-secondary schools according to their previous school background shows that about one-third of students come from grammar schools and approximately two-thirds come from secondary technical and vocational schools regarded as adequate.

# VII

## PART-TIME STUDY

In the early post-war period, interest in part-time study became increasingly apparent when a considerable number of people already engaged in the labour force were seeking ways of continuing their education. Part-time students started to enrol mainly at Faculties of Law, Arts and Letters, and Economics, and at Teacher Training Colleges. This was understandable in view of the fact that teaching at such institutions was mainly theoretical and thus students could easily study independently either from textbooks, mimeographed lecture notes and/or other sources, without attending lectures and seminars regularly. The growing importance of this form of study was soon realized, and became regulated by laws, statutes and rules of study. For example, the already-mentioned Federal Assembly's Resolution on Technical Personnel paid special attention to permanent education, in-service education and part-time study, and the Federal General Law on Education devotes a separate article to the possibility of part-time higher education at post-secondary schools, Colleges, Art Academies, and Faculties. Similar stipulations are found in Higher Education Acts of the different Yugoslav Republics, while the statutes of individual institutions of higher learning lay down detailed conditions and organisation of this form of study.

Part-time study is open to the economically active population of Yugoslavia and to those who, though unemployed, are genuinely unable to enrol as full-time students. Of course, the applicant must also meet all other conditions required for full-time studies.

Statistics on enrolments show that the number of part-time students at two-year post-secondary schools is rising steadily. The last few years (see Tables 6, 7 and 8) are an exception.

The majority of part-time students are enrolled in post-secondary schools of economics and commerce and in teacher training schools;

a somewhat smaller number are found at post-secondary schools of law and public administration and at different types of technical and engineering schools.

Post-secondary schools enrolling part-time students provide a certain number of facilities enabling them to study more easily. In most cases, special classes are held to introduce them to different subjects and to teach them methods of independent study. Some schools also run special afternoon or evening courses for part-time students or invite them, at regular intervals, to come for intensive courses or seminar work. Laboratory work and practical exercises for part-time students are usually shorter but also more intensive than for their full-time colleagues. Like lectures and seminars, they are arranged to suit students' free time. Teachers meet students individually or in groups in pre-examination periods and during the preparation of seminar papers and reports.

Some post-secondary schools are seeking new ways of developing contacts with their part-time students and improving the system of part-time study as a whole. The Merchant Navy Post-Secondary School of Piran, for example, has introduced a correspondence course for its first-year students; the Two-Year Post-Secondary School of Economics in Varaždin offers a correspondence course for both years of study in some of its departments. Plans are now under way for a correspondence course with programmed textbooks.

Since most part-time students live and work outside the place where their school is situated, post-secondary schools often set up special "Part-time Study Centres" in places where there are sufficient numbers of part-time students in need of assistance. Such centres are usually organised and run in conjunction with large business organisations, institutions, professional societies, some schools, and adult education centres of the region (People's and Workers's Universities, etc.).

Schools usually appoint one teacher, or a panel of teachers, responsible for the work of local centres.

The number of local centres for part-time study is fairly high and their network is well developed. In 1965/66 there were 236 such centres throughout the country and they offered assistance to over 12,000 part-time students. The highest proportion of local centres was run by post-secondary schools of economics and commerce, followed by teacher training schools and technical schools of different kinds.

The high number of part-time study centres in large and small towns in different parts of the country is a sign of the growing desire of people already employed to seek further education; it is also a sign of the important role played by the two-year post-secondary schools in meeting this need. The rapid growth of such centres has however sometimes resulted in inadequate working conditions: some centres lacked the necessary material and professional support and the quality of their work was rightly criticized. On the other hand, there are numerous centres which have done excellent work in training part-time students and which can serve as models of organisation.

It is generally agreed that in the field of higher education two-year post-secondary schools have done the biggest job in providing education for those already in employment. They are still seeking new forms of part-time education that would meet the needs of the economy and the aspirations and motivations of the students themselves. In this, they have to struggle with time and distance; they have to adjust their programmes of instruction to the needs and abilities of students; and they have to bear in mind modern principles of adult education.

It cannot be claimed that part-time post-secondary education has reached maximum efficiency:the proportion of part-time students who complete their studies in time is still below expectation, and many students prolong their studies considerably. A certain number of part-time students, like those enrolled at Faculties, drop out before they reach the end of the prescribed course of study. The reasons given for drop-out are varied: poor health, family obligations, difficulties in the job, lack of understanding and support in the firm, loss of motivation for study, etc. However, it can probably be said that even a few semesters of part-time study and a few successful examinations may widen the students' horizons and enable them to do better in their jobs.

There is no difference in curricula between part-time and full-time studies: students in both categories study the same subjects, have the same number of practical exercises and seminars, the same number of examinations, are required to write the same seminar papers and reports and expected to possess the same amount of knowledge at final examinations. That is why no distinction is made between graduates who were part-time students and those who studied full-time.

In addition to being an important form of personnel upgrading, part-time study also offers, in many cases, the only opportunity for improving the qualification structure of the labour force in particular sectors. This is precisely why many business and social service organisations have attached a great deal of importance to part-time study and have been ready to help both schools and students engaged in this form of education.

Students are often relieved of some of their duties at work in order to attend lectures, seminars, tutorials, or practical exercises. In other cases they are allowed to work shorter hours, work in the shift that is most convenient to them, or take unpaid leave. Some firms pay their employees' travel expenses and daily allowances to go to school. Others pay their tuition fees, buy them books and other supplies. In some cases, part-time students are allowed to work shorter hours or stay at home for a few days in the period before examinations and for the preparation of papers and reports.

These benefits naturally vary from company to company, depending on their personnel and training policies and on the general attitude towards skilled people and education.

# VIII

## RELATIONS BETWEEN POST-SECONDARY SCHOOLS AND SOCIETY

We have already noted that the encouragement given to form a network of Two-Year Post-Secondary Schools came originally from the Yugoslav Federal Assembly as an expression of the country's need for technical personnel with this particular level of qualification

Although the rapid expansion created numerous problems, the general conclusion remains that the majority of these schools have fulfilled society's expectations. This can best be seen in the increased employment of post-secondary school graduates, since this reflects clearly the needs of society for specialists trained in such schools.

### Employment of post-secondary school graduates

The employment of post-secondary school graduates can be followed throughout the period beginning 31st March, 1961, (date of the census) and ending in 1968:

Table 14 shows that the increase in employment was fastest for the category of employees with post-secondary school qualifications. Their proportion in the total labour force increased correspondingly during this period: in 1961 they accounted for 2. 1% of the economically active population; the percentage rose to 2. 5% in 1966 and 2. 6% in 1967, to reach 3. 3% in 1968. (The proportion of people with university qualifications was 4. 9% in 1968.)

In view of this trend and the large number of people (in absolute terms) with such qualifications, it is justifiable to stress the economic and social relevance of this type of education.

Another indicator of the importance of post-secondary education is the number of jobs for which this education is required (Table 15).

Table 14. NUMBER OF PEOPLE EMPLOYED (IN THOUSANDS)

| CATEGORIES OF EMPLOYEES | 1961 | 1966 | 1967 | 1968 | INDEX 1968/1961 |
|---|---|---|---|---|---|
| Total employed .... | 3,313 | 3,351 | 3,529 | 3,508 | 105.9 |
| University qualifications ..... | 122 | 152 | 158 | 173 | 141.8 |
| Post-secondary qualifications ..... | 69 | 88 | 93 | 116 | 168.1 |
| Secondary qualifications ..... | 361 | 425 | 434 | 475 | 131.6 |
| Highly skilled workers .......... | 160 | 206 | 199 | 234 | 146.9 |
| Skilled workers ... | 760 | 839 | 851 | 895 | 117.7 |

SOURCES: 1961 and 1966 - Statistical Bulletin published by the Federal Bureau of Statistics;
1967 - Census of population gainfully employed;
1968 - Statistical Yearbook of Yugoslavia, published by the Federal Bureau of Statistics (1970).

A certain reduction in the number of jobs requiring post-secondary school qualifications is the result of changes in the level of employment. Comparing these figures with those given in the preceding Table 14, we note that 41% of jobs requiring post-secondary qualifications remained vacant in 1966; in 1969, the percentage was reduced to 24%.

Apart from the social science graduates, all other types of graduates - particularly those coming from technical and medical schools - are in much greater demand than before. In 1968, graduates from teacher training and medical schools were employed mainly in the non-productive branches (i.e. social service organisations); those from social science schools were evenly distributed in the productive and non-productive branches, while other categories of graduates were employed mainly in the productive branches of the economy (Table 17).

We see that the demand of the economy and social services for two-year post-secondary school graduates grew over the period under review, with the exception of social science graduates, where the demand declined. Available data do not allow a more detailed analysis of the structure of demand; such an analysis would possibly modify the

Table 15. NUMBER (IN THOUSANDS) AND PERCENTAGE OF JOBS REQUIRING DIFFERENT LEVELS OF QUALIFICATION

| REQUIRED LEVEL OF QUALIFICATION AND SKILL | 30.9.1966 | | 31.3.1967 | | 31.1.1968 | |
|---|---|---|---|---|---|---|
| | NUMBER | % | NUMBER | % | NUMBER | % |
| University qualifications .... | 207 | 5.8 | 224 | 6.4 | 218 | 6.2 |
| Post-secondary qualifications .... | 149 | 4.2 | 159 | 4.5 | 152 | 4.3 |
| - in the economy .. | 69 | 2.3 | 70 | 2.5 | 66 | 2.3 |
| - social services . | 80 | 13.4 | 89 | 13.4 | 86 | 13.3 |
| Secondary qualifications .... | 499 | 14.1 | 533 | 15.1 | 530 | 15.1 |
| Highly skilled workers ......... | 319 | 9.0 | 328 | 9.3 | 318 | 9.1 |
| Skilled workers .. | 1,002 | 28.2 | 1,059 | 30.0 | 992 | 28.3 |

SOURCES: 1966 - Statistical Bulletin No. 488.
1967 - Census of population gainfully employed.
1968 - Statistical Yearbook of Yugoslavia (1970).

Table 16. NUMBER AND PERCENTAGE OF POST-SECONDARY SCHOOL GRADUATES IN THE LABOUR FORCE - BY TYPE OF SCHOOL

| MAIN GROUPS OF POST-SECONDARY (FIRST-LEVEL) SCHOOLS | 1966 | | 1968 | | INDEX 1968/1966 |
|---|---|---|---|---|---|
| | NUMBER | % | NUMBER | % | |
| Teacher training ... | 32,757 | 41.7 | 41,557 | 39.8 | 127 |
| Social sciences ..... | 6,634 | 8.5 | 5,761 | 5.5 | 87 |
| Technical and engineering ........ | 6,263 | 7.9 | 9,254 | 8.9 | 148 |
| Agriculture ........ | 1,633 | 2.2 | 2,178 | 2.2 | 133 |
| Medical ........... | 3,705 | 4.7 | 5,187 | 4.9 | 140 |
| Other schools ...... | 27,511 | 35.0 | 40,423 | 38.7 | 147 |
| Total .............. | 78,503 | 100.0 | 104,360 | 100.0 | 133 |

Table 17. EMPLOYMENT OF POST-SECONDARY SCHOOL GRADUATES BY TYPE OF SCHOOL AND SECTOR (1966-1968)

| MAIN GROUPS OF POST-SECONDARY SCHOOLS | 1966 | | 1968 | | INDEX 1968 | |
|---|---|---|---|---|---|---|
| | PRODUCTIVE | NON-PRODUCTIVE | PRODUCTIVE | NON-PRODUCTIVE | PRODUCTIVE | NON-PRODUCTIVE |
| Teacher training ........ | 1,053 | 31,704 | 1,224 | 40,273 | 116 | 127 |
| Social sciences ......... | 3,253 | 3,381 | 2,933 | 2,828 | 90 | 84 |
| Technical and engineering . | 5,291 | 972 | 7,721 | 1,533 | 146 | 158 |
| Agricultural ............ | 1,361 | 272 | 1,822 | 356 | 134 | 131 |
| Medical ............... | 103 | 3,602 | 233 | 4,954 | 226 | 137 |
| Other schools[1] ......... | 15,136 | 12,375 | 21,771 | 18,654 | 144 | 151 |

1. "Other schools" include industrial organisation and public administration schools; their graduates are at present in high demand due to the great efforts of the economy at modernization and implementation of a programme of economic and social reforms.

SOURCES: Statistical Bulletin, No. 490 for 1966, and unpublished data for 1968 supplied by the Federal Bureau of Statistics.

general picture to a certain extent. But the general conclusion remains that the highest demand is for technical and engineering school graduates, a pattern characteristic of the Yugoslav economy in recent years.

Post-secondary school graduates occupy important managerial positions in industry and other branches of the economy. A rough indicator of this situation is obtained through an analysis of reappointments of general managers of various business firms in 1966 and 1968 (general managers of Yugoslav firms are subject to reappointment at regular intervals). In 1966, 1,077 general managers were reappointed; their qualification structure was as follows (cf. Statistical Bulletin, Nos. 447 and 570); 188 (17.4%) had university backgrounds, 188 (17.4%) had post-secondary school backgrounds, while 741 (65.2%) had other types of qualification. In 1968, 2,727 general managers were reappointed, of whom 566 (20.8%) were university graduates, 369 (13.5%) were post-secondary school graduates, and 1,792 (65.7%) belonged to other categories of qualification.

One concludes from such figures that the number of post-secondary school graduates among general managers of Yugoslav enterprises is about 15%, which is a pretty high figure considering that post-secondary graduates compete for these jobs with university graduates. Another interesting illustration is given by the results of a recent survey by the Market Research Institute of Belgrade in 16 Serbian business firms (the results refer to the situation at the end of 1969). The sixteen firms had 490 people in managerial and executive positions; 209 of them (42.7%) had university qualifications, while 60 (12.2%) had post-secondary qualifications.

Data are also available on the number of unemployed post-secondary school graduates: in 1965, there were 407 of them, in 1967 there were 1,520, in 1968 3,101, and in 1970 4,504. (Cf. Bulletins of the Federal Employment Office for these years.) The unemployment of post-secondary school graduates at the time when many jobs requiring such qualifications remain unfilled is most often due to the fact that some business organisations remain closed to qualified people, particularly young specialists. *

It is interesting to observe the distribution of unemployed graduates by types of schools from which they come:

* This apparently illogical unwillingness on the part of industry must be considered at the macro-level: as each enterprise works as an economic unit, autonomous in the economic and self-managemental sense, the employment of a new member in the unit apparently decreases the overall income of the unit which has therefore to be divided among a larger number of recipients. This is often the main reason to the resistance to new job openings.

Table 18. UNEMPLOYMENT OF POST-SECONDARY SCHOOL GRADUATES

| TYPES OF POST-SECONDARY SCHOOLS | 30.6.1968 | 30.6.1970 | INDEX 1970 |
|---|---|---|---|
| Technical and engineering .......... | 242 | 258 | 106.6 |
| Economic and commercial .......... | 756 | 611 | 80.8 |
| Public administration .. | 280 | 369 | 131.8 |
| Social work .......... | 116 | 157 | 135.3 |
| Teacher training ..... | 428 | 1,587 | 371.7 |
| Other schools ........ | 1,280 | 803 | 62.7 |
| Total ................ | 3,101 | 4,505 | 145.2 |

While the unemployment of economic and commercial school graduates is on its way down and that of technical and engineering school graduates shows a mild upward trend, the unemployment of graduates coming from post-secondary teacher training schools shows a dramatic increase. This can be explained by the fact that many types of schools employing such graduates have either closed down or cut down their activities, but it is still noteworthy that at the end of 1968 there were over 6,000 unfilled jobs in various cultural and social institutions for which teacher training school graduates were well qualified. The number of unemployed graduates coming from "other" post-secondary schools is reduced, owing to the fact that such schools have adapted to the needs of the economy and social service organisations. *

The unemployment of post-secondary school graduates - like the unemployment of other types of manpower - also has its marked regional characteristics, as can be seen from the Table 19, which gives the regional breakdown of unemployment for post-secondary teacher training school graduates.

* It can also be argued that the main cause of discrepancy between job openings and unemployment of graduates of the two-year post-secondary schools is the fact that the majority of the graduates want to stay in the bigger cities where they have studied and are unwilling to go to the regions and villages that most feel the need for teachers and other experts.

Table 19. NUMBER OF UNEMPLOYED TEACHER TRAINING SCHOOL GRADUATES AND AVAILABLE JOB OPENINGS, BY REPUBLICS AND AUTONOMOUS PROVINCES, 30th SEPTEMBER, 1969

| REGION | (1) UNEMPLOYED | (2) JOB OPENINGS | (2-1) DIFFERENCE |
|---|---|---|---|
| Bosnia and Herzegovina .......... | 84 | 80 | -4 |
| Montenegro .......... | 23 | 3 | -20 |
| Croatia ............. | 405 | 65 | -340 |
| Macedonia .......... | 245 | 32 | -213 |
| Slovenia ............. | 29 | 141 | +112 |
| Serbia proper ........ | 570 | 76 | -494 |
| Voivodina ........... | 107 | 14 | -93 |
| Kosovo ............. | 12 | 12 | 0 |
| Yugoslavia .......... | 1,475 | 423 | -1,052 |

Table 19 shows that Slovenia, for instance, has a shortage of teacher training school graduates - judging merely by the demand recorded in municipal employment offices. In Kosovo, too, there are as many job openings as there are unemployed graduates, and the excess number of graduates in Bosnia and Herzegovina and Montenegro is negligible. The problem of finding jobs for such graduates is thus confined to the remaining four parts of the country, and particularly to their cities. In Serbia, for instance, Belgrade, Kragujevac and Niš record 324 unemployed graduates and only 32 job openings; in Croatia, the cities of Zagreb, Rijeka and Sisak have 259 unemployed graduates from post-secondary teacher training schools and only 8 vacant jobs.

The present discrepancy between increased demand for two-year post-secondary school graduates on the one hand and their growing unemployment in recent years on the other, could be removed by filling all jobs requiring post-secondary qualifications with adequately trained people, by effecting a certain amount of re-orientation in the schools and by their better regional distribution. If this could be done Yugoslavia would have a shortage, rather than a surplus, of post-secondary school graduates. The shortage would be particularly pronounced in the technical and engineering, economic and commercial branches, and in some other types of specialist training.

## Types of co-operation between Two-Year Post-Secondary Schools and the economy

In order to improve the relations between two-year post-secondary schools and the economy, the Federal Chamber of Commerce has made a survey of the existing types of co-operation between such schools and the economy. The interesting results of this survey are presented here in summary form.

The survey covered 95 business organisations and 41 two-year post-secondary schools. Of the 95 business organisations from all parts of Yugoslavia, 75 were industrial, 6 agricultural, 3 trade organisations, 4 building and 7 transport organisations. Of the 41 schools, 8 were social science schools, 24 technical and engineering, and 9 agricultural schools.

### 1. Results of the survey in schools

According to the results of this survey, co-operation between post-secondary schools and business organisations exist in the following spheres:

a) financing;

b) personnel training and permanent education;

c) exchange of experts;

d) research and development activities;

e) participation of representatives of business firms in schools' bodies of self-government;

f) scholarships.

Most schools have developed some form of co-operation with the economy but very few of them have formal bodies entrusted with this function, such as joint committees or groups of teachers: only 3 schools included in the survey had joint committees, and 4 schools had groups of teachers for contacts with business organisations.

#### a) Financing

The figures show that the total income in 1969 was about 24% more than in 1968. Except for the grants from scientific research funds, which were reduced, income from all other sources was higher in 1969.

The funds provided by educational financing associations represented 64. 7% of the total income of two-year post-secondary schools in 1969;

the comparable figure for Faculties was 80%. It is also important to note that the relative importance of this source is decreasing, while that of industry and individuals who pay their own tuition fees is increasing. This is explained by the large number of part-time enrolments in post-secondary schools: since educational financing associations do not pay as much for part-time study as they do for full-time, business organisations (and individual students) have to pay the difference.

Table 20. SCHOOL INCOME BY SOURCE (IN THOUSANDS OF DINARS)

| SOURCE | 1968 | | 1969 | |
|---|---|---|---|---|
| | NUMBER | % | NUMBER | % |
| Educational financing associations .......... | 26,192 | 66.7 | 31,315 | 64.7 |
| Business organisations ........ | 6,823 | 17.5 | 8,950 | 18.4 |
| Students' fees ........ | 3,661 | 9.3 | 4,411 | 9.1 |
| Government agencies and social service organisations ........ | 390 | 0.9 | 615 | 1.2 |
| Revenue from school publishing activities ... | 818 | 2.3 | 1,494 | 3.3 |
| Grants from scientific research funds ....... | 24 | 0.0 | 13 | 0.0 |
| Other sources ....... | 1,308 | 3.3 | 1,590 | 3.3 |
| Total ............... | 39,216 | 100.0 | 48,388 | 100.0 |

The distribution of the main sources of income varies considerably according to the type of the post-secondary school, as shown in Table 21.

The table shows that social science and economics schools get a much lesser percentage of their income from educational financing associations than technical, engineering and agricultural schools. It is also clear from this table that business and industrial firms and private individuals paying their own tuition fees contribute much more to social science and economics schools than they do to other types of schools.

Table 21. SCHOOL INCOME BY SOURCE AND TYPE OF SCHOOL (1968)

Thousands of dinars

| SOURCE | SOCIAL SCIENCE | | TECHNICAL AND ENGINEERING | | AGRICULTURAL | |
|---|---|---|---|---|---|---|
| | AMOUNT | % | AMOUNT | % | AMOUNT | % |
| Educational financing associations ...... | 4,618 | 37.5 | 20,668 | 73.8 | 6,029 | 77.6 |
| Business organisations ..... | 4,292 | 34.9 | 3,618 | 12.8 | 1,040 | 13.4 |
| Students' fees .... | 1,909 | 15.5 | 2,071 | 7.3 | 431 | 5.6 |
| Government agencies and social service organisations | 44 | 0.3 | 563 | 2.0 | 8 | 0.1 |
| Revenue from school publishing activities. | 1,253 | 10.2 | 224 | 0.8 | 18 | 0.1 |
| Grants from scientific research funds ............ | - | - | 10 | 0.0 | 3 | 0.0 |
| Other sources .... | 193 | 1.6 | 1,150 | 4.1 | 247 | 3.2 |
| Total ............ | 12,309 | 100.0 | 28,304 | 100.0 | 7,776 | 100.0 |

b) Personnel training and permanent education

This form of co-operation involves training programmes, occasional seminars and symposia, on-the-job training for students during the summer, organisation of special courses at the request of interested business organisations and preparation of plans for manpower training. The following results have been achieved through these forms of co-operation:

1) Specialist programmes were organised by 4 two-year post-secondary schools for 499 participants;

2) occasional seminars and symposia were organised by 15 schools; 52 seminars were attended by 1,245 participants;

3) on-the-job training was organised for 2,151 students during the summer months by 19 schools in 1968/69;

4) 57 subjects were introduced into the curricula of 8 schools at the request of industrial and business organisations; technical schools were particularly active in this form of co-operation;

5) manpower training schemes were developed by 15 post-secondary schools in co-operation with the economy.

c) Exchange of experts

1) Use of experts from business firms as lecturers or auxiliary teachers in post-secondary schools.

Of the 41 schools covered by this survey, 39, of which 31 were technical schools, used professional people from industry as their part-time lecturers or auxiliary teachers; 312 professional staff from industry were employed as part-time lecturers and 138 as auxiliary teachers. The average for all schools was 8 industrial experts employed as lecturers and 4 as auxiliary teachers per school.

2) Re-training and specialization of post-secondary school teachers in industrial and business organisations.

In the course of 1968 and 1969 12 two-year post-secondary schools sent their teachers and auxiliary teaching staff to industrial and business organisations for periods of specialization; 43 teachers were involved in 1968, 52 in 1969. The numbers are growing in social science and economics schools and decreasing somewhat in technical and engineering schools. This form of co-operation is still inadequately developed and further efforts will be necessary.

d) Research and development activities

This form of co-operation is not as extensive with post-secondary schools as it is with Faculties, which can be regarded as natural in view of the fact that post-secondary schools are primarily teaching and not research institutions.

In 1968, 11 two-year post-secondary schools concluded contracts with business organisations for 67 research projects; the number of projects in 1969 was 94. A more detailed analysis of these contracts would probably show that they were for smaller projects and practical analytic work, rather than for large-scale research projects. But even smaller projects such as these are useful for both industry and schools and should be encouraged.

Most of the research contracts with business organisations were concluded by social science and economics schools. Thus, in the year

1969, 8 of these schools concluded 49 contracts, while 24 technical and engineering schools concluded only 25.

The number of teachers and auxiliary teaching staff from schools engaged in research projects was much smaller than the number of those actually qualified to do such work. In 1968 only 54 post-secondary school teachers were engaged in research projects; the corresponding figure for 1969 was 64. Admittedly, some teachers were engaged as researchers in their individual capacities: about 100 in 1968 and about 120 in 1969. Teachers from technical and engineering schools led the way, both in collective arrangements and as private individuals.

The figures of the survey show clearly that two-year post-secondary schools have both the physical and human potential to undertake applied research of value to the economy and to society as a whole. The schools covered by this survey had 6 institutes, 8 laboratories, and 1 computer centre; a total of 23 out of the 41 schools examined had facilities which could be profitably exploited by the economy. These facilities existed mainly in technical and agricultural schools but were also to be found in other types of establishment.

There is no doubt that this type of co-operation benefits all parties concerned and therefore needs to be encouraged and planned in such a way that scarce resources are used efficiently and rationally.

#### e) Participation of business firms' representatives in schools' bodies of self-government

At the time of the survey, 25 schools had 120 representatives of business and industry in their self-government bodies. This form of participation was best developed in technical schools, while it was less satisfactory in other types of schools, and there is a growing feeling that more attention should be given to it.

#### f) Scholarships

A considerable proportion of students in post-secondary schools were recipients of regular scholarships provided by business and industrial organisations. In thirty out of the 41 schools 2,330 students were receiving scholarships (1,052 of them full-time, 1,278 part-time). Scholarships were most frequent at schools for economics and commerce. These figures refer only to regular scholarships and do not include various occasional grants or subsidies given to part-time students by their firms. Nor do they include numerous other material benefits that part-time students frequently receive.

2. Results of the survey in business organisations

The 95 business and industrial organisations included in the survey employed 392,400 workers and employees. Their qualification structure was as follows: 2.8% with university qualifications, 1.68% with post-secondary qualifications. The highest number of people with post-secondary qualifications were employed in trade organisations (4.4%), followed by agriculture and industry. The percentage of employees with university and post-secondary backgrounds ranged from 0.2 to 15.5% of the total labour force of the different organisations under review.

No special analysis need be made of the forms of co-operation between these organisations and post-secondary schools; a sufficiently clear picture was given above.

Co-operation with two-year post-secondary schools in 1969 involved the following:

- 228 contracts for research projects were signed with two-year post-secondary schools and faculties, with 286 experts from these firms taking part in the research;
- 224 experts from these firms served as part-time lecturers or auxiliary teaching staff at post-secondary schools;
- 520 employees of the firms were doing post-graduate work; 1,121 attended specialization courses; 557 attended various courses and symposia organised by two-year post-secondary schools and faculties; 3,842 people from these firms were part-time students; 4,194 students spent varying periods of on-the-job training in these firms during vacations;
- 40 of the firms under review were involved, in one way or another, in the preparation of training programmes and curricula for faculties and two-year post-secondary schools; 17 firms established their own personnel training and development programmes in co-operation with appropriate post-secondary schools and faculties;
- 89 out of the 95 firms included in the survey provided 8,132 scholarships for full-time and part-time students;
- 178 faculty and post-secondary school representatives were included in workers' management bodies of ten of the business and industrial firms;
- 29 firms allocated special funds in 1969 for the purchase of equipment for faculties and two-year post-secondary schools;
- 25 firms were making plans to allocate considerable funds for these purposes in 1970.

3. Summary

Even from this fairly small sample, and considering the relatively short period of observation, it can be concluded that there is active collaboration between the economy and post-secondary schools. What is needed now is a more careful evaluation and generalization of positive experiences to strengthen this relationship and give it a more permanent character.

The different types of co-operation are still rather limited in number, and it is to be hoped that closer links will follow the integration process now under way between business and industry on the one hand and post-secondary schools on the other.

The comparatively limited involvement of experts from business and industrial firms and from post-secondary schools in research projects, permanent education schemes, and self-government bodies of the schools means that much more should be done to strengthen relations between educational institutions and the outside world on the basis of the principles stated by the Federal Assembly Resolution on Technical Personnel.

The economy quite rightly expects the two-year post-secondary schools to become much more actively engaged in seeking solutions to certain vital issues such as personnel planning and training or optimum utilization of production capacities, etc.

The present analysis, however, shows that it is also up to the economy to try to combine its own educational effort with efforts made by educational institutions. Close co-operation is indispensable if the present economic reform is to succeed.

Support for the development of close links and co-operation between the economy and the educational system should, in its own interests, be the responsibility of society as a whole. The economy and higher education should be united by the common need to develop and acquire knowledge, and this must be done both in institutions of higher learning and in business and industry. The only questions that remain are those of organisational mechanisms, of material possibilities, of realistic assessment. Such questions can be resolved jointly by schools and business organisations, with the support and encouragement of various social and government bodies.

# IX

## CONCLUSION

The introduction of new technologies, organisational growth and new methods of work have necessitated further specialization and permanent education for many of the existing jobs; at the same time, many new jobs opened for which new skills were needed at different levels of qualification.

In seeking new forms and methods of education, two-year post-secondary schools have proved to be the most convenient type of educational institution. By offering an intermediary level of education, between the secondary school and the university, the two-year post-secondary school facilitates the choice of studies in accordance with individual aspirations and abilities.

The legal status of post-secondary schools is regulated by Federal and Republican legislation. This legislation makes such schools an integral part of the Yugoslav higher education system; in practice, too, they have become recognized as institutions of higher learning performing a most useful function for the economy and social services.

The training programmes and curricula of these schools reflect the need of society and the economy for new types of skills. The programmes and curricula are highly adaptable to the specific requirements of business, industrial, and social service organisations. They are also adapted to the needs of the particular regions in which the schools operate. They follow very closely new developments in science and technology and are subject to continuous modification and modernization.

Admission requirements to two-year post-secondary schools are very similar to those for other types of institutions of higher learning. Owing to their better geographical distribution, these schools have a much better regional and social distribution of the student body than have the universities. Part-time study is also more developed in these schools than is the case at universities. Their contribution to an improved qualification structure of the Yugoslav economy by adult and permanent education of those already employed has been considerable.

The teaching staff of post-secondary schools comes from existing faculties or colleges or is recruited from among the prominent specialists in economic or social service organisations. Appointments and promotions are regulated by law and by the statutes of individual schools. Recently, there has been an increase in the number of teachers with doctoral or master degrees, and the teacher/student ratio is also improving. The widely accepted view is that it is useful to have a certain number of part-time teachers, who will enrich teaching by their practical achievements and experiences.

The increased number of schools and their more even distribution throughout the country has resulted also in the establishment of closer ties with business and industry and with various school social service organisations, which have thus found themselves in a position to influence education in the direction of their own needs. The same fact has contributed also to a better distribution of qualified graduates in different parts of the country and different branches of the economy.

Following a period of rapid expansion of higher education, including post-secondary education, a new process of consolidation and rationalization has now set in. Some institutions of higher learning have merged; a certain amount of rationalization has been introduced in the system of study and in the organisation of teaching.

The place and role of two-year post-secondary schools in the system of higher education is now better understood than it used to be: they are recognized as very useful institutions for the successful education of skilled personnel needed by modern society.

# IV

## Place and role of university institutes of technology (IUT) in the new French universities

by

Jean-Louis Quermonne
Président, Université des sciences sociales
Grenoble (France)

## CONTENTS

Introduction ........................................ 215

I. The place of IUTs in the universities ............ 219

II. The role of IUTs within the universities ......... 225

III. Obstacles to be overcome in achieving IUT integration into the universities ................. 231

# INTRODUCTION

The main forms of short-cycle higher education in France are now centred in the IUTs. This paper will therefore deal only with the latters' relations with the universities.* It should be remembered, though that they have not always enjoyed this monopoly. Before 1966 the science faculties offered preparatory courses leading to the Diplôme d'études supérieures techniques (DEST), and the technical lycées provided - and in many cases still do provide - post-Baccalauréat classes for higher technicians leading to the brevet de technicien supérieur (BTS). In addition, the law faculties offered students not holding the Baccalauréat a two-year course called the capacité en droit, and this has been continued by their successors, the unités d'enseignement et de recherche (UER).

Finally, while the term short-cycle is generally taken to mean a two-year cycle of higher education, it should not be forgotten that in the old universities the faculties and institutes offered three-year courses which were quite separate from the now classic two, four and six-year curricula leading to the DUEL (Diplôme universitaire d'études littéraires) or DUES (Diplôme universitaire d'études scientifiques), the Master's degree (Maîtrise) and the Doctorate. This was and still is true of the institutes of political studies - coupled with centres preparing for careers in public administration - and of the science and arts degrees preparing for the teaching profession (Licence d'enseignement) with a three-year course of study. It was also the rule in the law faculties before the 1956 reform which extended the Licence course to four years. It is the lengthening of studies in general that is responsible for the trend that gradually led the faculties to opt in favour of long cycles.

* For a fuller understanding of this paper, foreign readers unfamiliar with French terminology and the French system of education and administration may need to refer to other documents, such as the Higher Education Orientation Act and Michel-Yves Bernard's book "Les Instituts universitaires de technologie", Dunod, 1970.

Since three-year courses can hardly be assimilated to real short-cycle courses, this study is confined only to short-cycle courses in the strict sense of the term, i. e. those organised in the IUTs. Although of recent creation, these establishments existed before the new universities were established under the November 1968 Higher Education Orientation Act - hence the problem of their relationship with these universities, involving the familiar issue of "association" versus "integration".

Admittedly, the Decree of 7th January 1966 creating the IUTs established them from the start as university institutes,* but there can be no doubt that the universities at that time were no more than an administrative framework, not an educational structure. The faculties and institutes which were formally part of the university were, in fact, autonomous. For almost four years, therefore, the first IUTs operated without having to take account of any university policy; the constraints on them were due to the centralized structure of French higher education and arose at Ministry level (central government and advisory bodies) and at the Académie and Rectorat level. ** The change brought about by the Law of 12th November 1968, establishing the new universities as public establishments of a scientific and cultural nature, therefore posed a twofold problem: that of the place and role of the IUT vis-à-vis or within the universities.

With regard to this problem, the pluri-disciplinary universities would either at last provide an appropriate structure within which the IUT, receiving the status of UER, would be able to achieve full development - Michel-Yves Bernard writes: "IUT is the unit in the new university naturally designed to provide training for higher technicians"*** - or, dominated by the traditional disciplines of the old faculties, they would appear as an additional constraint designed to submit the specific role of the IUT to the uniformity of traditional higher education and would force them to move backwards.

Faced with this question, the Government decided to try the experiment of incorporating the IUTs in the new universities, while at the same time protecting them against the above-mentioned dangers by provisions derogating from the law applicable to UERs. This is the significance of the Decree of 20th January 1969, which, while it did not confer on IUTs the status of a public corporation independent of the universities,**** did establish them as "derogatory" UERs and kept them to a certain extent under a priori State control.

* Michel-Yves Bernard, Les instituts universitaires de technologie, Dunod, 1970.

** Michel-Yves Bernard, op. cit., pp. 47 and 55.

*** Michel-Yves Bernard, op. cit., p. 130.

**** Unlike the instituts d'études politiques, some schools of engineering and medical UERs, the IUT have not acquired even the status of public establishments attached to the universities.

This policy still constitutes the legal basis of the IUTs in the new French universities. An attempt will be made to try to assess the effect not so much with respect to the law or administrative regulations, as in the light of experience. The problems raised by this situation will be analysed with reference first to the place and then to the role of IUTs in the universities. A few suggestions on how to improve the situation will also be made.

# I

## THE PLACE OF IUTs IN THE UNIVERSITIES

According to their initial statute, (Decree of 7th January 1966) the IUTs were originally set up as university institutes; the Decree of 20th January 1969, which amended this Decree, established them as UERs "as defined in Article 3 of the Act of 12th November 1968". As already indicated, IUTs are therefore not autonomous establishments in relation to the universities. The Decree of 20th January 1969 merely left open the possibility of making them public establishments of a scientific and cultural nature attached to the universities. However, so far the Government has not made use of this possibility and for the time being does not seem to want to do so. As UERs, on the other hand, IUTs are subject to derogatory provisions, and this "protectionism" gives them a unique position within the universities.

This derogatory situation first of all concerns the creation of IUTs. While the common-law UERs are created, on the initiative of the university, by Decree of the Recteur d'Académie, it is the Government, on the recommendation of the Conseil national de l'enseignement supérieur et de la recherche, that is responsible for establishing IUTs. In addition, the curricula offered by IUTs and their corresponding internal structure are laid down by Decree of the Ministry of Education. This shows clearly that, a priori, State control continues to exist.

The administration of the IUTs constitutes also an exception to the common law governing UERs. While the maximum number of members on the respective UER and IUT Councils (40 for the former, 39 for the latter) is almost exactly the same, membership of the IUT Administrative Councils is governed by a common regulation prescribing, in particular, the presence of outside members. In common law UERs this presence is optional. In addition, the Recteur plays an important part in deciding from which sectors these members should come and in designating the persons themselves. The proportion of elected members on the Council (teaching staff, students and administrators) may also differ from

UER common law, and teaching staff may serve on the Council of another UER at the same time. Contrary to common law, the Chairman and Vice-Chairman of IUT Administrative Councils cannot belong to the establishment. In the same way, the status of the Director of an IUT is not the same as that of the Director of an UER. Instead of being elected by the Council, the Director of an IUT is appointed by the Ministry of Education on the Council's recommendation. The appointment is for four years (instead of three) and is renewable only once.

Finally, IUT internal structure differs from that of the common-law UER in that considerable independence is left to the departments within the establishment. Moreover, the university does not have the power to define the aims of IUTs or to establish or abolish them.

The administrative autonomy of IUTs must also be assessed in the light of an unusual administrative system. Under the Higher Education Orientation Act, UERs depend for all their resources on the university to which they are attached. In other words, the Central Government makes overall appropriations to the universities in respect of teaching and administrative staff, overtime, premises and operating credits, and they are then responsible for distributing these resources freely among UER and their associated public establishments.

This is not necessarily true for IUTs. Article 8 of the Decree of 20th January 1969 specifies that: "unless a specific request to the contrary is made by an IUT, equipment grants, operating credits and the number of posts for each IUT are determined by the Ministry of Education after consulting the Conseil national and the conseils régionaux de l'enseignement supérieur et de la recherche".

This situation was originally due to the fact that the Decree of 7th January 1966 was published before the creation of the universities. It was feared that most of these, largely "traditional" UERs, would attribute a relatively small amount to the IUTs, especially since the latter's initial equipment and staffing ratios were far superior to those of faculties. It is not made less paradoxical by the fact that IUTs do not have financial autonomy, while the associated public establishments which do have an independent budget have their resources allocated by the university to which they are attached.

It is true that once confidence has been established between IUT councils and university councils, the article in the above-mentioned Decree would allow the IUTs to be governed on this point by the common law; their councils need only make the request. As far as is known, no request of this nature has yet been made.

The rules for admission to IUTs also differ from those in force for the common-law UERs. Admission to the latter, in principle, is open to all candidates holding the Baccalauréat or an equivalent qualification, although the universities are entitled to require these students to attend guidance classes (Article 21 of the Orientation Act). Entrance to the IUTs, on the other hand, is based on selection.

According to Article 6 of the Decree of 20th January 1969, "admission to university institutes of technology depends on verification of the candidate's level of attainment, in accordance with the regulations in force at the date of publication of the Act of 12th November 1968" (i. e. in accordance with the initial Decree of 7th January 1966). In practice, this means that a "numerus clausus" is imposed on the bodies responsible for checking the candidate's attainment, since no IUT department can recruit cohorts of more than 150 students. On this basis the admission boards give their decision after examining the candidate's record; the Baccalauréat is not always required.

In fact, this procedure raises a series of objections which will be examined later, and a number of practical difficulties which must be mentioned now. Because they are afraid they may not be accepted, many students apply to several IUTs and often enrol at the same time in other UERs. They delay their final choice until the last moment, sometimes without warning the IUT administration. Each department, therefore, has to draw up a final list of admissions and a supplementary one, and only as the defections become known can the real numbers in the department be established. This situation considerably reduces the advantage of determining admissions in July, because the defections occur just before the beginning of the academic year. In this way they help to aggravate one of the main obstacles to the growth of IUTs in France, namely, that not all the places available in the departments are filled, although in July a large number of students have to be refused.

Lastly, for the recruitment of teaching staff, the IUT appears as a UER with derogatory status. From the start, and in accordance with a deliberate policy on the part of the Ministry of Education, IUT teaching staff included teachers from higher and secondary education and qualified persons from industry. This situation made it difficult, at least for the last two categories, to make the recruitment of IUT teaching staff subject to university common law. Article 9 of the Decree of 20th January 1969 therefore stipulates that: "on behalf of the university institute of technology having the status of a public establishment of a scientific and cultural nature, or on behalf of the public establishment of a scientific and cultural nature to which the university institute of technology belongs, the Director shall appoint staff receiving fees and staff paid on a contractual basis". This applies to the majority of teachers coming from industry, with the exception of those with the status of professor, "maître de conférence", maître-assistant" or "assistant associé".

All other teachers, that is to say almost all permanent teachers, whatever their origin or status, are appointed by the Minister according to common law. However, instead of being selected by the restricted university council consisting of professors or assimilated members, after consultation with the UER and expert commissions, they are chosen by the Director of the IUT "on the basis of a recommendation by a commission appointed by the Council (of the IUT) and composed of representatives of the teaching staff and persons from outside". This situation has provoked considerable opposition. On the one hand, the teachers' unions are very reluctant to see "persons from outside" sitting on this commission, since their presence does not conform to the general rule that teaching staff are selected by their "peers". They also have reservations about the purely advisory functions of the commission which leaves the power of decision in the hands of the Director appointed by the Minister.

Finally, IUT teaching staff from higher education feel "segregated" insofar as they are not recruited in the same way as their colleagues in other UERs. They are afraid of not being recognized by the university as full-time teachers and so risk being restricted to the first cycle and prevented from working in the other university cycles. They also feel that they may be less well treated than their colleagues by the departments of the Comité consultatif des universités responsible for proposing to the Minister names for selection or promotion lists.

This feeling of frustration is made more acute by the fact that the IUTs do not officially recognize research as a vocation. Sub-paragraph 3 of Article 9 of the Decree quoted above states, however, that: "full-time established staff with the status of higher education teachers are also assigned, on their request and in respect of their research activities, to one of the units of the university when assigned to an IUT". This would appear to conflict with the recruitment system in force, insofar as it operates outside the university.

Apart from the above derogations, which constitute a fairly notable body of exceptions, the IUTs have the same status as UER within the universities. They are, therefore, represented on the university councils in the same way as the other UERs with equal participation in the various managing bodies: permanent and disciplinary sections of the Councils, conferences of UER Directors, advisory commissions, etc. The teaching staff coming from higher education may also be called upon to sit on the "conseils scientifiques" in a personal capacity.

There is no text on the position of university presidents with respect to the IUTs. Since the Decree of 20th January 1969 made no mention of this point, it is usually agreed that, like the Recteur, they should attend sessions of IUT Administrative Councils in an advisory capacity.

Generally speaking, correspondence from the IUTs to the Central Government is sent through the university president, and the IUTs' accounts are attached to the accounting department of the university. Presidents have the same authority over the IUTs as over other UERs, particularly with regard to law and order.

The fact remains that the State still has a much greater control over the IUT than over the common-law UER. This is demonstrated, as has been seen, by the a priori control over resource allocation and the powers of the Recteur, which in many ways are a survival of the old status of university institutes.

The third part of this paper will examine how practice and regulations may gradually alter this initial situation. Meanwhile, it is important to define the role of IUTs within the universities.

# II

## THE ROLE OF IUTs WITHIN THE UNIVERSITIES

It is probable - and in any case desirable - that the disruption of the French university system caused by the events of May 1968 and the Orientation Act will lead to a radical change in the role of IUTs within the universities. Their old "peaceful co-existence" with the other UERs might thus give way to active co-operation, heralding the beginning of a process of integration.

### Before 1968

As university institutes, the IUTs were set up in order to bridge a serious gap that the earlier introduction of the DESTs in some science faculties and the "Instituts nationaux de sciences appliquées" (INSA) had not succeeded in filling. The aim was to provide university training for higher technicians in the secondary and tertiary sectors. As this had not been undertaken by the faculties, the State decided to set up the IUTs which were to be parallel to, but outside, them. In so doing, it was resorting to a fairly well-tried method, based on the Decree of 31st July 1920 which made university institutes responsible for meeting new requirements in higher education as and when they arose.

The State had already used this method in other fields: for example, in creating the Ecoles nationales supérieures d'ingénieurs (ENSI), or in training senior civil servants (in 1945 the "Ecole libre des sciences politiques" was nationalized and decentralized in the provinces in the form of instituts d'études politiques). This "stratification" policy consisted of duplicating the faculties by university institutes which were intended to make good their deficiencies. It resulted in the gradual emergence of a second university system, parallel to but more flexible than the traditional system, and separate from and in fact fairly independent of the faculties.

By abolishing and dividing up the faculties, the Orientation Act of Higher Education made it possible to integrate these two systems. Since 1968, the transformed university institutes have therefore been placed on an equal footing in the new universities with the UER derived from the old faculties. In practice, of course, this is more a trend than a reality. The two old systems - faculties and university institutes - can be integrated only gradually, and some universities still retain relics of this "double sector". This is largely due to the derogatory statutes given in 1969 to most of the old university institutes converted into UER, first and foremost of which are the IUTs.

In deciding to commit itself to the process of integration recommended by Mr. Edgar Faure, the Government of Mr. Couve de Murville intended to proceed with the utmost caution during the years 1968-69. This attitude explains the derogatory statutes conferred on the former institutes under a series of "protectionist" Decrees. The future will tell whether these "safety locks" are destined to burst. They will certainly burst all the more rapidly if the new universities adopt the attitudes which, from 1920 to 1968, prevailed in the creation of the old university institutes, and if they reject the frequently conservative and corporatist habits of the old faculties.

For purposes of clarity we shall adopt as a working hypothesis the assumption that the process of integration under way will be gradually achieved. This analysis of the specific role that IUTs could play within the universities presupposes eventual success.

Nobody disputes the fact that in this case the IUTs might be the best possible framework for initial and continuing short-cycle syllabuses designed to train higher level technicians.

This means, in the first place, that they are mainly intended to provide a two-year terminal course. The meaning of this term should be explained. Clearly it does not mean that students who have opted for this course will be obliged to stop their training at the end of the short cycle. On the one hand, the staffing ratio and the special educational methods in IUTs have been so designed that students entering employment on leaving them have received an education combining the necessary technical skill with an adequate general training. In addition, various "bridges" to long-cycle higher education should enable some of them to continue their studies in other UERs at the second-cycle level. Above all, well-organised continuing training programmes should offer others the opportunity to return to the university as full-time students after a few years of professional life.

Before 1968 the IUTs and the second cycle of the UERs were so isolated from each other that links between the two systems of higher education were difficult. Certain regulations had indeed established "bridges", but without adequate co-ordination. This led to the idea of creating "universités de technologie" where courses started in IUTs could be continued beyond the first cycle.

In view of the independence of the new universities, this project would now appear to be superfluous. Proper integration between IUTs and other UERs should allow the IUTs to keep their initial objective and guarantee that their students and teaching staff will not feel that they are living in a "ghetto". *

Of course it will still be necessary to co-ordinate links between the terminal short-cycle courses in the IUTs and the first-cycle introductory courses leading to long-cycle courses in other UERs. Here we find the familiar problem of co-existence or interpenetration, or even merging, which occurs in connection with the American Junior Colleges.

Experience with the interdisciplinary first cycles created in the new French universities to promote new training channels is still too recent to be conclusive on this point. ** Nevertheless, as a simple working hypothesis we might briefly outline the suggested organisation of first-cycle courses in a fully integrated university. Three main types of first-cycle courses might co-exist harmoniously:

- terminal, mainly vocational, short first cycles of the IUT type which would absorb about one-third of first-year student enrolments;

- one or more interdisciplinary first-cycle introductory courses designed to guide students towards diversified second cycles or towards one year of further technical training in an IUT; these might also absorb about one-third of new enrolments;

- specialized first cycles leading directly to studies focused on the knowledge and practice of a particular discipline or training, designed for strongly motivated students but nevertheless allowing for some possibility of reorientation; these might account for the remaining one-third of first-year university enrolments.

It would obviously be premature to try to apply this working hypothesis systematically. Personally, however, we think that it would be unwise, mainly for educational reasons, to place much hope in the establishment of general-purpose first cycles that would be both terminal

* Practical solutions to this problem have already been found, particularly at the Université des sciences sociales de Grenoble, where there are bridges between the IUT and the Institut d'études commerciales (Maîtrise de sciences de gestion), the UER de sciences économiques (Licence de sciences économiques) or the Institut d'études politiques (Centre de préparation à l'administration générale).

** Cf. Livret de l'étudiant 1971-72, Université des sciences sociales de Grenoble.

and introductory to a second cycle. We therefore think it preferable to develop within the university two cycles, i.e. terminal and leading on to longer courses, provided that they complement each other and that two-way traffic between them is possible. *

Let us examine what will be the future of the partly vocational and certainly technically oriented IUT courses in the university framework.

Undoubtedly the first few months of collaboration between IUT and academic-type UERs within the same universities have been, and will continue to be difficult. As a result, they may either ignore or oppose each other but, in our view, the role of the IUT can and must be decisive if the new universities are to observe the spirit and the letter of the Orientation Act and help to create a modern culture based on the necessary alliance of science and technique, general training and technological know-how. Only if this objective is not achieved would it be necessary to establish or extend universities of technology.

We may therefore think that, without acting as a matrix, the IUTs can exert considerable influence on the development of the structures and aims of the interdisciplinary UERs and the universities. Their influence is already perceptible. It may be seen in the external membership of university councils, in the recruitment of associated or fee-paid teachers from industry and in the practice of active and audio-visual teaching methods.

At the same time, the IUTs can benefit from the best of university tradition for the recruitment of permanent teaching staff, strict scientific method and the necessary liaison between teaching and research. The result will be a true symbiosis and, where it is successful, the IUTs will be able to achieve their aims completely.

We must however be realistic. Such success implies that the universities themselves are not purely and simply a conglomeration of faculties disguised as UERs when their unity is retained, or "bits" of faculties when they are split up. Success will occur only if the new public establishments of a scientific and cultural nature have a carefully defined coherence and are able to conceive and apply a university policy. This necessarily involves the determination to impose on the classical UERs a transformation which, far from mutilating them, is the only means of securing their future. It implies the promoting of technology to be among the objectives of university education and research.

If these conditions are fulfilled, the IUTs can retain their specific character. Their task will be to provide short-cycle courses training

* Some IUT departments already organise one-year courses for students holding a diploma awarded after two years of academic higher education.

higher technicians for the secondary and tertiary sectors. But they can add other tasks to this initial activity, the most important being further education for adults already in employment. * In addition, IUT students will not find the door to further study closed. Adequate bridges will enable those with the necessary ability to go on to appropriate second-cycle courses. At the same time, the IUTs can offer one-year courses for students who have begun long cycles but wish to change over to work for a DUT (diplôme universitaire de technologie).

Teachers - especially those in higher education - will be able to divide their time between the IUTs and other UERs and will certainly not have to demand longer IUT courses so that they can teach beyond the first cycle or take part in collective research.

The IUTs themselves, instead of forming a cluster of small establishments subject to the uncertainties of local politics or private pressures, can find support in the universities. And by this means we may hope they will overcome the obstacles deriving from their specific character and which tie them down owing to the uniformity of central government structures and the traditionalism of academic bodies such as the University Consultative Committee. Consequently, provided that this gradual integration into the universities is well-designed and properly carried out, the IUTs can only benefit from it.

* This is already the case in Grenoble, for teachers in special schools, commercial agents and data processors.

# III

## OBSTACLES TO BE OVERCOME IN ACHIEVING IUT INTEGRATION INTO THE UNIVERSITIES

The generally optimistic tone of the foregoing analysis should not delude us, for the reality does not yet correspond. We merely wish to show that there is no fundamental incompatibility between the IUTs and the new universities - which could not be said of their relations with the old faculties - but merely administrative and psychological obstacles, which we shall now consider.

The first of these obstacles is a statutory one, and will surely be the easiest to overcome. The Decree of 20th January 1969 is earlier than the university legislation and should be adjusted. It would be sufficient to introduce into the necessarily derogatory statutes of the IUTs the elements resulting from the establishment of university bodies. In addition, where the university authorities have understood and genuinely accepted the specific tasks of the IUTs, the IUT Councils might make use of the possibility available under Article 8 of the Decree to entrust resource allocation, at first for a given period and then permanently, to the university bodies responsible for making allocations to the other UERs. This should at the same time lead to a gradual relaxation of central government control and of intervention by the rectors.

It will be more difficult to co-ordinate conditions of admission for students of IUTs and other UERs. The situation is paradoxical to start with, for IUT recruitment is based on an examination of the candidate's record, while the common-law UERs generally admit all Baccalauréat holders.

This absurd situation - which was necessary as a status symbol at the time the IUTs were set up - need not, of course, be reversed, but a more adequate adjustment will have to be made.

In the meantime, it is essential that in one way or another the IUT departments should "fill up" to capacity. New IUTs should also be set up, preferably with traditional channels, in medium-sized towns where there is a demand for higher education establishments. It would also be essential to provide university students with information and self-guidance facilities permitting a better distribution between IUTs and other first-cycle courses.

Later the IUTs might conceivably abandon selection - while still strictly observing the staffing ratios - in favour of a general guidance system enabling any candidate to be admitted to a university provided he freely adjusts his ambitions to his abilities and to an objective knowledge of employment opportunities. This ideal situation would inevitably lead to an expansion of the IUTs which should then accept about one third of students enrolling.

The situation of teaching staff in the IUTs is perhaps even more complex. Their present status and in particular their mode of recruitment are not it seems satisfactory. This is true mainly for secondary level teachers, and a national solution to their difficulties must be found. But it also applies to higher education teachers, which is paradoxical. One might, of course, legitimately consider that an IUT commission, or better still, its restricted council comprising only teachers of equivalent or higher categories should continue to express a reasoned opinion on the recruitment of new teachers. Not everyone is suitable for IUT posts. And technology is not a sufficiently widespread "approach" for this point to be disregarded.

But with this reservation it seems essential that IUT teachers should be recruited in the last resort - possibly after consulting an expert committee - by the university council restricted to teacher members. In an early stage at least, the IUT council might conceivably have an exclusive right of proposal, in order to avoid the appointment of teachers not trained in the special pedagogics of short-cycle education. There can be no real objection, subject to this important reservation, to leaving the final choice to the university council. The issues here involve not only teachers' career development and their mobility in higher education, but also their prestige and therefore the prestige of the IUTs themselves.

This reform must be accompanied by another. While there are some teachers whose lasting ambition is to teach first-cycle students, they are in the minority. Most of them also wish to teach - with the same qualifications - second and third-cycle students and to engage in individual and collective research. It must therefore be agreed that IUT teachers from higher education can be appointed to university posts. In terms of teaching requirements and teacher aspirations, their service might be divided between the IUTs and the other UERs either by teaching alternate years in each or by time-sharing. This condition is necessary to permit a university teacher serving in an IUT to have effective access to university research centres and teams on the same footing as his colleagues assigned mainly to the second cycle or, a fortiori, the third cycle.

Once these reforms have been achieved, the IUTs could retain their essential individuality and at the same time be integrated into the university. It will be all the easier to achieve this, as we said above, insofar as technology itself will acquire a higher status in the other cycles and applied research.

Naturally, one may legitimately prefer to this integration a different system leading to the parallel establishment of cultural universities and technological universities incorporating IUTs.

Apart from the fact that this policy, if systematically applied, would be contrary to the Orientation Act, it involves the risk of re-establishing at a higher level a "double sector" which has already failed in secondary level education in France.

Let us keep this alternative in reserve as a last resort in case the pessimistic assumption which we refused to consider should materialize. But subject to the establishment of a few "prototype" universities of technology, let us cherish the hope that the French universities as a whole will succeed in effectively constructing the alliance between science and technique.

It is hard to see how universities which are determined to meet the challenge of these final years of the twentieth century would wish to do otherwise.

# V

## Teachers in non-university Higher Education
## A British Case Study

by

Gareth Williams, Associate Director

and

Alice Crampin, Research Officer

Higher Education Research Unit, London School of Economics and Political Science (Great Britain)

# CONTENTS


| | | |
|---|---|---|
| Summary | | 239 |
| I. | The teaching situation | 241 |
| II. | Teaching staff: problems and issues | 247 |
| III. | Conclusions - Further education's self-image | 261 |

## SUMMARY

In this paper we suggest that many of the issues and problems connected with teachers in advanced further education (the nearest British equivalent of Short-Cycle Institutions) result from the diversity of the institutions themselves and the ambivalence of their situation within the educational system.

Until recently the further education colleges formed a part of the educational system that was almost entirely separate from the traditional academic secondary schools and universities. They were geared very largely to the provision of part-time training for the needs of the local economy. Their teachers and students may have cast envious eyes at their more favoured counterparts in the grammar schools and universities, but since there was virtually no movement between the two sectors further education became almost self-sustaining in providing its own teachers.

The recent rapid expansion of higher education, together with changing political and educational philosophies, have brought the two systems into much closer contact with one another. This has highlighted the ambiguity of the position of teachers in further education. At one end of the spectrum the colleges compete directly with universities for highly qualified academics ; at the other they employ those who would otherwise teach in secondary schools. Along another dimension, they employ staff who have had considerable experience in industry and commerce, rare in both schools and universities.

However, the concentration of growth in the further education sector has meant that the colleges have increasingly had to compete with universities for staff. In comparison with the universities, however, their pay scales are lower (except for teachers below the age of 30); their prestige is much less; they have a much more diverse student body comprising a high proportion of part-time students; they have to offer a wider range of courses; promotion prospects are worse; they offer few possibilities of achieving distinction, and consequent rapid advancement, through research and other non-teaching activities; their staff are treated as local government employees, whereas universities are self-managing institutions; their curricula are much more prone to outside control and they have much less financial freedom.

In these circumstances, if the colleges compete with the universities for staff, they will inevitably remain institutions of second choice even in a less expansionist period. Present policy seems destined to follow the previous pattern of making them more like universities. In doing so, however, much that is valuable in the old technical college tradition - particularly part-time studies and adult education - is in danger of being lost.

# I

# THE TEACHING SITUATION

## 1. Description of short-cycle institutions in Britain

Higher education in Britain takes place in three different types of institution: universities, colleges of education (where teachers are trained), and the further education colleges.

It is this third category that corresponds most nearly to the short-cycle institutions of many other OECD countries. The similarity does not, however, result from the fact that their courses are of short duration: the majority of them offer courses that are as long as or longer than, British university degree courses. The justification for treating them as short-cycle institutions is rather that they are based in a technical practical tradition that in many ways runs directly counter to the more academic and theoretical ethos of the university.

Further education colleges were founded by local initiative rather than by central government. They were developed to cater for the needs of local youth, training them to fit their local labour markets. Naturally, the needs of industry gave these "vocational" courses a bias towards technology and commerce, which remain predominant. The level of the courses varies very much according to college and area, and many colleges provide a great variety of courses at all levels, in response to local demand. They were never designed to provide education at one level only. However, in the post-war period, the growth of advanced work within the colleges has been stimulated by the enormous expansion in the demand by students for higher education, at the same time as scientific and technical advances enhanced the need for highly trained manpower in industry. University expansion did not keep pace with the demand and so colleges that could organise the requisite courses were well attended. Eventually, the phenomenal growth of higher education led to attempts to plan it as a whole and the place of the further education sector in the tripartite system of higher education was recognized.

However, it is from this very recognition that spring most of the issues andproblems facing teachers in further education today. They are responding to the challenge of initiating courses of university level wherever need arises. At the same time, educational planners are attempting to tidy up the further education field by creaming off certain institutions for the development of higher education and discouraging it in others. This is done by granting special privileges to those colleges where most advanced work is concentrated at present, thus conferring upon them university or quasi-university status.

Within further education there are many different types of institution, including national colleges for certain special subjects, "major establishments" and evening institutes. There used to be three types of "major establishments": local, area and regional colleges. These were designated according to the size and population of the areas from which they drew their students. They provided the bulk of the vocational courses offered within further education, including courses in art and design as well as science and commerce. Not surprisingly, it was in the big regional colleges that most of the advanced work developed. Students began to be drawn to some of them from beyond the bounds of their own regions, so that these colleges came to resemble universities in catering for national rather than local needs. Increasingly, as a result, their students have become full-time. (It should be noted that the situation described here applies to England and Wales; but in main essentials Scotland and Northern Ireland are similar).

The local colleges provided, and still provide, mainly part-time courses, few of which are at the level of higher education and many of which form an integral part of local apprenticeship schemes. This was the function for which they were set up and to which they still adhere. The area colleges, however, fell somewhere in the middle with varying amounts of advanced work and varying numbers of part-timers.

In the years following the 1956 White Paper on "Technical Education", ten of the regional colleges were designated Colleges of Advanced Technology (CATs) which were to provide only courses at an advanced level, including post graduate and research work. These colleges were subsequently transferred from local authority control to direct control by the Department of Education and Science as their status as national, rather than regional, institutions became clear. Later, they were granted full university status. Meanwhile other regional colleges were developing more and more advanced work. This movement was furthered by a new scheme whereby colleges could prepare students for a national degree examination administered, independently of the universities, by the Council for National Academic Awards, a body set up for the purpose.

In the mid-1960s the binary policy for higher education was introduced. This focused on the further education colleges as the most rapidly growing sector of higher education, rather than the universities. In particular, the policy proposed that this growth should be concentrated in 30 polytechnics. These were to be formed, often by amalgamation, from those regional colleges that were making the greatest contribution in the provision of advanced courses. Thus the binary policy, in attempting to counter the dominating influence of the élite university sector, created a new élite within the further education sector. This was done by obstructing the process by which colleges had previously upgraded themselves from a concentration on mainly non-advanced work to an emphasis on advanced work. The words "élite" and "upgrade" are used advisedly, since the desire to achieve parity with the universities was one of the mainsprings behind the colleges' drive to innovate. The binary policy has frustrated such aspirations in colleges other than the polytechnics. A question that remains unresolved is whether those further education colleges that provide higher education do it best by aiming to become indistinguishable from universities, or whether they can achieve parity of esteem while fulfilling independent educational objectives. This ambiguity in the position of the colleges is acted out in the day-to-day life of their teachers.

## 2. The nature of courses in advanced further education

As a result of their rapid development, a great variety of courses are taught in further education colleges. At the summit are the new CNAA* degree courses which are intended to be equivalent to the university honours degree. The range of subjects is being rapidly extended and now embraces three main disciplines: science and technology; business studies; and arts and social sciences. There are also interdisciplinary courses. B. A. and B. Sc. degrees are offered for undergraduate courses; M. A. and M. Sc. degrees for post-graduate courses and M. Phil. and Ph. D. degrees for research work. Undergraduate degrees are offered at both honours and ordinary levels. The courses are designed by the teachers in the colleges and then submitted to the CNAA for approval. The bulk of this work is done in the polytechnics where there are now some 500 approved courses. However some are done in other colleges (about 100 courses have been approved) although their future is not altogether clear. Twenty thousand students are now enrolled in these courses. In addition some colleges still prepare students for the external examinations of the University of London, teaching from a prescribed syllabus and with no means of influencing course content.

* Council for National Academic Awards. Unlike the universities which award their own degrees, the colleges can award only degrees that are authenticated by this national council.

Set slightly below honours degree level, much of the teaching in advanced further education prepares students for the examinations for the Higher National Certificate (HNC) and the Higher National Diploma (HND). Higher National Diplomas are regarded as approximately of pass or ordinary degree standard and are full-time or sandwich courses, lasting three years. Higher National Certificates are two-year courses which are part-time and are consequently of a somewhat lower level.

These examinations are often set internally by the colleges but assessed externally by the relevant professional institution, for they are very closely tied to the needs of a particular profession and are in that sense strictly vocational (although an element of liberal studies has been introduced in recent years).

The colleges also prepare students for a great many other professional examinations, such as those of the institutes of professional engineers and the Royal Institute of Chemistry, for example. They also provide, increasingly, training courses for further education teachers, training for the Diploma in Art and Design, and for certificates for computer personnel, such as those administered by the City and Guilds Institutes.

They are, therefore, even at the advanced level, providing a direct service to the industrial community. The teachers must work closely with a number of outside interests and, even when they can design their own courses, they do not have the autonomy of their colleagues in a university to decide, uni-laterally, what courses they wish to teach and how they wish to teach them. In comparison with the flexibility offered by the much vaunted academic freedom of university teachers, this is often very irksome. As the CNAA degrees become more widespread, many of the miscellaneous qualifications for which the colleges offered instruction are being converted into degree courses or, alternatively, into Higher National Diploma courses. However, the fact that degrees are becoming increasingly widespread has led to the downgrading in esteem, and possibly in content, of some of the other advanced courses that lead to qualifications that are not titled degrees. Many of the professional institutes expect bachelor degrees as the minimum entry qualification granting exemption from some of their own preliminary exams, and are less willing to recognize HNCs or even HNDs.

This has caused considerable difficulty and insecurity in the colleges. Many of the teachers have long experience in teaching these courses, which still form a large part of the colleges' advanced work in terms of enrolments. Many believe that these courses have particular merits in catering for young people, and even adults, who are working in industry and who gain their qualifications as part-time students.

The mixture of courses that any one teacher teaches depends on the particular mixture offered by his college. This in turn depends on the kind of college and the locality. Teachers who occupy the same rung of the career hierarchy may be doing very different kinds of work. Official statistics at present give information only about the aggregate of all teachers in further education, (advanced and non-advanced). Teachers' professional organisations, wishing to forward the interests of the whole group, prefer to consider the work of the colleges as a whole, rather than to deal separately with the different sections of their membership. For these reasons it is virtually impossible to separate information about those teachers who teach mainly advanced courses from those who teach mainly non-advanced courses. In any case the overlap is considerable, with many staff teaching both kinds of courses.

3. The organisation of teaching

The traditional method of teaching in a further education college was an adaptation of schoolroom techniques. Pupils were taught or "overtaught" in classes with the teacher going through the syllabus material and then setting exercises on it. Full-time students were spending on average 23 hours per week in class. (This compares with about 15 hours formal teaching per week received by students in universities of which, however, only 8 are formal lectures and the remainder various kinds of discussion group and practical work.) It is widely believed that there is waste in the deployment of staff and that the changes favoured by the CNAA, whereby teachers' commitments are reduced and small group discussions introduced, should be accelerated in all colleges. This would bring the practice in the colleges more into line with the universities' systems of lectures supplemented with seminars, tutorials and private reading and essay work by the students.

The colleges, apart from the polytechnics, are hampered in their experimentation with university teaching methods by the lack of flexibility in their accommodation and by the regulations laying down the minimum enrolments necessary before a new course can be approved. These regulations* apply to the number enrolled in a course, not to the actual size of class taught and there are some exceptions made for the approval of certain advanced courses. They are however a much more stringent and direct form of control than is found in the universities, where staff-student ratios can vary very considerably from faculty to faculty. In colleges of further education, permission to appoint staff

* Committee on Technical College Resources: Report on the Size of Classes and Approval of Further Education Courses, HMSO, 1966.

is given on the basis of the numbers of students in advanced courses for which a department caters. It is therefore only possible to build up temporary underemployed capacity in the full-time teaching force for experimentation when the project is specifically approved by the local authority.

Although sandwich courses, in which full-time education is interspersed with periods of industrial experience, are not an entirely new innovation, their incorporation into the CNAA degree (and its forerunner, the Diploma of Technology) has led to their increasingly wide acceptance as a legitimate means of gaining a degree. They are a pioneering feature of the colleges' approach to higher education.

Many of the teachers in further education are firmly committed to the sandwich arrangement as an invaluable means of integrating theory with practice in the vocationally orientated courses they aim to teach. Nevertheless, they impose a considerable extra responsibility on the teachers, for on them falls the burden of providing the link between the student's year in industry and the rest of his course in college. Existing research shows that the experience of students in industry has not always been successful,* and that the role of the teacher who is the student's industrial tutor is of paramount importance. To fulfil this role satisfactorily requires great skill on the part of the teachers as organisers and liaison officers.

The extra strain on those students who are studying part-time, together with their status as mature adults, requires a special approach from the teaching staff. The teachers have to sustain the students' motivation and help them to gain the most from college life in the limited time at their disposal. Wastage is of course a particular problem in all forms of part-time education with a high proportion of mature students. Colleges building up advanced courses and able to attract full-time students from far afield are often tempted to drop the more demanding part-time work. Many teachers however remain firmly convinced of the importance of nurturing such courses, if the college is to retain its close links with, and service to, the local community in both secondary and higher education.

* M. Jahoda, The Education of Technologists. Tavistock Press, London, 1963, and J. Heywood: "The Effectiveness of Undergraduate (Dip. Tech.) Industrial Training", in Journal of Engineering Education, Vol. 5, pp. 281-289, Pergamon Press Ltd., London, 1967.

# II

# TEACHING STAFF: PROBLEMS AND ISSUES

## 1. Who are the teachers?

### i) Background and training

It has already been made clear that the teaching done in further education is very varied in character. It ranges from upper secondary level to the most advanced levels of higher education. Thus the teachers can be compared with teachers in secondary schools, at one end of the spectrum, and with teachers in universities at the other. In addition, their close ties with industrial work makes mobility between the two sectors particularly common, and there are many part-time teachers from industry and commerce. Indeed it has been pointed out* that many teachers of the most industrially orientated subjects think of themselves primarily as practitioners of that subject who happen to be teaching, rather than as career teachers. They are more likely to see teaching as one of the multiple roles which they are called to fill in the course of their careers.** Those recruited directly into teaching advanced courses, immediately after gaining their own degrees, tend, especially in the polytechnics, to identify with their contemporaries teaching in universities. Consequently, current attempts being made to unify the profession and to prescribe the training necessary for a teacher in further education lead to many stresses and strains. The academically orientated teachers would regret any move that might lessen the mobility of staff between the further education and university sectors. Nevertheless, it is the policy of the professional bodies representing the members of the profession to seek to introduce a form of training for teaching as a condition of service in further education colleges. This

* Ethel Venables: The Young Worker at College, Faber and Faber, 1967, pp. 219-220.

** P.F. Payne: "Multiple Roles", The Technical Journal, May 1967, pp. 9-10.

was recommended by a government committee,* which during the 1960s issued a series of reports on the training of teachers for further education, but the recommendations were subsequently rejected by the government of the day.

At present there are only five technical teachers' colleges, offering one-year courses to train already qualified teachers, or people from quite outside the profession, as further education teachers. One scheme allows for already practising further education teachers to do a sandwich course consisting of part course work and part teaching practice under supervision, in the college where they are already working. The technical teachers' colleges' extra-mural activities include organising short courses for in-service teachers in nearby further education colleges.

About a dozen university education departments offer teaching practice in colleges of further education to their students. One or two joint degrees in education and science or technology are being pioneered which give syllabus space to further education. There is also a CNAA part-time degree course in social science for teachers. A few of the polytechnics have departments of education. However, so far, they have chosen to become affiliated to their local university departments of education, rather than join the CNAA, and they are training school teachers.

Hendon College, part of a polytechnic designate, has introduced a sandwich course for training full-time teachers in service, in conjunction with one of the technical teachers' colleges, and it is believed by many that it is in this sort of scheme that the way ahead for training technical teachers lies. This would be a way of bringing into the scheme not only new recruits to the lower rungs of the teaching profession, but also those who entered higher up the ladder and who would not be prepared to suffer the drop in salary that taking time off for training would mean.

Unless the position within the universities is changed, an anomalous situation might well be created where the two halves of the binary system were distinguished on a new count. The teachers in the universities would remain untrained whereas the teachers in the polytechnics would be trained. This might affect the relative attractiveness of the two professions and put further obstacles in the path of mobility, unless steps were taken to recognize the training financially.

At present (1969 figures), only about a third of the teachers in further education, graduate and non-graduate are trained. The proportion

* Report on Teachers for Further Education, HMSO, 1961. Report on the Supply and Training of Teachers for Further Education, HMSO, 1966.

is very similar for both groups but non-graduates are slightly less likely to be trained than graduates at all levels of the career structure. Those on the higher rungs of the career ladder (that is for the most part the older teachers) are slightly less likely to be trained than their juniors for both graduate and non-graduate groups.

ii) Career structure

Graduates make up 34% of the total teaching force but they are disproportionately represented in the upper levels of the profession. This is true for both men and women as Table 1 shows.

The corresponding career structure for university teachers is shown in Table 2.

The comparison between teachers in further education and university teachers is not unambiguous as the grades do not correspond exactly. If, however, principals, vice-principals and heads of departments are considered the equivalent of professors and principal and senior lecturers, it is clear that the career pyramid for graduates in the two sectors of teaching is not dissimilar. Whether these comparisons are, however, the right ones depends partly on salaries and as will be seen in the next section the salary progression of university teachers differs markedly from that for teachers in further education.

Within the colleges there is a certain amount of stress involvec in using the same hierarchy of posts for both graduates and non-graduates. The result is that good graduates tend to be appointed at a higher rung of the ladder than non-graduates - they may start at Lecturer Grade II level - and to be promoted younger.

The consequences of the "pressure at the top" from the young ambitious entrants to advanced teaching in polytechnics, that is created in this way, are discussed later in the paper.

iii) Mobility and recruitment

The number of graduate teachers leaving their jobs in advanced further education reflects to some extent the volatility of the current phase of this evolving career structure. Of the male graduate teachers aged between 25 and 29 in the spring of 1968, 10.6% had left by the following spring; for those aged 35-39 the figure was 6.6%. These figures compare with 7.3% and 5.3% for non-graduate teachers and less than 4% for university teachers of similar ages. However, 88% of the graduates leaving further education for other occupations return to this profession later in their careers. No directly comparable figures are available for

Table 1. GRADES OF TEACHERS IN GRANT-AIDED ESTABLISHMENTS FOR FURTHER EDUCATION

Percentages

| | MEN | | WOMEN | |
|---|---|---|---|---|
| | GRADUATES | NON-GRADUATES | GRADUATES | NON-GRADUATES |
| Principals ...... | 3.0 | 0.9 | 0.4 | 0.7 |
| Vice-Principals and heads of Department .... | 8.9 | 3.7 | 1.6 | 3.8 |
| Principal lecturers ....... | 4.9 | 1.4 | 1.0 | 0.3 |
| Senior lecturers . | 19.8 | 10.0 | 7.3 | 3.1 |
| Lecturers Grade II ........ | 34.8 | 29.1 | 27.0 | 17.1 |
| Lecturers Grade I ........ | 25.5 | 44.9 | 50.6 | 53.0 |
| Assistant lecturers ....... | 3.1 | 10.0 | 12.1 | 22.0 |
| Total ......... | 100.0 | 100.0 | 100.0 | 100.0 |

SOURCE: DES Statistics of Education 1969, Vol. 4, Table 31. Women make up 13% of the graduate teaching body, 15% of the non-graduate and 14% of the whole.

Table 2. GRADE OF STAFF IN UNIVERSITIES

Percentages

| | MEN | WOMEN |
|---|---|---|
| Professors ........... | 12 | 1 |
| Readers/Senior Lecturers ............ | 19 | 10 |
| Lecturers ............ | 63 | 72 |
| Below lecturers ........ | 6 | 17 |
| Total ................ | 100 | 100 |

universities but apart from an exceptional period between 1964 and 1966 when they were growing at about 20% per year, the universities have recruited very few staff from other economic sectors. A picture emerges, therefore, of the further education sector having much more mobility of staff with other economic sectors than the universities - a situation which has both advantages and disadvantages.

Further light can be shed on the people moving into the further education sector, to take over the expansion of advanced teaching, by the history of the development of the Colleges of Advanced Technology from big colleges of further education to special institutions for advanced work, and on to become technological universities. The scale of the development is shown by the fact that in 1956 there were fewer than 350 full-time staff in eight CATs. By 1966, there were over 2,500 in the ten CATs. At the same time, however, there was decrease in total student numbers (though of course most of those who disappeared were part-time).

Whenever higher education has been extended in the further education sector, great stress has been laid on the importance of recruiting highly qualified staff comparable to university personnel.* This was supposed to mean that staff must have the ability to teach "and to relate their industrial experience to their teaching work", but in effect it meant that young graduate staff replaced older non-graduates with other professional qualifications.** At first there were few women recruits, until the introduction of social science departments increased their number. Increasingly, too, staff came in with higher degrees, so that qualifications were much more like those of university staff.

The erosion of the industrial bias of the staff background is shown by the fact that in 1956 nearly 60% of the staff in the first eight CATs came from outside the educational sector, half of them from industry. Very few (9%) were receiving their first appointment, 22% came from elsewhere in further education, 11% from schools, and only 8% from universities. By 1966 the picture had changed in so far as universities now supplied 15%, technical colleges 15%, and schools only 5%. First appointments had risen to 13%.

The figures for new recruits to the CATs during this period show the same trends more clearly. Whereas in 1957 37% of recruits came from industry, and in 1962 42% did, by 1966 the proportion had fallen to 29% while that coming from universities had risen from 8% in 1956 to 24% in 1966.

* NCTA: Memo on the Recognition of Courses in Technical Colleges leading to the Diploma in Technology, 1955.

** See T. Burgess and J. Pratt: Policy and Practice; the CATs, Allen Lane, the Penguin Press, 1970, for a much fuller discussion of this and the following points.

Nevertheless when they became universities, the CATs still recruited their staff from a wider range of people than did the other universities at the time. Since 1966 their recruitment policy appears to have been almost indistinguishable from that of other universities.

In summary, the experience of the CATs suggests that the more advanced work is developed in the further education sector, the more the staff in that sector take on the characteristics of the university sector.

It has yet to be seen whether the polytechnics will develop distinctive staff characteristics of their own, but present indications are that they are recruiting essentially the same type of graduate as the universities.

2. Pay and prospects

i) Pay

The pay schedules for the different grades of full-time teachers in further education are negotiated, as are those for school teachers, by the statutory "Burnham" Committees, on which are represented the teachers' organisations and the local education authorities who pay teachers. These agreements, once reached, are mandatory.

Lecturers Grade I, and Assistant Lecturers are concerned in the main with non-advanced work. Assistant Lecturers' salary structure is directly equivalent to that of teachers in schools. Grade II Lecturers do mainly advanced work with some of the associated preparatory courses (e.g. ONC and OND). Senior Lecturers and above are appointed on a quota system, depending on the amount of advanced work being carried out in a department. Therefore, there are fewer such posts available to the teachers in colleges and departments which are not doing advanced work. Thus, the lower rungs of the career structure are likely to be career grades for these people and probationary grades for those teaching advanced courses. This makes it difficult to say which grades are analogous to those in universities since the same grade is occupied by people doing very different things. At present both the Assistant Lecturer grade and that of the Lecturer, Grade I, are long grades allowing for 15 annual increments. Financial recognition is given to a degree, and more to a good honours degree, as with school teachers. It is argued, however, that in further education more attention should be given to other relevant professional qualifications. No financial allowance is made for training, but there are special "responsibility allowances" as in school teaching. Lecturers, Grade II, have a shorter scale with ten increments. For those graduates who start work in this grade, it commands a very advantageous starting salary (in 1969 about £ 2,000), compared with the bottom of the University Lecturers' scale of £ 1,500. However, the University Lecturer scale rises to £ 3,400 with an efficiency bar at £ 2,450. The further education college Lecturer, Grade II, rises only to about £ 2,700. Senior Lecturer and Principal Lecturer are both very short grades with three and four increments respectively which, at the maximum, can give a salary of about £ 3,800. In universities, a Senior Lecturer can go up to £ 4,400. Heads of Departments in the colleges can reach a salary of more than £ 4,000 only in the departments doing most advanced work. Only Principals and Vice-Principals can reach salaries of £ 5,000 - £ 6,000 and then only if they are in the biggest colleges, where they have to take the most responsibility. University Professors have a starting salary of £ 4,500, which, in further education can be reached only by a few heads of college departments. The university professorial average salary of £ 5,600 is equalled by only a few College Directors.

It appears, therefore that the equivalence between university grades and college grades suggested in the previous section is supported by the salary scales. To summarize this evidence, a good graduate who enters further education can expect to earn more than his university counterpart during the first few years of his working life. However, after about the age of 30 he will rapidly fall behind. At the top end of the spectrum about 30% of university staff are earning more than £ 4,000 a year, a figure equalled by less than 12% of college staff. The same information is shown in a different way in Chart I which indicates age earning profiles of graduate staff in universities and further education colleges in 1967.

When the CATs were assimilated on to the university salary scale the transfer was very complicated because of the universities' system of fixing senior staff's salaries individually, within given ranges, and because of the difficulty of aligning the colleges' career grade, the assistant lectureship, with the universities' career grade which is the lectureship. The result was that assimilation led to very large salary increases of about 20% over the decade 1956-66. This was nearly twice as fast as the increase of any other major income group in the country, and illustrates the financial advantages enjoyed by university teachers over college teachers.

ii) Career prospects

The current salary structure has led to the situation where an able entrant to a polytechnic can start at a high salary but has a salary scale in front of him which climbs slowly and is likely to peak much sooner than that of his contemporary in a university.

Chart 1

AGE EARNINGS PROFILE OF GRADUATE STAFF IN COLLEGES OF FURTHER EDUCATION AND UNIVERSITIES

1966 - 1967

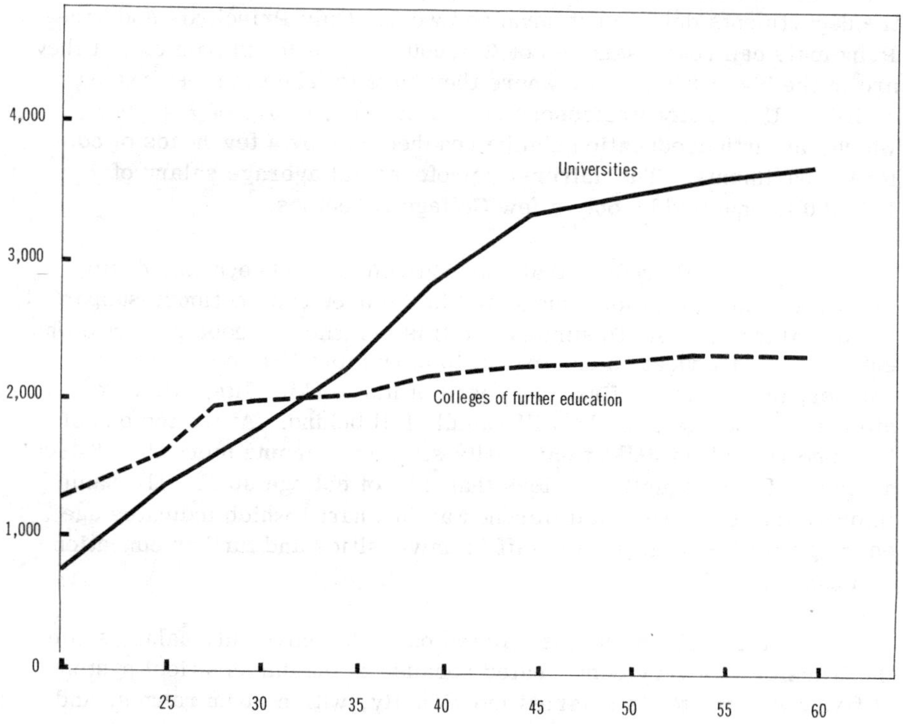


*Source :* "Rewards and Careers" by John Bibby, *Higher Education Review*, Autumn 1970.

The consequences of this situation have been mitigated only by the rapid expansion of the colleges' advanced work which has created new senior posts in the newly designated polytechnics. These posts have been filled by young men to whom the salary they offered was attractive. However, only a high rate of premature leaving from these posts would open up comparable promotion prospects to their successors. Some anticipate that such a high rate will develop and persist so that the colleges will continue to be staffed by young people who make teaching in them their career until middle age. This, however, presupposes that a well-paid market will be maintained for ex-college teachers approaching middle age. This seems unlikely since such a market would be most probably another educational sector. The only one more attractive financially would be the universities and current policy appears to be to keep the colleges, not the universities, as the main growth sector.

More fundamentally, the universities have their own promotion bottlenecks approaching as a result of their own explosive growth of the mid-sixties. Moreover, the universities have shown so far no great enthusiasm for recruiting senior staff from other economic and educational sectors, especially the less prestigious colleges, and it is very unlikely that they will start to do so in the foreseeable future.

## 3. Conditions of work

### i) Teaching load

The working day in the colleges can last from 9 a. m. to 9 p. m. at night. In many colleges there is a presumption that lecturers will be willing to do some work in the evenings. This applies to many of the polytechnics as well even though they may have a majority of full-time students and do less evening work. In addition, the college year is usually longer than that of the universities, and the organisation of sandwich courses may make for broken vacations. The college year is usually about 36 weeks long, compared with 30 weeks in most of the Universities. Recently, a government committee investigated the organisation of the college year and recommended that, in the interests of efficiency in the use of plant, the college year be extended beyond 36 weeks. * The Secretary of State reacted with alacrity to this proposal and sent a circular to local education authorities asking them to examine the introduction of a college year of more than 36 weeks. The Committee distinguished between "college years", "teacher years" and "student years" and made it clear that it did not wish to increase the

* Committee on the More Effective Use of Technical College Resources: A Report on the Pattern and Organisation of the College Year, HMSO, 1970.

burden of the second of these. Nevertheless the teachers' organisations were alarmed at the proposals and were very keen to secure a national agreement on the conditions of service before the committee's recommendations were implemented.

At present the number of hours that a teacher actually spends in front of his classes varies from about 22 to 14 per week, depending on the teacher's grade. The total official working week is about 30 to 32 hours. The rest of the time is spent on administration, research or tutorial work. The Assistant Lecturer' teaching load which is the maximum found in the colleges is roughly comparable with the average school teacher's. University teachers, on the other hand, devote on average about eight hours per week to direct teaching duties and a further six to preparation. However, their total working week is over 40 hours. This figure is derived from estimates made by the teachers themselves whereas the college figure refers to statutory hours. Teaching loads in the CATs were reduced during their transition from college to university, possibly owing to the introduction of seminars and tutorial teaching methods. It appears that this process may also be underway in the polytechnics. * Their staff-student ratios are generous at the moment because they have been encouraged to start new degree courses in the anticipation of rapidly increasing demand from students.

ii) The problem of research

One of the big differences between higher education in the universities and higher education in the colleges is the amount of research work that the staff carry out alongside their teaching duties. Traditionally, very little was carried out in the colleges, but with their increasing stature as institutions providing higher learning has come the demand that they, like the universities, should devote a substantial part of their efforts to research. The proponents of this view suggest that research in the colleges might well be more problem-orientated and of more immediate practical application than much of that done in the universities, because of the colleges' practical traditions. ** The opponents of research in the colleges see research as likely to raise unit costs unnecessarily, so preventing the college from providing a solution to the problem of increasing student numbers.

At present, the staff may claim a few hours a week as research time, provided they can offer some evidence of their research activities.

* For further discussions of the effects of expansion and of efficiency in the deployment of teachers, see G. Wilson and P. Lewis "Cost Studies in Higher Education", Higher Education Review, Vol. 2, No. 2, Spring 1970.

** See: Eric Robinson: The New Polytechnics, Cornmarket Press, London, 1968. for a forceful exposition of this view.

No such formal control exists in the universities. In addition, since 1967, it has become possible for establishments which are doing a considerable volume of research to appoint people to a new staff grade, that of Reader, to direct and supervise such research. The Readers do little teaching and command a salary within the range of that of heads of departments. The relationship between teaching staff and full-time research personnel has yet to be worked out, but it would be in keeping with the policy of the teachers' professional organisations to seek to keep the two functions separate as far as policy on appointments and salaries is concerned.

It is notoriously difficult to make a direct comparison between the expenditure per student in the colleges and in the universities on facilities such as books and equipment, because of the large element of research expenditure included in university costs. Nevertheless, there are many indications that teachers in universities can rely on more ancillary facilities than can their counterparts in the colleges.

In 1964-65 the UGC statistics showed that the five new universities had an average library stock of 67,000 volumes and an annual expenditure on books and periodicals of £ 44,000. A survey carried out by college librarians for the same year reported that 18 regional colleges had an average book stock of 18,000 and annual expenditure of £ 5,000.

The provision of other facilities varies from college to college, depending on how much money each has been allowed for the development of advanced courses. Often laboratories in polytechnics are newly built and lavishly equipped, but other parts of the college will be cramped into old fashioned classrooms dating from the days when it was a technical institute with very different expectations. The colleges are small units and hence at a disadvantage when it comes to the purchase of large items of equipment such as computers. As will be seen in the next section, they do not have the power to decide to pool their resources and share. In comparing their material resources with those of universities, whose incomes have in the past so greatly benefited from private endowments, the college teachers feel considerably under-privileged.

## Teachers and Authority

Colleges of further education are controlled by local authorities which receive their money from local taxation and from central government subsidy. The finance committee and the education committee of the local authority then allocate each college its budget. The central government subsidy is fixed biennially so there is, in effect, a two-year planning horizon for current expenditure. Building programmes have to be specifically authorized by the central government and are budgeted separately. A loan is raised and the cost of servicing and repaying it charged to the colleges. The finance for advanced courses is drawn from a pool into which all the local authorities pay. The local authorities draw out of it as and when they wish to build up the advanced work in their colleges. Even in the case of advanced work the decision is taken by the education committee rather than the college staff. In comparison with the autonomous guilds of dons in the universities,* the principal of a college and his staff are quite explicitly employees of the local education authority. This has led to extreme frustration among the staff in some cases. Complaints about the bureaucratic nature of decision-making are rife and the staff feel that the rigidity of the system is crippling. The colleges must specify in detail how they arrive at their estimates for the following year's expenditure and each item has to be approved separately. Once the funds are allocated, the colleges have no power to make adjustments between different expenditure heads by, for instance, using the money saved on teachers' salaries to buy extra books, nor can they unilaterally decide to economize on books bought in one year to save up for an item such as a slightly bigger computer than their current allocation permits. As the colleges gain in standing and prestige so their staffs increasingly resent the hold which the "amateurs" on the education committee have over them. All staff appointments are controlled, so that new courses can be introduced only if the local education authority favours them. One loop-hole exists: part-time staff can be employed on the colleges' initiative alone and this accounts for their continuing important role in the colleges.

The polytechnics cast increasingly envious eyes on the greater degree of self-government that university staff enjoy. Universities' freedom in financial matters is much greater. Their recurrent expenditure is determined for five years at a time and, once it is determined, they are free to distribute it internally entirely as they wish. The internal government of most universities is fairly democratic in so far as staff representation is concerned. Proposals are afoot to liberalize the position in the polytechnics. ** These colleges are to be given all possible freedom in managing themselves with the minimum of detailed control by the local education authorities. The authorities will still settle the broad range of courses to be provided and they will still approve the colleges' annual financial estimates. The authority of the head of the college is to be increased by giving him the power to choose his own staff. The head or director, as he is to be called, will be a member of the governing board and the academic staff will be able to elect some of its members. However, a large majority of the members will continue to be local dignitaries.

* <u>The British Academics,</u> by A.H. Halsey and M. Trow, Faber, London, 1971.

** <u>Notes for Guidance on the Government and Academic Organisation of Polytechnics,</u> sent to local authorities by the Department of Education and Science, April 1967.

The governing body will submit financial estimates to the local authority but once the amount of money is approved it will be free to make adjustments in the detailed allocation of funds. This will overcome one of the colleges' main difficulties, but some staff in the colleges feel that control by such a broadly based body still effectively denies autonomy to the colleges.

The academic staff are to be members of an academic board as in the universities. The board, subject to the ultimate authority of the governing body, will have responsibility for academic matters such as the curriculum and examinations. It is yet to be seen how these new provisions, to be incorporated into the articles of government of the polytechnics, will work out in practice. At present the staff are still very conscious of the continued operation of the old system, with close supervision from the local authorities as well as closer control by central government than is found in the universities.

In addition to the financial control which the central government ultimately exercises over the local authorities, the colleges' prospects are directly affected by central government pronouncements about policy. The reports of the Committee on the More Efficient Use of Technical College Resources have already been mentioned. These with their pronounced cost-effectiveness bias would scarcely be tolerated in a university. This approach was, in the past, much more acceptable to the staff of the colleges for it is in keeping with their practical "hard headed" traditions. Nevertheless the Committee's reports have aroused resentment as unwarranted interference by outsiders.

The polytechnics are creatures of the government, and their increasing independence from local authority control is through government favour. The government's aim is to create in them institutions more responsive to the dictates of public policy than are the universities. This in itself, however, creates a worse situation for their staff than that in the autonomous universities. The staff of the polytechnics look with envy at the buffer systems designed to protect the universities from direct control by the State. The University Grants Committee acts to preserve the universities from direct dealings with the Department of Education and Science. Although its independence has been slightly eroded it is still regarded as a bulwark against direct state control. In addition to local and central government control, the colleges are subject to surveillance in a third way that is not experienced by the universities. It has already been explained that the curriculum of the colleges' degree courses is submitted to the Council for National Academic Awards. The purpose of this scheme was to allow the staff of the colleges greater freedom in the design and examination of courses than had been possible under the old arrangements, where students were prepared for external degrees of London University. Although most teachers applauded the innovation, in practice there have been complaints that the system leads to inflexibility, since any change in the syllabus must be submitted for approval. This may involve a visit of CNAA personnel to the college and considerable delay before the change can be implemented. Moreover the strong university representation on the Council has been criticized by some college staff who would prefer to see the Council a more exclusively college affair with the university members playing a more peripheral role. The domination of the CNAA by university members, and the importance of the Council in authenticating the degree courses offered by the colleges, is perhaps the best example of all of the inferior status of their staff in comparison with those of universities.

# III

## CONCLUSIONS

### FURTHER EDUCATION'S SELF-IMAGE

Much of what has gone before has listed the grievances felt and expressed by those working in further education. It is clear that the majority of the grievances arises from the unfavourable comparisons made by the college staff between their working conditions and those of their colleagues in universities.

The admission of these grievances as legitimate, presupposes that the answer to the question: "Why should staff in short-cycle institutions have working conditions similar to those in universities?" is "Because they fulfil the same role". As any economist knows, the labour market tends to equalize the net advantages obtained by similar types of labour in different parts of the labour market. If the net advantages of college teaching are lower than those in the universities, the staff they recruit will also be inferior. This will prejudice the future of the institutions if they strive to become "centres of excellence", in competition with the universities.

In the past, this answer to the question did not command the same general acceptance as it does now. The college staff saw themselves as fulfilling an entirely different role, providing education at a variety of different levels on a relatively <u>ad hoc</u> basis, in response to local needs. Nevertheless, they thought of themselves as on an educational escalator and expected to move up it. After all, many of the universities had started as technical institutes and had risen to become civic universities through local pride and endeavour. This provided a satisfactory present and exhilarating future for the colleges. The pace of change was gradual enough for the more irreconcilable elements in this self-image to co-exist. The imposition of the binary policy on the colleges at a time of rapidly rising expectations, however, changed the controversy into open conflict about what traditions should be retained and what jettisoned. The escalator has been abolished and the universities and colleges set side by side. The prevailing political and educational philosophy seeks to ensure "parity of esteem" between all sectors of higher education. Rightly, the teachers argue that such parity of esteem will be difficult to achieve if teachers in the advanced part of further education continue to view their position, in terms of prestige, status and salary, as inferior to that of their university counterparts. However, the more fundamental problem posed by the policy for the teachers is that of finding a real reason for continuing a separate existence as equal but different. Before, they were different and had aspired to be equal, now they have to be both simultaneously. Moreover, if they are to see the realization of the projected redress of the balance in the distribution of state funds between the universities and themselves, they must take the offensive in proclaiming the virtues of their type of education.

The consequences of this for the teacher's self-image are only just beginning to emerge. However, we are beginning to see the old traditions of further education described in this paper presented as the pillars of a new theory of higher education. The form of education that served the local community is elevated to provide the system supposedly best able to cope with the demands of mass higher education. The theory now concentrates on how to serve the interests of the national community, as opposed to the local one, where further education's tools were forged. The claim made for further education is that its pragmatic tradition can best provide the education necessary to equip the population for a world where rapid change makes flexibility and adaptation to new roles necessary within the span of one lifetime. The universities, of course, disagree.

There is disagreement over which type of education provides "a truly liberal outlook", is "narrowly vocational" or "narrowly academic", "subservient to the demands of industrialists" or producing "an élitist band of scholars". It seems that there are two camps in the colleges: those who would like to be more equal than different, and those who are determined to be different; but both argue as if their view should prevail over the whole educational system. The freezing of the system within its component parts has intensified the debate over what a unified system should be like. It is the teachers in the colleges who find themselves bearing the brunt of the debate, for it is they who are seeking to establish themselves, and they who are expected to be the innovators.

# VI

## Teaching learning approaches in Short-Cycle Higher Education

by

Guy Berger
Professeur, Université de Vincennes (France)

## TABLE OF CONTENTS

Introduction ........................................... 267

I. STATING THE PROBLEM ........................ 269

II. CHARACTERISTICS OF THE STUDENT POPULATION 271

III. PEDAGOGICS OF THE TRANSMISSION OF KNOWLEDGE AND KNOW-HOW ..................... 275

A. Elements of analysis ........................ 275

B. Elements for a solution ..................... 278

IV. GENERAL PROSPECTS FOR HIGHER EDUCATION .. 279

## INTRODUCTION

Economic, demographic or institutional studies dealing with the growth of post-secondary education have often done no more than show the emergence of mass higher education without proposing any real possibilities of intervention or even prediction. Such studies point out the difficulties most national economies encounter in absorbing new graduates or simply in bearing the cost of higher education, and show how little forecasts of manpower requirements actually affect "human resources planning".

Educational growth is a largely spontaneous process, in which little account is taken of forecasting policies, particularly employment policy. The result of this "spontaneous" development is that the educational system responds each time by partial measures and contingency decisions to pressure which it does nothing to resist.

This characteristic of educational growth must be taken into account in any attempt to organise short-cycle higher education and, more specifically, its relationship with long-cycle higher education. In our view, no planning policy at present enables either qualitative or quantitative trends in higher education to be forecast with a sufficient degree of accuracy.

Most of the choices made in orienting growth are based on ideological rather than on really scientific premises. Since ours is a technical civilization in which humanistic educational values appear to have been rejected, it is decided that short-cycle higher education shall be "technological". As we see it, however, technology seems to be an umbrella term used to qualify almost anything (this being the case, for example, of certain French University Institutes of Technology or of certain American colleges). Because the development of our societies seems to be directly connected with that of scientific thought, it has been decided that encouragement should be given to the advancement of studies in the field of the fundamental and applied sciences, but at the same time it is clearly the number of applicants for literary or related studies which generally grows fastest. The duration of studies is said to be too long, but almost everywhere it tends to become still longer. This means working from within the system itself and thinking out the kind of teaching structure for higher education that will make it able to respond to changes we are unable to control. It also means that educational systems should not be permitted to grow by providing partial, ad hoc remedies designed to limit the extent of the damage rather than solve the problems.

From this standpoint France appears to be a significant example. Owing to the pressure of demand, new structures were set up, in particular the University Institutes of Technology (IUTs). As the pressure continued to increase, more or less artificial devices were invented such as "passerelles" (bridges), allowing access from the newer to the older structures, although for neither is this really possible. In some countries, owing to the effect of various types of extensions, short-cycle education becomes as protracted as long-cycle education, but is then called an "other" type of education. Short-cycle higher education does not even fulfil the function of democratizing education which it was intended to do. Its very success means that middle-class students are frequently attracted to it because of more definite vocational prospects.

We have tried to analyse these questions in the perspective of a transformation of the entire system of higher education.

The comments which follow are working hypotheses - sometimes of a contentious nature - which should be confronted with the individual situation in each country as well as with the very different sets of problems found in each discipline.

In most countries, "university" is a term which still does far too much to conceal the real variety of education streams, and if our proposals are deliberately very general in character it is because they should lend themselves to considerable adjustment in order to meet specific requirements.

# I

## STATING THE PROBLEM

The introduction of new post-secondary teaching structures for the purpose of short-cycle higher education encounters so many difficulties as to pose a virtual dilemma.

Either the short-cycle is regarded as an independent entity directly orientated towards certain types of vocational practice, or else it tends to resemble the first stage of long-cycle education. In the first case, from a university standpoint, it is a sort of dead-end failing to offer the ablest or most highly motivated students any access to the long university cycle; both students and teachers consider it to be of little value; nor does any structural change result in the university system as a whole. From an economic standpoint, it is true that in the immediate future it can somewhat reduce the inflow of students and enable certain manpower requirements to be met. But since it is a closed cycle, it is rather an extended secondary vocational school and merely reflects the general trend to prolong studies without opening up new prospects for higher education.

In the second case (where it tends to resemble the first stage of long-cycle education) the short-cycle has the following disadvantages:

- it no longer bears any relation to its vocational function;
- most of the students normally want to transfer to the long-cycle;
- insofar as it is still directed towards concrete and practical questions, it slows up the students who plan to continue, since the second stage of the long-cycle is designed as an extension of the usually wholly theoretical first stage;
- insofar as the short-cycle emphasizes the theoretical aspects, it becomes part of the university system, gradually loses all individuality and wholly fails to reply to the problems it was initially supposed to solve;

- last, and we think by no means least, by gradually assuming the form of a first cycle of long education, short education may fail in its "ideological function" which was to revalue vocational and specialized practices as such by considering them as the means and form of "general" training.

From a teaching standpoint, we believe there is no way of resolving the dilemma unless a number of premises implicit in higher education are understood and unless proposals opposed to these implicit premises are formulated.

It is these premises and proposals that we shall attempt to express. They cover the characteristics of the student population upon leaving secondary or intermediate school, the pedagogics of the transmission of knowledge and know-how, and the general prospects of higher education.

# II

## CHARACTERISTICS OF THE STUDENT POPULATION

As higher education was for long designed to recruit and teach an élite, it apparently considered "traditional" students as possessing a number of homogeneous characteristics, such as a taste and capacity for abstract thought, a "general culture", the need to understand the theory of a subject before acting upon it, etc. The increase in student numbers was accordingly seen as expressing access to universities of a new population with diametrically opposite characteristics for which new streams had to be created. The selective nature of higher education, as well as of the entire educational system, therefore long prevented any awareness of how ill adapted this system was to student populations, since failure was supposed to penalize, and in fact did penalize the recipient of education, and not what was taught.

Actually, all recent studies show that, regardless of the method of recruitment, and in particular whether it is selective or not, the student population entering higher education is extremely heterogeneous. Even where, as in most Latin countries, national examinations based on national curricula are used, mental profiles, motivations, knowledge, and levels of intellectual or emotional maturity vary widely. Possession of a baccalauréat, an Abitur or any similar diploma is not sufficient indication on which to base forecasts. When university admission is based on the passing of some final secondary school examination, one is too often apt to forget that this refers to a concept of average and that an infinite variety of profiles are covered.

We therefore feel that it is impossible to define a priori any rigid curricula based on the organisation of knowledge or of the vocational practices which must be learned without allowing for this initial diversity. Paradoxically, however, in most university systems the lower cycle is very rigidly structured, few channels are offered, and greater freedom of choice is only progressively granted to the student, as though needs were homogeneous, and levels comparable. It is thus far easier to define the terminal cycles with accuracy, even though the diversity of vocational practices makes them very numerous, than the initial cycles. At the end of higher education it may be assumed that certain disparities in the level of knowledge have been corrected, that as objectives upon graduation are more clearly specified motivations get clearer, that intellectual and emotional maturity has had more time to develop and that a fair degree of homogeneity has thus been achieved.

Most systems of higher education thus offer a tree-like structure, consisting at first of a minimum number of streams which then steadily proliferate. By definition, there is then a contradiction between the poorly diversified first stage of long-cycle education and the necessary variety of short-cycle education.

But more serious still, there is a contradiction between the first stage of the long-cycle and the population it is supposed to serve, since its structure is based on a number of assumptions concerning the necessary organisation of knowledge rather than of those of the processes of apprenticeship.

We believe that the "tree-like" structure which is now characteristic of long-cycle higher education should be replaced by what for the sake of convenience we shall call a "double-funnel" structure, which can be outlined as follows:

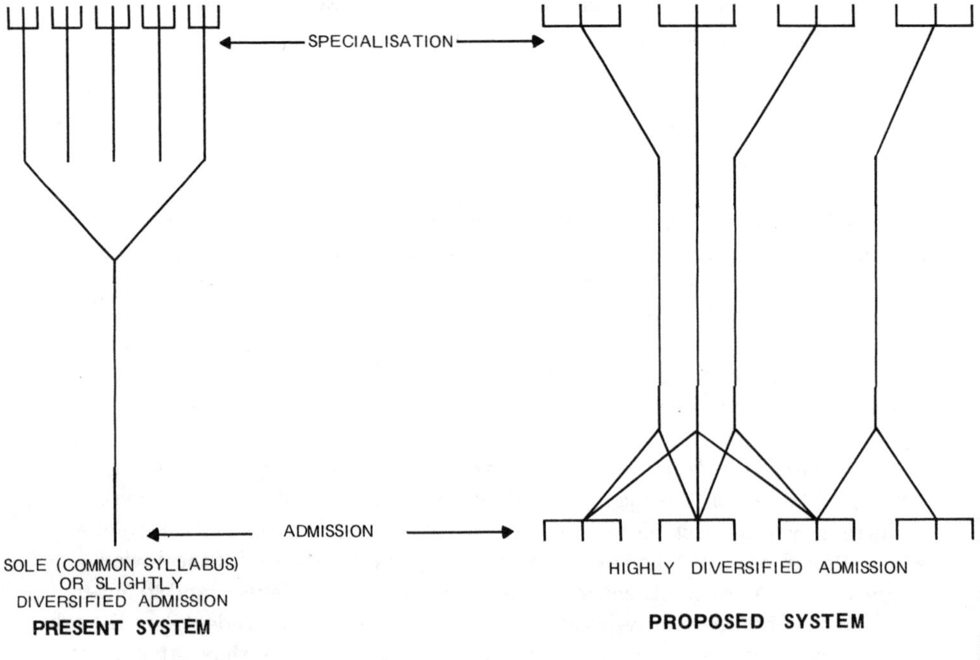

We believe this scheme:

- takes more into account the true nature of the student population;
- effectively provides for various orientations and, if necessary, for orientation without loss of time;
- in certain cases avoids the bottleneck of the first year (as all students follow exactly the same study circuit, the first year is necessarily the one in which the bottlenecks occur);
- allows the problem of transfer from short-cycle to long-cycle higher education to be stated very differently.

Again in the context of the psycho-sociological characteristics of the student population, we think that is is necessary to distinguish the following sub-groups:

- A small number of students (growing smaller all the time, it would appear) have definite ideas about a vocation as soon as they enter higher education. Whether they follow a family tradition or have been clearly oriented, they are generally disappointed by long-cycle higher education, which nearly always delays their entry into a professional career. They do not see why they should make a detour through theoretical training for which they do not understand the need. At best they accept the detour passively. At worst, the length of their studies "disorientates" them and they will be finally disappointed in their job;
- most students have no definite ideas about a profession. They therefore have no reason, other than economic, to choose a short-cycle. But the university system, and especially the first cycle will offer them no help in making up their minds; all it does is to allow a longer period of indecision or ignorance. When they finally enter their professional career, it will nearly always be too late and the best students will extricate themselves, if they have choosen a wrong career, only by undertaking further studies and accumulating superfluous diplomas.

Independently of the above considerations, the choice of the long-cycle may often be said to show that the student is hesitating to choose a definite career, or desires to delay entry into active life for as long as possible, rather than a capacity for theoretical reasoning.

Whether short-cycle or long-cycle education is concerned, whether the student does or does not know what he wants to be, whether the purpose is to confirm the choice of some or enable the hesitant to choose, we think higher education should act promptly in helping students to encounter the actual situations they will later meet in their careers.

The problem is not to create a higher vocational education (which exists, incidentally, in the form of long-cycle education in medicine) but to bring certain vocational practices into the whole of higher education.

This of course once more raises the overall problem of links and modes of transfer from short-cycle to long-cycle education.

# III

## PEDAGOGICS OF THE TRANSMISSION OF KNOWLEDGE AND KNOW-HOW

### A. ELEMENTS OF ANALYSIS

The organisation of higher education and the establishment of short-cycle parallel to long-cycle education are based on a number of implicit cultural and pedagogic premises.

The first premise is the radical opposition between general and vocational training. Experience shows that it is those the nature of whose training is regarded as being more "general" ("Humanities" as opposed to "Science" students, "Pure Science" as opposed to "Engineering" students, etc.) who have the "narrowest" profiles and the least opportunity of changing their job or of applying the knowledge they have acquired in some other area. In present-day society the most likely fate of the mathematician is to become a teacher of mathematics, while the engineering graduate may become an economist, a manager, or a specialist in branches far removed from his original background. The concept of "instrumental disciplines" which is later discussed perhaps accounts for this opposition.

The second premise, one moreover related to the first, corresponds to a certain image of "science classification", as understood in both a chronological and logical sense. Such a premise allows one to disregard completely all that is known about apprenticeship processes, the role of motivation or simply the real interest of secondary school leavers. It is as through the higher education structure, in the name of orderly learning, demanded patience and submissiveness on the student's part while requiring him to make intensive use of his mental faculties.

In education the notion of basic knowledge is often confused with that of knowledge "which chronologically comes first". The fact of doing "first" what is to be used "later" triggers off mechanisms of rejection, loss of memory and of motivation. The need for such fundamental knowledge is often not perceived by the student until he reaches a certain practical level, or else certain theoretical levels in other disciplines.

A careful study might show that, apart from their selective function, the first year or two of higher education serve little purpose, and that the knowledge acquired must later be "relearnt" almost entirely (see the first year of medical study in most countries). This diagnosis may seem harsh but is almost always confirmed.

We therefore propose to undertake a more operational analysis of the types of disciplines (or knowledge) actually dispensed by higher education systems. This analysis shows that while the method of combining the various disciplines is actually different in short-cycle and long-cycle education, it cannot take the form of a simple sequence over time.

We propose to distinguish:

1. Instrumental disciplines. These are the disciplines whose inherent objectives do not match those pursued by the student during his studies but which must be learnt for professional purposes or for other openings; e.g.

- correct use of a foreign language;
- knowledge of elementary statistical instruments;
- methodology of clinical observation, of experimentation, of operations research.

The time at which these instrumental disciplines are learned is relatively unimportant, so long as it precedes the period of professional activity:

- to crowd them in at the beginning would be unrealistic;
- to group them at the end would prevent the student from getting to know the actual conditions of his future career.

These fields of study can be found in both long-cycle and short-cycle education.

2. Basic subjects, are those whose content is not the same as that of the subject selected by the student but a knowledge of which is necessary for a proper understanding of his own subject; e.g.

- knowledge by the psychology student of biological mechanisms;
- knowledge by the medical student of molecular chemistry and of the elementary organisation of matter;
- knowledge by the social science student of fundamental economic laws.

These subjects should be "integrated" as far as possible. As pointed out earlier, it is usual to begin with them, but:

- this is debatable from a pedagogical standpoint;
- this makes it impossible to articulate the short-cycle with the long-cycle: e.g. after two years of study a medical student knows nearly nothing of what a nurse knows and vice versa. Paradoxically, what the nurse knows would be of use to her only at the end of any medical studies she might undertake. On the other hand, a medical student dropping out after four years of study would have received no really thorough vocational training. In France many of these drop-outs become travelling salesman for leading pharmaceutical firms: they have, in fact, learned to talk about medicine, about which they know nothing.

3. Theoretical subjects. Apart from the basic subjects which are usually theoretical for pedagogical reasons the dialectics of a theoretical versus a concrete approach must be taken into account, in both the long- and short-cycles. Above all it is necessary for students who stop at the short-cycle to be able to acquire an overall understanding of the practical side and for all students to have a few minimum intellectual tools:

- mathematics,
- model construction,
- systems analysis,
- elementary anthropology.

4. To these subjects should be added the body of knowledge making up the actual substance of the studies chosen, and which presumably can hardly be identical either in size or approach for short-cycle or for the first stage of long-cycle higher education. We are speaking here only of "disciplines" and knowledge in the traditional sense of these words. These frameworks should be completely thought out again and the problem of the vocational approach put separately. We are confining ourselves here to a common minimum for short- and long-cycle education.

## B. ELEMENTS FOR A SOLUTION

In view of the above distinctions, two methods should allow short-cycle and the first stage of long-cycle education to be articulated with sufficient flexibility.

1. From the strictly practical point of view, we think that the first element of a solution would be the introduction of the "credit" system. "Credits" would be considered as integrated, that is as centred on an "objective" (and not on some aspect of a method or practice) and should at the same time include an analysis of the objective and all the theoretical and concrete approaches to it (see so-called "integrated" instruction in medicine). This system should allow the acquisition of a "university capital", a wide variety of first-year curricula, a real approach to the actual conditions in vocational practice at all levels and the possibility of a minimum amount of theory at all levels. Only by "destructuring" higher education as it exists, particularly in the European universities, can we apparently get out of the dilemma described at the beginning while allowing the permanent tasks of education to be carried out.

2. We believe that in both short-cycle and the first stage of long-cycle higher education students should be in contact with vocational practice and actual working conditions, which are often the same whatever the level of the graduate. This should take place no later than the end of the first year in order to allow for orientation. Previous working experience could also be evaluated by this system by the use of equivalences or lower value credits.

The need for a number of "instrumental disciplines" must moreover be insisted upon. These will in fact be the starting point for transfer to the long cycle or for the resumption of study after a period of professional activity. It is very difficult, we think, to go much further, especially as regards the purely scientific disciplines where the problems of "knowledge organisation" are still of major importance, but a combination of the two proposals should reduce "wastage" and "redundancy" to a minimum if the student resumes his studies.

# IV

## GENERAL PROSPECTS FOR HIGHER EDUCATION

1. As a result of the trend in teaching, of student demand, of the existence of "educational media", of the growth of knowledge, etc, two changes appear to be characteristic of university systems:

- the transition from "teaching" to "learning";
- the transition from a system of knowledge transmission to a system of knowledge production.

The two processes, which only partially overlap, nevertheless have the effect of:

- increasing the student's autonomy;
- causing motivation to be taken into account;
- radically altering the "pace" of learning, in the sense that pace becomes relatively individualized.

This change should particularly affect the "instrumental disciplines", which would lend themselves to "independent" modes of access and therefore in some measure to any sort of order in the curriculum, through the use of such educational media as:

- programmed instruction,
- computer-assisted instruction,
- audiovisual aids,
- language laboratories,
- small discussion groups at the same level.

(It is a paradox that the greatest efforts now being made in producing educational media concentrate on complex and hence "rare" types of knowledge, except perhaps as regards modern languages.)

Our belief is that this dual change, taken in association with the organisation in terms of credits or "unités de valeur" as earlier described, can reduce the disparity between the short cycle and long cycle, especially by making the latter more flexible. The essential difference is that the long cycle, owing to its very length, should lead to greater individualization, to wider acceptance of individual learning patterns and hence to more flexible programming, whereas short-cycle education should impose greater constraints, since it must more promptly succeed in producing an organic, professionally utilizable whole.

There can therefore be no question of making the short-cycle into the first stage of the long-cycle, nor can two years in the short-cycle establish access to the third year of the long-cycle. But there is little reason why the knowledge acquired and the "time spent" should not be fully integrated into the long-cycle, and that the "cost" of the transfer be thus reduced to a minimum.

2. The distinction between short- and long-cycle education should be made part of a broader scheme, one which in particular would enable initial training to be distinguished from continuing or further training. Here again the two sets of notions are not at all clear. A subject now taught in refresher courses for long-cycle graduates may well have already been taught to others in the short-cycle. (For example, continuing education for secondary school teachers generally consists of the sort of vocational training that primary teachers receive in the short-cycle, while in continuing or extended training the latter take the language or mathematical courses already taken by former in the long-cycle.)

The previous example shows the absurd nature of a system which contradicts its own postulates on the organisation of knowledge and prevents transfers in practice.

What makes higher education so difficult to organise at present is the small amount of concrete information available on occupational profiles at various levels and on what graduates subsequently become. For lack of such information or lack of interest for it, we continue to reason in artificial terms based on a pseudo-rational vision of the articulation of knowledge and on a simplified view of professional practices. It would not be realistic to expect very clearly defined occupational profiles from those professionally concerned since their exigencies are necessarily contradictory.

A better knowledge of the student population, of what graduates subsequently become, of changes now taking place in actual or potential teaching practices in higher education, based above all on a comprehensive grasp of the factors conducive to the sort of university training which can be used at different professional levels, will allow us to express the problems of higher education as a whole, and hence of the possible linkages between short-cycle and long-cycle higher education.

Only later can these problems be dealt with profession by profession and discipline by discipline, since we consider that any structural solution which might be imposed on actual knowledge or practices cannot provide the answer to the problems we have raised.

# VII

## Problems of employment for graduates of short-cycle higher education and French experience with University Institutes of Technology (IUTs)

by

Michel-Yves Bernard, Professeur au Conservatoire national des Arts et Métiers, Paris and Conseiller technique au ministère de l'Education nationale (France)

## TABLE OF CONTENTS


Introduction .......................................... 287

I. Various forms of short-cycle higher education ....... 289

II. Employment for short-cycle higher education graduates: qualitative aspect .................... 295

III. Employment for short-cycle higher education graduates: quantitative aspect .................. 301

IV. Employment for short-cycle higher education graduates: the socio-psychological aspect ........ 307

Conclusion .......................................... 311

# INTRODUCTION

The concept of short-cycle higher education is gaining ground in almost all countries. Young people entering higher education are offered a choice between two separate cycles of different duration (the long cycle generally lasting four to five years and the short cycle two to three years). France was somewhat late in adopting this idea and in that country short-cycle higher education began only in 1966.* It is provided in the University Institutes of Technology (IUTs) which, as their name indicates, are a branch of the French university system (more precisely, to use the statutory term, a Unit of that system).

The object of this paper is to consider the problems posed by the employment of short-cycle higher education graduates: it would indeed be meaningless to organise a system of education leading to a degree if the graduates of that system are unable to find a place in the labour market corresponding to the training received and offering prospects for promotion. The problem, however, must be considered as a whole and one should refrain from conceiving education merely as a means of preparing narrow specialists who can be immediately productive in the present occupational context. Rather, education should train people for the society of tomorrow. It would be a serious mistake to define employment possibilities in terms of a list of current occupations, to be filled quantitatively and qualitatively. A prospective approach is needed, which we have attempted to follow in this brief outline of French thinking on this issue during the setting-up of IUTs.

To examine the employment outlets for an educational system and then take action to adjust that system to the outlets desired means

* A preliminary experiment was tried in 1952 for students enrolled in courses leading to the brevets de techniciens supérieurs (higher technicians' certificates). We shall revert to this experiment in Chapter I.

tackling not only an economic problem but also, and above all, a sociological one. While occupations may be similar in all countries of comparable structure and climate, and their distribution more or less determined by the gross national product, this does not hold for the educational system, which is closely bound up with a country's civilization; the extent to which it may be adapted is often very limited, mainly because of sociological constraints. We shall therefore study the employment problems of short-cycle higher education graduates as they arise in France, a temperate country with a population of 50 million, a gross national product of about $ 2,600 per capita and specific educational structure. Since the reforms made under Napoleon at the beginning of the 19th century, education at all levels has been considered by the French as a public service which the State must provide for all citizens with absolute equality and therefore absolute uniformity. The consequences of this standpoint are many: we shall concentrate on the main one:

> Access to higher education in France is open to all students who have completed their primary and secondary schooling (a period of 12 years) and have passed a school-leaving examination (the Baccalauréat). All types of Baccalauréat are EQUAL before the law, although they do not imply the same curriculum; and the holder of a Baccalauréat is automatically allowed to enrol at the university in those courses which he feels capable of undertaking.

This constraint obviously has a fundamental effect on the problem of employment. This problem would not be approached in the same way by a country with a tradition of strongly diversified, independent higher educational establishments which are competitive, operate at different levels and are selective in their entrance requirements. It is therefore highly dangerous to study a problem connected with the educational system while ignoring the attitudes of the people of the country, their traditions and the structure of the society they have gradually built up.

Forecasting is an excellent practice, akin to the art of prediction, derived from the decision-makers's desire to feel morally "secure". Only when the time comes to draw up the balance sheet is it possible to judge what the forecasts are worth. Studies have been undertaken in order to evaluate French experience of short-cycle higher education, and we refer our readers to them. Our essential aim in the present paper is to outline the forecasting methods used in France in order to compare them with those applying in other countries and thus provide a basis of discussion.

# I

## VARIOUS FORMS OF SHORT-CYCLE HIGHER EDUCATION

Short-cycle higher education may, conceivably, take various forms, each with its corresponding types of employment possibilities. Hence the need first to establish a classification.

By definition, higher education is designed for young people aged about 18,* who have just completed their secondary schooling. The "traditional" form of higher education consists of courses which in France used to last between three and four years, and which now often take five years. This extension is a disquieting development difficult to combat. The first two or three years of the course are generally devoted to acquiring a sound foundation of general and relatively abstract knowledge (e.g. engineering students study mathematics and physics). This period of basic education tends to become longer. The final years are devoted to the study of concrete problems connected with the professional activities of future graduates. But, owing to the growing importance of the basic theoretical instruction, techniques which should be practical tend to be taught in a formalized way (e.g. mechanics which tend to become "rational") and often become abstract. It is therefore necessary to add some years of practice at the end of the course, and this is a further cause of extension. The diagram in Figure 1 shows this progression from the abstract to the concrete. In this way, specialists are trained whose action is solidly based: they are "adaptable" and "capable of synthesis". They know how to proceed from the abstract to the concrete, which is an essential characteristic of the senior executive.

Failures in long-cycle higher education are frequent. Over half of the entrants do not stay the course and therefore receive a "truncated"

* Schooling begins at the age of 6 and young people should therefore logically be 18 years old when they enter the university. However, many repeat a class and the real average age of entry is between 19 and 20. Longer secondary schooling makes a systematic study necessary of the ways and means of shortening higher education.

Figure 1

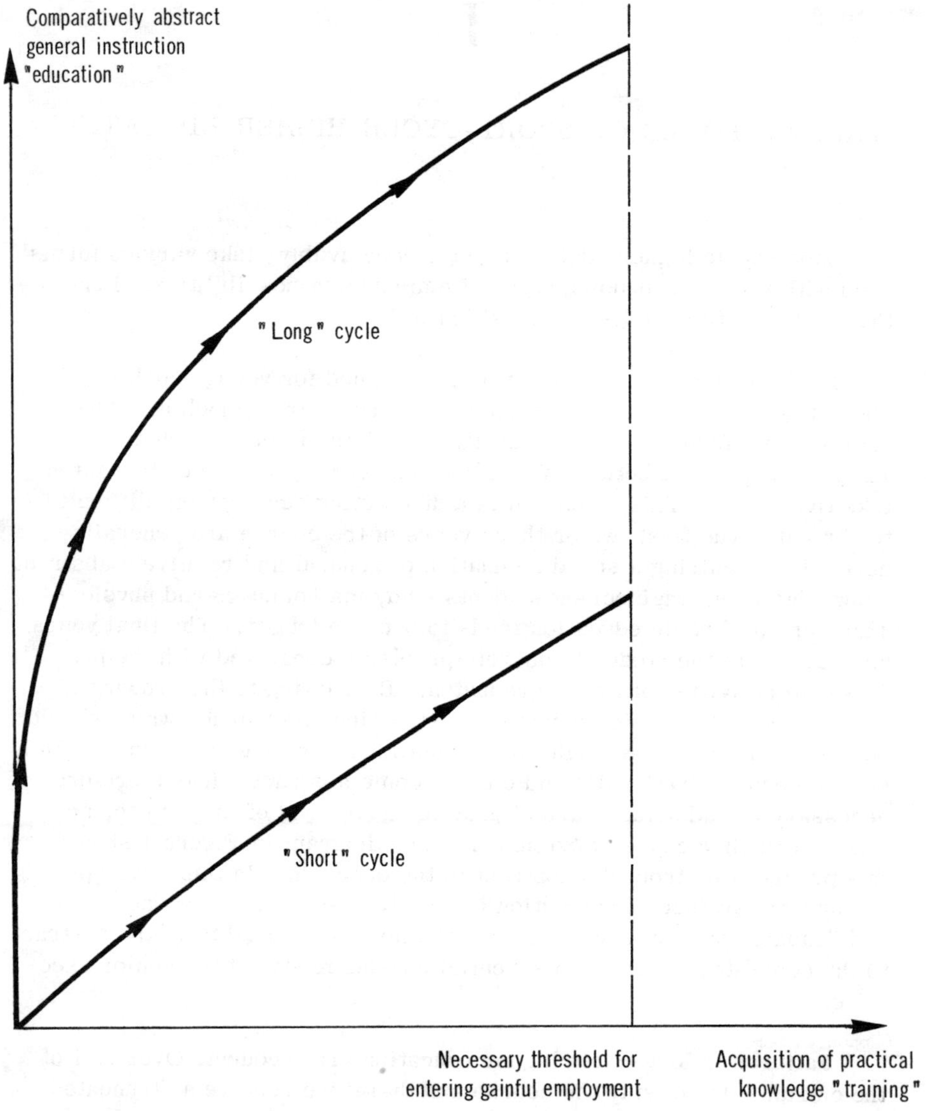

Comparatively abstract general instruction "education"
"Long" cycle
"Short" cycle
Necessary threshold for entering gainful employment
Acquisition of practical knowledge "training"

long-cycle education for which there are no employment possibilities. Students who are apprehensive of long-cycle courses, which are useless unless they are completed, should be advised to choose an alternative where methods are different (otherwise they will have the feeling of being cheated, since they are bound to encounter the same difficulties). The solution adopted in France is a short-cycle education mainly directed towards practical training. The students acquire useful, practical knowledge based on a less extensive general education than in the case of those taking long-cycle courses. This "concrete", practical education can be shorter than the normal university course since, from the beginning, it imparts utilisable knowledge. A man may be considered utilisable in society when he has reached a certain threshold of practical training. However, practical knowledge, although utilisable, is often not very formative; it is also "perishable". Once the threshold in practical training needed for a job has been attained, employment should be sought. As will be seen from Figure 1 progress along the vertical axis is always rewarding if it is possible. Horizontal progress is irrelevant beyond a certain efficiency threshold.

This kind of short-cycle higher education may be provided in several types of institutions:

a) Institutions of university status with their own autonomy, their specific rights and their types of personnel. This is the solution adopted in France; it has the advantage of giving the same status and therefore the same prerogatives to all young people of the same age and to all their teachers. It avoids segregation and removes a number of pitfalls in the search for employment since for all the professions concerned a "university background" will be included which, righly or wrongly, will raise their status. The same institution will include departments providing short-cycle courses and others enrolling long-cycle students. It is not easy to foster symbiosis between these two types of departments, owing to the prejudices and the pretentions of certain academics and many students. But it is possible, and in certain French universities this fusion is beginning to be achieved. Several university presidents or vice-presidents come from the short-cycle University Institutes of Technology (IUTs).

b) "Secondary school" type institutions specializing in short-cycle higher education courses. The training provided here is even more practical and this is no doubt an advantage in the search for immediate employment. But this training often produces specialists who are not easily convertible. Furthermore, this method leads to a regrettable segregation of students: only the "élite" taking long-cycle higher education enjoy the benefits of the university system; the "common herd' taking the short-cycle courses continue to be subject to secondary school discipline. Such segregation of students - and also of teachers - should be avoided.

Figure 2

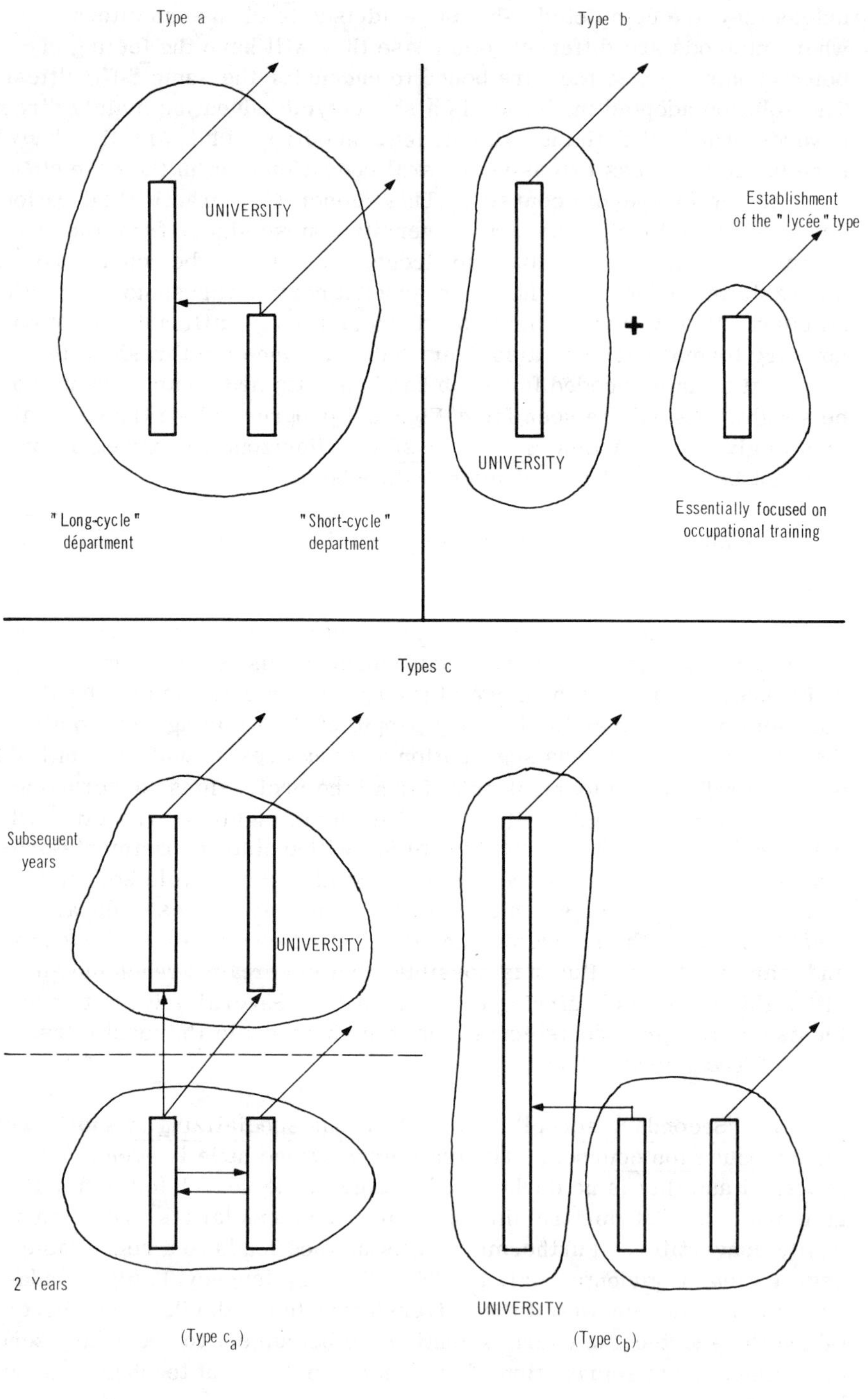
Type a
Type b
UNIVERSITY
"Long-cycle" department
"Short-cycle" department
UNIVERSITY
Establishment of the "lycée" type
Essentially focused on occupational training
Types c
Subsequent years
UNIVERSITY
2 Years
UNIVERSITY
(Type $c_a$)
(Type $c_b$)

Courses leading to the brevet de technicien supérieur (higher technician's certificate) constitute in France an example of this type of training.

c) Independent institutions providing courses in higher education covering the first two years irrespective of subsequent options. These are establishments which provide for students who intend to take the long cycle, which they will finish elsewhere, and for those who will enter the labour market at the end of their two-year course. This is the system of the "Two-Year Junior Colleges" in the USA and of the CEGEPs in Canada. But a distinction must be made between a system in which all students have to go through such an establishment (as in Canada) and one in which they can go directly to an establishment providing the complete long-cycle course (as in the USA).

Figure 2 illustrates these different possibilities. It would be interesting to compare the effectiveness of these systems, but the political and sociological context cannot be disregarded. Alternative "$c_a$" was envisaged in France by a study group (the 1962 Commission presided over by M. Boulloche, former Minister of Education). But the solution was dropped, despite its probable educational efficiency, because of the political problems it raised.

In the light of conditions in France, we shall now examine the short-cycle higher education provided by certain parts of the university which, like the rest, admit students holding the secondary school leaving certificate. Their objective is to provide practical training better suited to certain students than the theoretical instruction provided by most departments. Because it is essentially practical, such training may be short; theoretical instruction is bound to be long and must of necessity end with a period of practical training. In no case does the short cycle constitute part of the long cycle,* but it is a type of university education. Finally, we assume that, in accordance with French legislation, a student entering the university chooses freely between the short and the long cycles: he would be given advice but remains free to make his own choice. We shall see how the employment structure is linked with this free choice.

* An educational stream should prepare young people for entering employment: in this respect part of the long cycle, i.e. particularly the first part, which is the most abstract (statistics, physics, anatomy, biophysics, etc. for medical doctors), cannot possibly lead to employment possibilities. Certain departments of the (French) administration recruit young people who have completed only two years of the long-cycle studies, but they are then given "in-service training" where in fact they take the rest of the long-cycle course in a "spirit" adapted to the needs of the administration. Their total training is therefore equivalent to a long cycle.

# II

## EMPLOYMENT FOR SHORT-CYCLE HIGHER EDUCATION GRADUATES: QUALITATIVE ASPECT

It is impossible to identify the employment problems of short-cycle higher education graduates without making a brief analysis of the functions performed by men in society on the basis of the knowledge they have acquired. This leads to a distinction between science and technique.

Let us call "science" a body of knowledge logically classified in a theoretical framework which exists only because it is useful for classifying phenomena which are thus related to each other. For instance, we have physiology, linguistics, nuclear physics, neurology and the topology of functions. A man of science may be a disinterested aesthete who studies for pleasure. He may also be a researcher who studies to advance science. He may likewise be a teacher who studies to master his subjects and guide others wishing to learn it. It is obvious that the disinterested amateur will not concern us with reference to the problem of employment; the researcher, on the other hand, is useful to society, which is therefore likely to offer him employment if he has mastered his "science". He needs the longest possible period of study. As for the teacher, he may well lead his pupils astray if he has not mastered the subject he teaches and he too, therefore, needs a long course. In the field of science, it is difficult to see what employment opportunities (i. e. paid jobs offered by society) are available to short-cycle higher education graduates. The only conceivable occupation is that of science journalists or "rewriter". Although jobs are few, this occupation is important owing to its social impact, but it would not justify a special training and could not be the basis for a short-cycle course. In short, we may infer that there are not many opportunities in the field of science except through long-cycle training.

Let us now consider an entirely different way of classifying human knowledge, i. e. in terms of its usefulness in satisfying a human need (health, clothing, travel, shelter, communications). We then have various "techniques", e.g. pharmacy, civil engineering, law, electronics, accountancy. These techniques will vary in importance and thus give rise to different levels of action by those who acquire them. It is therefore in these techniques that graduates of short-cycle higher education must seek employment. It is clear that a technique must, above all, be useful and that it must be utilized. From these two concepts emerge the idea of utilization and the idea of improvement (by adding to or revolutionizing the technique). A man who may be expected to improve a technique will require a long training; he must be able to proceed from the abstract (knowledge of science) to the concrete (elements of science useful to the technique). But the man who has only to make use of the technique can quite well acquire his basic knowledge through a short training. This shows us a first type of outlet for short-cycle higher education; it will "produce" persons who have learned the rudiments of a technique and are able to utilize them to meet human needs, without aspiring in the first instance to improve the technique, but simply to "perform a service".

We must now draw up a list of the various techniques, which satisfy human needs. We can classify them in five categories:

Primary sector (mining, agriculture):

- agriculture, agronomy,
- agricultural machinery,
- horticulture, land use,
- animal husbandry,
- fishing,
- geological assistant.

Secondary sector (industrial production):

- public works,
- civil engineering, building,
- metallurgy, materials shaping,
- mechanical engineering,
- machinery and engines; motor vehicles,
- heating engineering; heating, air conditioning,
- electrical engineering, telecommunications,
- chemistry, pharmaceutical industry,
- laboratory technology; construction of apparatus,
- measuring instruments for physics, chemistry, biology,
- textiles, clothing,
- food industries.

Tertiary sector (services):

- data collection and processing,
- business management,
- publicity, marketing,
- local government,
- cultural promotion work,
- tourism,
- hotel and catering industries.

Public health sector:

- medical assistant, nurse,
- dental assistant, dental mechanic,
- X-ray technology and measuring instruments for doctors,
- biological analyses,
- optician,
- hearing aid mechanic,
- dietician,
- hospital management, social security.

Educational sector:

- primary school teacher,
- vocational guidance officer,
- education of handicapped children,
- nursery school teacher,
- welfare officer.

The above list, which might represent courses of short-cycle higher education, reveals the possibility of a classification into two categories. On closer examination, a technique will be found to be a set of miscellaneous elements whose conjunction is justified only by the possibility of meeting a human need. The action taken to meet this human need will be comprehensive, involving the combination of various components into a construction designed to meet the specification of the customer. Two possibilities may be considered in this context:

- Either the construction is on a small scale and requires only simple individual techniques which can be acquired in two or three years' study. In this case a single person can learn them and build the object or perform the service himself;

- or the construction is on a large scale and could not be handled by a single person. It will then call for an "architect", or leader, and a team of specialists, each with a perfect knowledge of some part of the technique.

Short-cycle higher education can lead to these two types of job which do not call for the same training. For comprehensive tasks involving simple techniques, it is essential to have the ability to synthesize, a good general education and a feeling for human relations, as the technician will be in contact with his "customer". A good example of this type of employment is transport management. Haulage firms (and incidentally many service enterprises) are anxious to recruit young people with a good general education and the right personal qualities. This implies short-cycle higher education comprising an introduction to the socio-economic problems of firms. Specific technical knowledge would be reduced to the minimum as in most cases graduates going into business will need only the rudiments of specific technical skills. This type of outlet exists in the tertiary sector, the service industries, and also in cultural promotion work, social work and vocational guidance, where personal qualities are more important than technical knowledge. Higher educational establishments catering for this type of employment provide a general education, instruction in "modern humanism" (communication sciences, social sciences, human sciences) and only a minimum of technical knowledge.

The second category is fundamentally different. The aim is to produce experts with a thorough knowledge of their subject and capable of working in a team. Here the educational establishment will provide a highly specialized curriculum, very detailed and with a relatively large scientific basis. The human aspect is less important, as the specialist will hardly be required to communicate with anybody except the team leader. Short-cycle higher educational establishments of this kind will mainly operate in the primary and secondary sectors, where techniques are highly sophisticated and generally consist of applied sciences.

Three points therefore emerge from this qualitative analysis of the problem of jobs available to short-cycle higher education graduates:

- An essentially scientific short-cycle higher education offers practically no prospects of employment;
- a short-cycle higher education must include a proportion of technical knowledge and may lead to:
  - the training of individuals to perform services on their own for other individuals, if the techniques involved are simple,
  - the training of experts able to use a specific technique in a team, working under a leader, if the techniques are complex and difficult to learn.

It may be claimed that the first years of long-cycle higher education also offer the training outlined above. In fact, everything depends on the spirit in which the training is provided and it is here that we return to the practical aspect. In two years it is possible to give a practical legal training geared to the problems of everyday life: the individuals thus trained will be of use to society and will render service. It is also possible to base the whole legal training on the history of institutions. After two years the students will not be utilisable but if they have survived they will be well equipped to continue their studies and become eminent jurists able to serve on the Council of State.

We must again emphasize the fact that theoretical instruction is bound to be long and gradually arrives at practical problems. An abbreviated long cycle is useless; while the short-cycle concentrates on practical instruction and for that reason can be short.

# III

## EMPLOYMENT FOR SHORT-CYCLE HIGHER EDUCATION GRADUATES: QUANTITATIVE ASPECT

It is not enough to define a function in the economy and the content of the corresponding training in order to resolve the employment problem; that is only part of the problem, and we must also know how many jobs corresponding to that classification will really be available. This is a very difficult question one which can be approached in various ways, none of which is satisfactory.

The simplest method, often employed, is to try to extrapolate on the basis of present and past situations. There are, of course, more sophisticated planning methods, but it is not certain that the results are any more convincing in the field of educational planning. In practice, surveys are carried out among employers to try to ascertain their manpower requirements, and the results are then assembled in huge tables and attempts are made to interpret them. This procedure has many defects:

1. As caution is essential in this field, the figures obtained will usually represent underestimations. An employer will tend to set his staff requirements low, because should economic progress be below expectations, he wishes to avoid being blamed, as he certainly would be, for having pressed for the training of specialists whom he does not need. It is easier for him to meet unexpected manpower needs by accelerated vocational training methods.

2. Extrapolation up to two or three years is possible, up to five years is doubtful, and up to ten years is fantasy. However, in order to set up the infrastructure needed for even short-cycle higher education, it is essential to be able to count on a running-in period of at least five years.

3. Extrapolation is obviously based on the present situation, and consists in modelling the future on the past, particularly where job

descriptions are concerned. Generally speaking industrial firms are well equipped for assessing the numerical trend of the specialists they employ at present, but have absolutely no means of predicting what new jobs will exist in ten years' time, and still less how many. Only a few very large firms may have at their disposal forecasting machinery capable of predicting what new jobs are likely to exist in ten years' time.

4. It must not be forgotten that one of the major preoccupations of heads of firms is to ensure good personnel management. In order to fill a given vacancy, the firm may either recruit a graduate from the educational system at the level of the job, or may promote a suitable staff member from a lower grade. The post then open to a graduate fresh from the educational system will be at a lower level than the vacancy which the firm needs to fill. This process of internal promotion is very difficult to quantify, as everything depends on the personnel resources available. It is a monumental error to try to determine the number of jobs available without taking internal promotion into account.

5. In a free economy, enterprises are independent and recruit their employees quite freely, just as they buy their raw materials or build their factories. It is difficult to define a general trend and still more so to lay down an overall policy. If the educational system is uniform and centralized, and therefore obliged to follow an overall policy, as it is in France, there is inevitably some incompatibility. Either the industrial system should be strictly planned or the educational system diversified.

In practice, the overall data regarding employment possibilities identified by this method do not measure up to the actual needs of the future economy, and cover only the "traditional" posts. On the other hand, the requirements of each enterprise are fairly well defined and can take internal promotion into account. The solution is therefore to leave educational establishments fairly free, while obliging them to keep in close contact with several industrial firms. It is locally, by links between a dozen industrial firms and a dozen short-cycle higher education establishments, that one can try to reach equilibirum between personnel requirements and resources in trained personnel. Short-cycle higher educational establishments must be well integrated into the economic community with the help of suitably constituted boards of management and the collaboration of specialists from local industry as teachers. Equilibrium will then be achieved gradually. There will nonetheless be errors, and we must expect either a slightly lower student intake than required or a risk of unemployment among surplus graduates. Below we shall see that there are other outlets for short-cycle higher education, which can be used to alleviate cyclical unemployment.

An educational system does not, however, exist solely in order to provide the economic system with the qualified specialists it requires.

Admittedly it must do this, or it has failed in its task; but it is not designed solely for that purpose. It must above all work to prepare the future society, which implies imagining what the future will be and directing its efforts along the lines it feels to be the best for all. In this field, an overall policy on a national scale is essential. In France, the Commissariat Général au Plan has carried out research on these lines, examining the evolution of an age group, i.e. a group of young people born in the same year (at present approximately 830,000 individuals). These young people enter the school system at the age of six and leave it after ten, twelve or fifteen years of education to join the active population. The Manpower Committee of the Commissariat au Plan has tried to fix the proportion of these young people which corresponds to the nation's future needs, and which ensures full employment for the workers.

Clearly the imponderables are very large; almost nothing is known of the phenomenon of workers' advancement within the firm, nor is it possible to compute the proportion of vacancies which will really be filled by external recruitment at the qualification level of the vacancy. Almost nothing is known about the female labour force, an appreciable proportion of which does not enter the economic sector on completion of education, but only later (when the children have grown up).

The results obtained by this Committee of the Plan are, in general, as follows:

- 25% of an age group (200,000 people, in France) may leave the educational system at the statutory school-leaving age and find employment as unskilled manual workers (without technical knowledge, vocational skill or know-how, but merely physical strength and ordinary common sense).
- 40% of an age group (350,000 persons, in France) enter the economic system only after learning a trade (manual skill, know-how); this is the skilled worker category.
- 25% of an age group (200,000 persons, in France) should continue their studies in order to acquire technical knowledge going beyond empirical "know-how", and human knowledge going beyond mere common sense. These will be the technicians.
- 10% of an age group (80,000 persons, in France) undertake long-cycle higher studies in order to master a subject and move straight into a post with professional status (engineers, doctors, teachers, researchers, lawyers, economists).

Difficulties arise if we try to define a more detailed structure within this breakdown. For technicians the Committee thought that 40% of posts might be open to external candidates who had completed short-cycle higher education, and that 60% might be filled by internal promotion This means that 10% of an age group, or approximately 80,000 persons in France, should start short-cycle higher education each year,* thus providing the material for direct recruitment of almost one-half of the technician vacancies available at this level. A subtle, and doubtless inappropriate distinction, has been made between technicians and higher technicians: a higher technician is either somebody who has completed short-cycle higher education or a technician without any higher education who has been given internal promotion.

The Committee then tried to break down manpower requirements among the various occupations. The results are approximatively as follows for short-cycle higher education graduates:

- 25% (or 20,000 persons) should enter occupations connected with production (agriculture and mining) and manufacturing, i.e. the primary and secondary sectors;
- 25% (or 20,000 persons) should go into the tertiary sector, i.e. services, management and organisation;
- 20% (or 16,000 persons) should go into the public health sector;
- 30% (or 24,000 persons) should go into education, socio-cultural promotion work, vocational guidance and welfare.

These figures are clearly very much higher than those corresponding to the present situation in France; the number of long-cycle higher education graduates, for example, is barely half the figure mentioned above; and for short-cycle higher education the difference is still greater. There is therefore no danger in increasing enrolments in short-cycle higher education by accepting additional students to keep pace with the population expansion and the democratization of education; there is still a margin. The problem of the quantitative assessment of outlets remains, however, and is not easily resolved. In a country with a free economy, there must be a close link between the various industrial and educational establishments in order to reach equilibrium locally by a process of trial and error. At the national level, tentative forecasts must be made, but it must be remembered that they are likely to be on the high side. They are very long-term evaluations which must be handled with some care when used in the medium term and still more in the short term.

A word should be added concerning a further difficulty in free entry systems like the French. In principal, a Baccalauréat-holder can enter

* 10% in short-cycle higher education and 10% in long-cycle higher education amounts to 160,000 persons in France. This is indeed the level observed; but failures are numerous. Less than one student in two actually completes the course he originally selected.

a university and choose any branch, long or short, and can specialize as he likes within this branch. There is a gradual weeding-out and, of course, considerable drop-out. Clearly this freedom is incompatible with any long-term planning. In practice, it quickly becomes clear that the system of free choice leads to a shocking imbalance, and gradually fairly strict rules of guidance have to be introduced. In France these rules have been in force since 1966 for short-cycle higher education; the University Institutes of Technology had a fixed number of places and selected their students in the light of expected employment possibilities. In fact, each Institute fixed the number of places in terms of the number of suitable candidates and the possible outlets. This procedure is not perfect and often leads to a Malthusian system. The long-cycle was not selective, however, and accordingly accepted the students rejected for the short-cycle; clearly this was leading to a serious disequilibrium, and this phenomenon was one of the causes of the university disturbances of May 1968. Since that time, legislation has provided for increasingly strict guidance, and even in some cases selection in all streams of higher education. If it is desired to ensure equilibrium between personnel requirements and graduate numbers, it seems necessary to introduce selective admission to the university.

This, however, does not resolve the basic problem of the democratization of education: if a youth wishes to study and there is no place to offer him in one of the streams he wants, what can he be offered instead? To cast into "outer darkness" those who are not accepted by a higher education institution is not, from a social point of view, a constructive solution. Once again we see that it is impossible to solve the problem of employment outlets on a purely economic basis; political and human factors must also be taken into account. The educational system may be regarded as primarily designed for people; it must therefore be wide open and try to allow each to rise as high as his particular abilities permit. On the other hand, education may be regarded as the furnisher of specialists for the economy and must provide those which it needs.

In the first case the economy, which takes second place, is likely to be faced with too many people trained for a given level; these will then be employed at a level below their qualifications; they may become embittered, but may also give good service to the community because of their over-qualification. In the other, the population takes second place, and is likely to include a large number of people who wanted a higher education, but were prevented because of the selection process. In theory there will be no over-qualification since each person is employed at his own level; but there will probably be a lot of discontent.

This brief analysis suggests that, in countries with a free economy, where the market-linked economic system and the population-linked education system are largely independent of each other, it is preferable to adopt the first system if the aim is economic prosperity. But we still have to answer the fundamental question: who is the more unfortunate: a well-educated man who can find work only at a level below his skill or a man who was unable to better his education because of a surplus of qualified manpower at the level to which he aspired? This is not a simple question and we shall revert to it in our conclusion.

# IV

## EMPLOYMENT FOR SHORT-CYCLE HIGHER EDUCATION GRADUATES: THE SOCIO-PSYCHOLOGICAL ASPECT

It is not enough, however, that there should be jobs; the students must also be willing to take them, i.e. to enter the labour market on completing short-cycle higher education. Experience shows that there is no natural motivation to do this, and that it must be created by trying to remove real or imaginary doubts on the part of the students.

We can pass rapidly over the first obstacle, which is a psychological one. With few exceptions, the student has lived in only one environment, that of the school; there he feels secure in surroundings with which he is familiar. He has learnt a certain way of life. To become an active member of the economy and take a job is for him a serious and complicated operation, akin to re-birth. At 24 years of age, at the end of a long cycle of education, the transition is unavoidable, but at 20 or 21 there is a choice between "taking the plunge" into the unknown economic sector and continuing his studies, with the short-term certainty of remaining in surroundings where he feels secure. The choice is an important one. For boys it is complicated by the military service obligation, an additional unpleasant obstacle in this process.

In order to try to motivate young short-cycle higher education graduates to become active members of the economy, it is first necessary to avoid making this transition inevitable. They must be offered a choice between:

- entry into working life;
- continuing their studies in a long cycle.

The choice must be put to them after they have been given detailed information about the economic world and about further studies. In France, in 1966, students were granted permission to continue their studies if they were deemed capable; and at the same time, short-cycle higher educational establishments were required to develop their contacts with employers. Experience shows that the proportion of students opting for immediate continuation of their studies soon became high, sometimes reaching 30%; it has since declined and in some sectors has become very small. After a transitional period, therefore, the motivation to take up employment on leaving short-cycle higher education was created; students remain free to decide, and the majority of them choose to start working. A recent relaxation of military service obligations will probably accentuate this trend. We may wonder what would have happened if the opposite policy of prohibiting further study had been adopted. It would probably have affected the recruitment of establishments thus transformed into "dead ends", but French policy, which has not changed, has always been to leave the student free to choose which establishment he will go to, and if we wish young people to go into short-cycle education they must not feel that they are in a blind-alley. Long-cycle higher education thus appears as one of the outlets for short-cycle higher education in the same way as employment in the economic sector. It is nonetheless a rather special form of employment and we may wonder whether short-cycle establishments ought to prepare students for it, as they cannot do everything. The position in France is very clear; short-cycle establishments must be oriented towards economic activity and must in no case be a "preliminary" to long-cycle higher education. This means that short-cycle graduates who choose the "job" of long-cycle higher studies will have difficulty in carrying on. It is a more difficult "job" to get than the others, which is normal as it opens up more favourable career prospects; experience shows, moreover, that this is not a serious handicap and that good results are obtained provided information is given and guidance dispensed wisely.

In conclusion, in a system where the choice is left to the student, short-cycle establishments must lead both to long-cycle education and to economic activity, but training is oriented towards the latter. An intensive campaign to inform and guide students is, of course, essential. This system has the advantage of providing a safety-valve for the placement of young people; if some outlets for short-cycle higher education are blocked because of market conditions, it is possible to increase the number of students continuing their training. This is far preferable to unemployment, provided that the job shortage is cyclical. It constitutes "intellectual investment" in the population.

Young people seeking employment are fortunately not influenced only by the immediate advantages (starting salary, daily tasks); they are also interested in career prospects possibilities several years ahead. But there is too often a regrettable correlation between the level of one's first job and career prospects. In France, this correlation is high in the public service, i.e. in a very large number of jobs. It is less marked, though still exists, in the private sector. There is in particular a subtle distinction between the concept of "executive" and "non-executive" posts, a "non-executive" grading involving various disadvantages ranging from a less favourable pension scheme to such minor vexations as signing the daily attendance sheet. The public service in France is closely linked with the concept of salary scales defining a young man's career once and for all on the basis of the level at which he entered. This correlation between career prospects and level at entry is clearly a disincentive for the short-cycle higher education graduate. He will try to continue his studies, or will go directly to a long-cycle establishment, with the risks of failure which this involves, if he believes, rightly or wrongly, that the level at entry will determine his career. Each one will try to start work at the highest possible level, or else combine with others to bring pressure to bear on employers to raise the starting-point for short-cycle graduates; and this will reduce the number of outlets.

There is only one solution, which is not easy to apply as it means revolutionizing personnel management and fighting the "graduate castes" with their established privileges; career development must be completely dissociated from the level at entry into that career, and this dissociation must be made known by clear example. This is, of course, a long-term policy, but should be undertaken without delay if we want short-cycle higher education graduates to go straight into active life. Their diploma should be a criterion of fitness only for a first job, because there are no other criteria; later a sounder assessment should be made of the worker's aptitudes and his diploma forgotten. The period during which level of salary and type of qualification are related should not exceed five years.

Even so, it is no use thinking that the individual on his own in active life will rise unaided, even if all the roads to interesting jobs are equally open to him. The young worker must be helped by making continuing education available to him. In France the Acts of 3rd December 1966 and 16th July 1971 allocated to short-cycle higher educational establishments the task of providing continuing education, to allow them to follow and assist their former students. Provision is made for paid leave to cover one year's training three years after graduation, so as to enable him to climb further up the career ladder. This system of advancement is essential if we want young people to take jobs; if they feel that they are leaving the university for ever, and are regarded as "emigrants" they will do everything to avoid going and will not leave a higher educational establishment until forced to do so. If, on the other hand, they know that the establishment which trained them will not abandon them, and that they may return for help and advice, they will more readily go into active life, no longer as emigrants but as explorers. They will, in fact, become "life members" of the establishment, from which they will obtain life-long training.

Finally, we have to ask whether we have the right to motivate people in this way. Is it normal to incite young people to leave the educational system when they could continue to advance, by influencing them to enter employment? It is certainly necessary, if society is to survive, that people of the highest competence should be found. But a society in which everyone wanted to do research or engineering, and nobody would accept a manufacturing job could not survive. There are, moreover, humble tasks which are nonetheless indispensable. A society which wishes to survive is therefore obliged deliberately to direct young people, by constraint or persuasion, into the jobs that need to be done. In order to avoid the social tensions which will inevitably result from the frustration felt by those leaving the university after a short course of study, however, we must make a clear distinction between general education and technical training or, to put it another way, we must distinguish between "homo sapiens and homo faber". Society must do everything possible to encourage access to education for all, and try to dissociate the purely cultural aspect from the purely technical knowledge aspect. This may seem Utopian, but it is nonetheless essential if we wish to justify ethically the necessary motivation of young people to work at the level where society needs them in order to function.

## CONCLUSION

Employment possibilities exist for those taking short-cycle higher education, provided that this consists of highly practical training, and not decapitated long-cycle higher education limited to its abstract parts.

The qualitative approach to the problem is simple and consists of listing the functions needed in modern society. The quantitative approach, on the other hand, is very difficult and seems capable of providing only local solutions, implying a danger of rigidity; an overall solution is practically impossible to envisage in countries where recruitment is linked to the economy's demands or the number of students trained to the population.

It is not enough, however, that short-cycle higher education should have outlets; young people must also be willing to take them. This presupposes a motivation, which is perfectly possible provided that short-cycle higher education institutions are not "dead ends" and have as "noble" a status as long-cycle establishments, both forming part of the university.

Whether this motivation is ethical is a question which is still open and touches on the relationship between social and individual ethics. Let us conclude on this note, recalling what we said at the beginning: that it is a serious error to reduce the problem of employment outlets for an educational system to a purely economic problem of job accounting. Unfortunately, the economic approach is relatively feasible, as we have tried to show in this paper; the socio-psychological approach is difficult and tends to be discarded. This leads naturally to a disaster which can be avoided only by trying to answer the question "Is the educational system a public service at the disposal of individuals, or at the disposal of society as a whole?" The answer lies, perhaps, in dissociating general education from technological training.

# VIII

## Outreach programmes in the United States Community Colleges

by

Dr. R.E. Schultz, Director,
International Office, The American Association
of Junior Colleges (United States)

## TABLE OF CONTENTS


I. Community service programmes ................ 317

II. Co-operative education programmes ............ 323

III. Developmental education programmes ............ 331

IV. Summary ....................................... 337

Selected bibliography ........................... 339

The term outreach as used in this paper refers to non-traditional programmes offered by junior colleges in the United States. These programmes attract students who would either not be served by such institutions or would be served in less effective ways. This paper treats three types of outreach programmes that are offered in our junior colleges. These are: 1) community service programmes, 2) co-operative education programmes, and 3) developmental education programmes. The treatment of each of these types of outreach programme includes a rationale, problems and issues, and potential for the future. While references are made to programme characteristics, no programme descriptions are provided. The focus of this paper is on public junior colleges. Outreach programmes are not characteristic of private junior colleges.

# I

## COMMUNITY SERVICE PROGRAMMES

Community service constitutes a basic function or purpose of comprehensive public junior colleges in the United States. (The terms "continuation education", "adult education", and "life-long education" are also used to designate this function.) Until approximately 15 years ago most community service programmes were administered by local secondary school systems and public universities through extension programmes. However, with the rapid expansion in the United States of public junior colleges beginning in the mid-1950s (from 336 in 1955 to 847 in 1970), responsibility for community service activities has been increasingly assumed by these institutions. This change is being reflected in their official names. Many have added the term "community" or substituted it for the term "junior" in their titles. In some states all such institutions are officially designated as community colleges and have such names as Harrisburg Area Community College, Portland Community College, and Kauai Community College.

This acceptance of responsibility for community services to junior colleges has occurred for several reasons. First, we have found that adults identify more readily with post-secondary educational institutions than with secondary schools. Another reason for the shift is that a junior college normally serves a larger geographic area than does a secondary school. This enables it to offer a greater variety of services and more specialized programmes. Also, the staff and facilities of a junior college make it better qualified than a secondary school to provide community services. Finally, except where very specialized expertise is required, a locally oriented junior college is able to assess and respond to the informal educational needs of its community more quickly than can a university. Where the expertise of a university is needed, a local junior college and a university sometimes co-operatively offer a programme. In such cases the junior college may provide the facilities and organise the programme while the university furnishes the instructional staff.

Community service programmes have developed and grown to the point where many junior colleges in the United States serve more adults on a part-time continuing education basis than they enroll in their regular full-time programmes.

## The Rationale for Community Service

These programmes can be placed into three categories in terms of the purposes served, namely, a) economic, b) social, and c) cultural-recreational. Since these purposes are the same as those frequently stated for traditional forms of higher education, each will be related specifically to continuing education.

### a) Serving Economic Needs

Preparing youth for initial job-entry employment is widely accepted as a function of junior colleges. Because of continuous technological changes, employment requirements are constantly undergoing change, with new jobs being created while existing ones are modified and eliminated. Junior colleges in the United States are playing an increasingly important role in assisting workers and industries of their communities which are affected by these changes. They do this by offering adult education retraining programmes.

Large corporations and industrial concerns sometimes operate their own retraining programmes. However, this is not practicable for many small companies and business concerns, or when relatively few workers of a particular type are needed by a large industrial concern. In many cases junior colleges perform this retraining function as part of their continuing education programme. Sometimes such programmes are offered on the premises of industrial plants. Those programmes also provide educational opportunities for workers who desire to up-grade themselves and/or qualify for promotions.

Programmes with an economic focus are not limited to employees. Junior colleges offer programmes for owners and managers of business and for salesmen. Sometimes a university co-operates in these programmes but many times a junior college offers them on its own. Basically such programmes have as their purpose the improving of the efficiency and/or profits of an operation.

### b) Serving Social Needs

Increasingly in the United States the view is held that the resources of locally oriented junior colleges should be used to help solve community social problems. At times this involves no more than making facilities available to community agencies and organisations, and at others junior colleges co-operate with such agencies and organisations by providing lecturers and consultants. In still other instances a junior college may assume exclusive or primary responsibility for alleviating a social problem.

The range of programmes which focus on social problems is extensive. The programmes cover topics ranging from a short course on child care for expectant mothers to language instruction for recent immigrants, to a series of films and lectures on pollution control or drug abuse, to an adult literacy programme. A programme may be as short as a single lecture or as long as a several-month course.

c) Serving Cultural and Recreational Needs

The amount of free time for working people is continuing to increase in the United States. For example, experimentation is now occurring with a four-day work week. The extent to which man benefits from this leisure time is determined in large measure by how he spends it. While specifying what is "good" in this respect involves a value judgment, cultural and recreational activities are generally considered personally enriching and beneficial. Voluntary participation (including attendance) in cultural and recreational activities requires two conditions in addition to having leisure time. One of these is their availability; the other is having sufficient background and/or skill in an activity to obtain satisfaction from participation. Junior colleges contribute to bringing about both these conditions through their community service programmes. Increasingly they are becoming the cultural and recreational centre of their communities, especially of communities which are located away from cities.

Community cultural and recreational opportunities are made available by junior colleges in a variety of ways. These consist of musical and dramatic productions which are increasingly performed jointly by the student body and adults of the community, artists' series involving outside talent, art exhibits, cultural films, book reviews, and so forth. They also sponsor athletic contests which are open to the public, and they make available their facilities, including the library, to youth and adults of the community.

Junior colleges also teach adults the skills and provide them with the backgrounds needed to obtain satisfaction from participation in cultural and recreational activities. This is done by offering evening classes in art, music, drama, literature, and the like.

## Problems and Issues Relating to Community Service

Despite the growing acceptance of community services as a major responsibility they still represent a marginal or emerging function for many public junior colleges in the United States. There are a number of reasons for this. Notable among them are difficulties encountered in a) identifying community needs and interests, b) establishing priorities, c) securing institutional commitment, and d) obtaining financial support.

### a) Identifying Community Interests and Needs

The decision to provide a specific service cannot be made satisfactorily by a college staff alone. It requires conferences and discussions with representatives of the community, surveys, and the review of information gathered by other agencies. Whether it is the junior college or some other community agency that takes the initiative in this process, it is imperfect at best. The larger and more complex the community, the more difficult is the undertaking. Many junior colleges appoint advisory committees comprised of representatives of the various groups and interests of the community for this purpose.

### b) Establishing Priorities

Once needs and interests are identified, it is necessary to determine which of them should be served by the junior college, since there are other agencies better qualified to meet some of these needs and interests. There is also the question of what constitutes an appropriate activity for an educational institution. We have pronounced differences of opinion on this point. Some junior college leaders contend that the choices need to be made with great care. Others maintain that a community-oriented junior college is obligated to attempt to serve any unmet educational need in the community.

### c) Securing Institutional Commitment

The commitment of an institution's governing board, its administrators, and at least a segment of the faculty is needed to have an effective community service programme. Governing boards sometimes raise questions as to the emphasis which a junior college should give community services. In other cases such programmes are promoted by administrators because of their public relations value rather than because of a desire to serve the community. When this happens the programme may be a thin layer of highly visible but superficial activities. Some junior college faculty members are more concerned with personal prestige than they are with service to the community. They prefer to emulate university professors rather than develop community-oriented programmes. In an effort to solve this problem, some junior colleges make a special effort to recruit faculty who have a strong commitment to serving the community.

d) Obtaining Financial Resources

Opinions on how to finance community service programmes range from the view that participants should pay the full costs to those who maintain that society as a whole benefits from these programmes and therefore the costs should be borne by taxpayers. Between these extremes are those who contend that the nature of a particular programme should be the determining factor. Among this group are those who maintain that if a programme helps resolve a social problem and thereby results in general community benefits, it should be supported by tax funds. Conversely, when the benefits are primarily to the individual, as in the case of cultural and recreational programmes, he should bear the cost.

Methods by which community service programmes are supported in the United States reflect these various viewpoints. In the case of manpower training and retraining programmes, the cost is frequently borne by the federal government. In other cases the cost is paid in part or entirely by business and industrial concerns. Local and state tax sources are also used for this purpose as are student tuition charges. Increasingly in recent years the federal government has supported social service programmes for underprivileged and minority groups. Still, many cultural and recreational programmes are financed by admission charges to participants. This has the obvious problem of denying participation to some who would benefit greatly from them.

## Potential for the Future

An adult education leader when addressing a group of junior college presidents challenged them to make their institution truly community colleges. He said that to accomplish this they must "... identify and capitalize on (the institution's) unique role and construct a programme, design an organisational structure, and employ methodology to fulfill that role rather than being content to remain an inadequate copy of patterns designed for other roles and other functions answering different needs". * That statement was supported by a recent nation-wide study of community service programmes in junior colleges of the United States. Based on the evidence obtained, the investigator predicted that the following trends will characterize the community service function of United States junior colleges in the years ahead:

* Verner, Coolie, "The Junior College as a Social Institution", Community Services in the Community Junior College, State Department of Education, Tallahassee, Florida, 1960.

- Institutions will develop aggressive outreach programmes designed to extend their campuses through their service areas;
- institutions will place increased emphasis on community education for all age groups;
- institutions will employ a greater diversity of media in meeting community needs and interests;
- institutions will utilize better their catalyctic capabilities to assist their communities to solve basic educational, economic and social problems;
- institutions will be increasingly concerned about the cultural growth of their communities;
- institutions will recognize the need for better co-operation with other community agencies. *

Whether these predictions are realized remains to be seen.

* Harlacher, Ervin, The Community Dimensions of the Community College, Prentice-Hall, Inc., Englewood, New Jersey, 1969, pp. 70-107.

# II

## CO-OPERATIVE EDUCATION PROGRAMMES

Several types of work-study arrangements are found in junior colleges of the United States. Basically these are 1) part-time employment which students secure, 2) alternate periods of study and work arranged by students, and 3) institutional co-operative education programmes. The primary objective served by the first two types is financial gain for the student rather than the educational benefits derived from the work performed. However, the importance of these two types of work-study arrangements becomes apparent when it is realized that a high percentage of our junior college students are married and support families. As many as 80 to 85% of the students enrolled in public community junior colleges are employed part-time. Alternate periods of work and study are also common. A student may devote three or four years to complete a two-year programme because of intermittent periods of study and work.

Selected for treatment in this paper is the third type of work-study programme - co-operative education. It overlaps the other two but is distinctive in that the primary purpose of the work is educational rather than financial. There may be remuneration and alternate periods of study and work but the work experience is provided because of its educational value. Co-operative education in this context can be defined as the association of an employer and an educational institution to prepare students for future employment.

### Rationale for Co-operation Education

There has been a substantial increase in co-operative education programmes in our junior colleges during recent years. This has resulted primarily from a desire to find more effective ways of providing employers with well-qualified workers and to add relevance to student learning. The results are advantages to students, the institution and the employers.

a) Advantages to Students

Co-operative education programmes give students an opportunity to bridge the gap between theory and practice. In addition to enabling them to gain skills and apply knowledge in actual work situations, these programmes afford students opportunities to test their interests and suitability for a particular type of work. Further, students are provided with educational experiences they would otherwise not receive because their work assignments give them access to materials and equipment which are not available in junior college classrooms and laboratories.

Students who have participated in these programmes make the transition from college to work gradually. They have a better opportunity than other students to comprehend the significance of formal learning for the world of work. Studies have shown that students who participate in co-operative education programmes, when compared with other students, excel in several respects. Their motivation to study is stronger, they are better oriented to the world of work, they obtain employment more easily, and they exhibit more job stability and satisfaction. *

b) Advantages to Institutions

While the major reason for junior colleges developing co-operative education programmes is better to serve students and employers, there are also advantages to the institution. The financial benefits can be substantial since the equipment required for some occupational programmes is very costly. Junior colleges which attempt to provide practical experiences in laboratories are frequently forced, for financial reasons, to use outdated equipment. Co-operative programmes enable students to learn using up-to-date equipment with comparatively small cost to the institution. Another type of economy provided by these programmes is that they enable a junior college to serve more students. While one group of students is engaged in a work experience, the institution's facilities and instructional staff can serve other students. In the case of highly specialized occupational programmes, the increased student output can be considerable.

Co-operative education programmes also serve to motivate instructional staff. The fact that students are being introduced to the latest techniques and developments provides an incentive for faculty to keep themselves current. These students also bring a measure of excitement and experience to the classroom. In addition, such programmes serve a public relations value by reducing the communications gap between the institution, the community and the students.

* Wilson, James W. and Lyons, Edward H., Work Study College Programs, Harper and Row, New York, 1961.

c) Advantages to Employers

Employers gain from participating in co-operative programmes because it gives them opportunities to evaluate prospective employees. A high percentage of junior college co-operative students obtain employment after graduation in the business or industry where their work experience is performed.

Another advantage to employers claimed for co-operative programmes is that students in these programmes have a positive effect upon regular workers. This is because such students are likely to be well-motivated and career-oriented, and they are sometimes more up-to-date in their fields than are regular workers. There may also be public relations benefits to employers from the publicity which they receive from the news media and press.

## Problems and Issues Relating to Co-operative Education

Though co-operative education programmes have the merits which have been mentioned, they are no panacea. Like most other endeavours, they are no better than the time, effort and leadership which go into them. Some of the problems and issues that affect the success of such programmes are as follows:

a) Organisation and Staffing

Junior College co-operative programmes sometimes encounter problems because they lack competent leadership. In some junior colleges responsibility for co-ordination and administration is assumed by each programme that provides work experiences.

This arrangement seems to be satisfactory where participation is limited. When extensive use is made of co-operative work experiences, however, an overall co-ordinator is needed.

For a co-operative programme to succeed, there must be a firm financial and philosophical commitment by both the institution and the co-operating business or industry. While such programmes can result in financial savings to an institution, funds are still required to staff them adequately. There are instances in which the junior college president's interests do not extend to the staffing level. The results are predictable.

Staffs for co-operative programmes function in a variety of roles. They serve concurrently as teachers, counsellors, supervisors and co-ordinators. It helps in their relations with officials in business, industry and government if they are knowledgeable about the world of work. At the same time, they need to possess a firm commitment to the educational concepts of co-operative work experiences. The problem of status can be somewhat alleviated when those who co-ordinate work experiences are assigned some regular teaching responsibilities and have regular faculty status.

b) The Work Experience

It was previously stated that the primary objective of co-operative work experiences is educational development - not immediate financial gain for either the student or the employer. Yet difficulty is encountered on this very point. The problem is not so much with top management as with students' immediate work supervisors. They may either not understand or simply reject the educational point of view.

Keeping the focus on educational development is more difficult when the student receives compensation. There are those who maintain that for this reason no salary should be involved. This gives the institution a greater degree of control over the work programme. Others disagree with this position both on the grounds that most junior college students need the money and that a salary adds reality and motivation to the experience. The prevailing practice in our junior colleges is for students to receive a partial salary for co-operative work experiences. They are given a special "trainee" status and receive none of the extra benefits of regular employees. Where a business or industry is unionized, it is frequently necessary to negotiate salary arrangements with union officials. In fact, in highly unionized occupations, the entire educational programme may be arranged with union officials rather than with management.

Some junior colleges, in co-operation with management and/or union officials, have established guidelines to help assure that the student's educational development receives primary consideration. Some examples follow:

- The assignment should provide opportunities for the student to apply classroom knowledge and/or acquire needed skills;
- the assignment should provide opportunities for the student to test career interest;
- the assignment should provide opportunities for the student to explore a variety of tasks in a number of departments or assignments;
- the assignment should provide for increased responsibility commensurate with the student's development.

Enrolment in a co-operative programme should not guarantee the student a work experience. An appraisal is needed in each case to determine if the student is ready to profit from and perform the duties which the work experience requires. Co-operating business and industries are apt to withdraw from a programme if inadequately prepared students are assigned to a work experience. There have been instances in which a business or industry (including labour unions) would not accept a qualified student for a work experience because of his race or colour. With our recent civil rights legislation, this type of discrimination is now relatively rare.

Misunderstandings are sometimes encountered in the supervision of work experiences. The best way we have found to avoid them is for the direct supervision to be done by the business, industry or agency which provides the work opportunity. College co-ordinators, in turn, work closely with these supervisors offering advice and direction as needed.

c) Evaluation

Students' co-operative work experiences are evaluated for two purposes. One is for feedback to facilitate improvement. The other is for assigning grades. The first type of evaluation is provided primarily by the student's immediate work supervisor. The second is done by the college co-ordinator with input from the work supervisor.

The unit credit system employed by our junior colleges confronts them with the issue of whether to assign units of credits for co-operative work experience. There are those who contend that credits should not be awarded when a student receives pay. Where that point of view prevails students may be given certificates as evidence of having successfully completed a co-operative work experience. Where credits are awarded, the number of units to be granted poses another problem. There are no established standards for doing this. It is a fairly common practice, however, to equate a half-day of work experience with half of a normal academic load.

We encounter a similar problem in assigning grades. There is objection to letter grades for work experience on the grounds that the judgements are subjective. Those who take such a view fail to realise that the same criticism could be made of most grading. Nevertheless, co-operative work experience is often graded as either "satisfactory" or "unsatisfactory" rather than assigned a letter grade of A, B, C, etc.

## Other Issues and Problems

It is sometimes contended that co-operative work experiences contribute to student dropouts. Evidence on this point is limited, but what there is indicates that just the opposite is true - it increases student retention in junior colleges.

A current concern in the United States is that our growing unemployment rate will result in employers withdrawing from co-operative programmes. This could happen because of pressure from labour unions and a reluctance by employers to create the impression that regular workers are being replaced by part-time students. These possibilities have posed no serious problem to date.

An important unanswered question in co-operative education is "How much?". It does not follow necessarily that because some experience is good, more is better. Obviously numerous factors affect what is an optimum amount with variations from person to person and field to field. There is almost no evidence on this matter. By and large, the amount of work experience provided in our junior college programmes is based on expediency and tradition.

Closely related to the previous issue is the question of what constitutes an effective combination of work and study for educational purposes. Here again there are no ready answers. In some cases concurrent work and study may be best. In other cases alternating periods of work and study or a single work experience at the end of the programme may be best. All of these approaches are used but there have been no well-designed studies to test their relative merits. By and large, expediency, habit and "hunch" provide the guidelines.

## Potential for the Future

It is generally accepted in the United States that co-operative education is viable as a strategy for learning. Further, it is agreed that the community junior college is well suited for offering this type of education. Even so, changes in co-operative education are likely to occur in the years ahead. As ways are devised to co-ordinate more effectively computers, tapes, film, and the like for instructional purposes, we can expect that simulators will become more common than at present. This may reduce the amount of direct work experience required and/or change substantially the nature of that which is provided.

Better advantage should be taken in the future of the fact that many students interrupt their formal studies for periods of full-time employment. Junior colleges could do more to assist such students to obtain employment related to their educational programmes and then co-ordinate the work experience. This would save the student time and be efficient for the institution.

Another "straw in the wind" for the future of co-operative education in junior colleges is work experience at locations remote from the campus. Some senior colleges and universities already do this. It is common in such fields as medical education, but rare in junior colleges. However, a few are doing this with an international twist. As an example, there are institutions which prepare bilingual secretaries and require, as part of the programme, work experience in a country that uses the non-English language that is being mastered.

Another feature [illegible] in the [illegible] for the [illegible] of [illegible]
among graduate colleges [illegible] work experience at locations [illegible] the [illegible]
the [illegible] more senior colleges and universities [illegible]
It is common in such fields as [illegible] education [illegible]
colleagues, however, [illegible] with an international [illegible]
As an example, there are institutions which have [illegible]
students [illegible] as part of the programme [illegible] work experience in a
country that [illegible] the [illegible] language [illegible].

# III

## DEVELOPMENTAL EDUCATION PROGRAMMES

Most public, and a considerable number of private, junior colleges in the United States have "open door" admissions - in practice if not in policy. This means that any high school graduate and, frequently, adults who have not completed high school are eligible to enroll. The result is a student body that is very heterogeneous in educational backgrounds, interests, and aptitudes.

In discussing programmes for these students terminology poses something of a problem. Several terms are used, frequently interchangeably, in the United States to describe such programmes. Until recently the term "remedial" was most commonly used and usually referred to "make-up" courses taken within a traditional academic department. During the past several years other types of educational endeavours have been employed in an effort to assist junior college students who have educational deficiencies. Among these are skill laboratories where students can work individually to remove weaknesses, special guidance services, and special academic courses. The generic term developmental education is increasingly used to refer to these various special services. Some writers and practitioners, however, continue to use the term "remedial education" to describe this broader scope of services.

### Rationale for Development Education

It is not the purpose of this paper to establish a rationale for the "open door" admissions policy of junior colleges. It is, rather, to treat one of the consequences of that policy - students who are educationally underprepared. Junior college teachers, administrators, and leaders are all challenged and perplexed by implications of the "open door" admissions policy. There is a growing recognition in the United States that it is professional irresponsibility to admit large numbers of students for whom there are no appropriate educational programmes. Those with responsibility for education planning are increasingly taking the view that public junior colleges should develop the same commitment, establish the same priorities, and show at least as much creativity in developing programmes and curricula for educationally disadvantaged students as they do for other students.

Apart from the growing philosophical commitment of providing realistic programmes for a diverse student body, another factor has contributed to the recent emphasis on developmental programmes in our junior colleges. Until the past few years our higher education institutions, including junior colleges, enrolled relatively few students from the Black, American Indian and Mexican-American minorities.

There were numerous reasons for this low minority enrolment, an explanation of which could be the subject for another paper. Suffice it to say that major efforts are now being made to enroll such students in junior colleges. Public policy-makers have taken the position that educating the youth of these minority groups is necessary if they are to move into the mainstream of American life where they can make the contributions of which they are capable. Further, these policy-makers have decided that our public junior colleges are an especially appropriate educational institution to serve that group. As a consequence, many more students with inadequate backgrounds attend our junior colleges now than in the past. This means that the need for special programmes to assist such students has become of prime importance.

Developmental programmes are intended to remove students' educational deficiencies and thereby salvage human resources. However, analyses of such programmes in junior colleges have frequently led to the conclusion that they primarily serve other ends. Such terms as "cooling out" and "custodial service" are used to describe what they find to be the actual outcomes.

The research on which such conclusions are based has been focused on traditional remedial programmes. The implied, if not the stated objective of those programmes is to prepare students for academic transfer courses in a traditional classroom setting. Students assigned to those remedial courses are often given the same material as regular students. Frequently, the only difference is that it is presented at a slower pace. It has been repeatedly demonstrated that the intended outcome is not obtained by this method alone. Few students who are assigned to such remedial courses complete a junior college transfer programme. Most of them drop out after one or two terms because of lack of interest and/or the failure to receive passing grades. They return to the streets with no more skills than when they entered the junior college; they are usually the last to find employment and the first to be terminated when work forces are reduced.

## Some New Approaches to Developmental Education

The failures of traditional junior college remedial programmes and the wastefulness that results both in human and financial resources have brought demands for more effective methods of assisting students who are educationally underprepared. The result has been a variety of new approaches and orientations. These recent efforts differ from the traditional approach to remedial education in several significant ways:

- The emphasis is no longer predominantly on preparing students to qualify for academic transfer courses. Experience has shown that the majority of students with pronounced educational deficiencies do not transfer to senior colleges and universities. As a consequence, the emphasis is shifting to reading, writing and computation skills which are needed successfully to pursue occupational and other types of non-transfer programmes.

- Account is taken of the fact that students who are deficient in a given area such as reading differ greatly from one another in the specific nature of their problems. Failure to take this fact into account is one reason why remedial courses have often met with so little success. They are organised and conducted on the premise that all underprepared students have the same inadequacies to the same degree and will respond to the same treatment. Increasingly, remedial programmes are being individualized. A student's weaknesses are diagnosed and specific activities are planned to remove them. The student then works primarily on his own to remove deficiencies as quickly as possible and/or as he chooses. Skills laboratories have been developed for this purpose. They are equipped with a variety of instructional aids and self-teaching materials such as programmed texts. The student spends as much time as he chooses in the skills laboratory. When he thinks he has removed the deficiency he so informs the faculty member who is in charge. A proficiency examination is held and the student's readiness to proceed to other courses is determined. The better developed of these arrangements represent sophisticated examples of individualized programme instruction - IPI. Some of our learning theorists are advocating that all instructional systems be organised in this way.

- Considerable attention is given to guidance and counselling. It has long been common knowledge that many students who enter junior college poorly prepared either lack long-range personal and occupational goals or have unrealistic goals. Developmental programmes place emphasis on guidance and counselling in an effort to deal with that reality. There is increasing recognition that unless changes occur in the self-perceptions and occupational goals of many students, little long-range benefit will come of any educational progress which they might make. Efforts are made to guide these students into occupational programmes where they can develop skills which enable them to obtain employment.

- An overall programme is planned for students with serious educational deficiencies. Many students from disadvantaged backgrounds have had poor elementary and secondary school experiences. In addition, they frequently come from families where the socio-economic level is low, with all that this implies. It requires more than a few remedial courses or time spent in a skills laboratory if such young people are to be salvaged. Our junior colleges are experimenting with a variety of comprehensive developmental programmes. One model that some institutions are using consists of three major aspects: a) courses in the humanities and social sciences developed and taught with the background of these students in mind; b) individualized programmes to improve reading, writing and mathematics skills; and, c) group guidance emphasizing human relations, supplemented with individual academic and non-academic counselling.

- Developmental programmes are being staffed by faculty who possess special skills and commitments. Remedial courses in our junior colleges have typically been assigned to the youngest and least experienced or to the incompetent older faculty members. Few of them have had special training, orientation or commitment for working with the educationally disadvantaged. Fortunately, that picture is changing. A recent survey found no difference in the age and experience of these instructors compared to those of other faculty members. Even more significant, 70% had either volunteered or been employed expressly for developmental teaching, and 85% had received special training for working with non-traditional students. *

## Evidence of Success

A direct comparison of broad-based developmental programmes with isolated remedial courses is difficult because the goals of the two are different. Developmental programmes are intended to serve multiple purposes, whereas remedial courses are usually limited to a single objective. While evidence comparing the two approaches is limited, that which we have favours the broad-based developmental programmes. A study was recently made of students in 40 junior colleges who had enrolled in developmental programmes. 47% of them subsequently went either into occupational or transfer programmes,

* Ferrin, Richard I., "Developmental Programmes in Mid-Western Community Colleges", Higher Education Surveys-Report No. 4, Collège Entrance Examination Board, 990 Grove Street, Evanston, Illinois 60201, p. 41.

12% left to enter employment, 25% discontinued because of lack of interest, progress or money, and 14% were still enrolled in the programme when the study was made. * Unfortunately, the study did not provide evidence on how many of those who entered occupational and transfer programmes completed them.

## Persistent Problems and Issues

It would be misleading to leave the impression that all is well with developmental education in junior colleges of the United States. There are issues and problems galore. Among the major ones are the following:

a) Agreement upon Purposes

While there is a growing acceptance of the need for developmental education, the latter by no means enjoys a secure "place in the sun". There are still many faculty members, administrators and public officials who are not committed to special programmes for students who are educationally underprepared.

b) Procedures and Methods

While progress is being made, we still do not have adequate instructional materials that are adapted to the learning problems of students with educational deficiencies. The same applies to teaching procedures. Seldom are the methods employed related to learning theory. Among other things, this makes it difficult to do research on the effectiveness of various approaches.

c) Credits and Grades

Our system of unit credits and grades poses an endless number of problems for development education. Public funds are frequently provided on the basis of student credit hours. Unless credits are awarded, public financial support may not be forthcoming. On the other hand, granting credit poses a philosophical issue. Many faculty members are uncomfortable awarding credit for sub-collegiate work. However, in addition to the financial implications, eliminating credits has an adverse effect on student motivation. For these reasons, the trend is toward awarding credits which may or may not be applicable to two-year degrees and rarely can be transferred to a senior college or university.

Closely related to the issue of granting credit for developmental courses is that of assigning grades. The trend is away from assigning

* Ibid., p. 44.

traditional "A" to "F" letter grades for such courses to a "satisfactory" or "unsatisfactory" designation, and more recently to so-called non-punitive grading. When non-punitive grading is used, if a student fails to achieve at least a passing grade in a course - usually "C" - reference to the course is placed on his record. He continues in the course until a "C" level of achievement is attained or until he chooses to stop trying.

d) Financial Support

Developmental education is expensive. Educational officials are not always willing to give these programmes a priority in their budget requests, nor do legislators always provide the funds requested. At the institutional level, administrators are sometimes reluctant to allocate the financial resources needed for a strong programme. Substantial federal grants have eased this problem in recent years, but that source of support cannot be expected to continue indefinitely at its present level.

e) Time and Effort

Closely related to the previous issue is that of how much time, effort and resources a junior college can justifiably invest in students. A frequently asked question is how many chances a student should receive. Those who hold to a liberal view contend that in the long perspective it is in the interest of all if every reasonable effort is made to assist such students. Traditionalists, on the other hand, contend that developmental programmes make a mockery of higher education and academic standards. Currently the tide is running against the traditionalists. Many institutions are hard-pressed however to present convincing evidence that their developmental programmes are successful in terms of student output - when completion of a junior college programme is used as the criterion.

Potential for the Future

The points just covered make it clear that problems face our developmental programmes in the future. It seems unlikely, however, that public junior colleges in the United States are going to retreat from their commitment to serve all students who enter their institutions. Progress has been too great to expect that they will revert to previous practices. What may happen, and what is occurring now in a few institutions, is the development of an IPI system for all students. If that occurs, developmental education programmes may lose their present identity. Each student, at whatever his level of educational attainment, will proceed through a programme limited only by his motivation and the time he wishes to commit to the undertaking.

# IV

## SUMMARY

These three outreach programmes represent efforts which are being made by junior colleges in the United States to provide non-traditional educational services. It is hoped that the impression has not been left that all junior colleges have developed these programmes to the extent that they might. There is, however, a growing commitment to them. Two closely related movements are gaining momentum in the United States, both of which may highlight outreach programmes and change the context in which they are offered - namely, the "school without walls" and "external degree" concepts. They may very well amount to more than passing fads.

## SELECTED BIBLIOGRAPHY

Community Service Programmes

Chernow, Burt. "The College Art Collection", Junior College Journal 39:14-16, September 1968.

Fightmaster, Walter J. Establishing and Expanding a Community Services Programme. American Association of Junior Colleges, One Dupont Circle, NW, Washington DC, 1969, 55 pp.

Goodrich, Andrew L. Community Services for the "New Student" at Inter City Community Colleges. Michigan State University, 426 Erickson Hall, East Lansing, Michigan, 1970, 32 pp.

Harlacher, Ervin. The Community Dimension of the Community College. Prentice-Hall, Inc., Englewood, New Jersey, 1969.

Myran, Gunder A. Community Services in the Community College. American Association of Junior Colleges, One Dupont Circle, NW, Washington DC, 1969, 60 pp.

Rollins, Charles and Appleton, Wallace B. "Accent on a Cultural Commitment", Junior College Journal 38:30-31, October 1967.

Work Study Programmes

Brown, Robert L. Co-operative Education. American Association of Junior Colleges, One Dupont Circle, NW, Washington DC, 1971, 32 pp.

Johnson, B. Lamar. Islands of Innovation Expanding: Changes in the Community College. Glencoe Press, Beverley Hills, California, 1969.

Lupton, D. Keith. "Campus Stretching Through Co-operative Education", Junior College Journal 40:37-39, February 1970.

Lupton, D. Keith and Wadssworth, R. B. "Junior College Co-op: Partnership and Practice", Journal of Co-operative Education, 5:50-57, May 1969.

Wilson, James W. and Lyons, Edward H. Work Study College Programmes. Harper and Row, Co. , New York, 1961.

Developmental Education Programmes

Chalghian, Sarah. "Success for Marginal Students", Junior College Journal 40:28-20, September 1969.

Ferrin, Richard I. Developmental Programmes in Midwestern Community Colleges. Higher Education Surveys Report No. 4, College Entrance Examination Board, 900 Grove Street, Evanston, Illinois, February, 1971.

Gordon, Edmund W. and Wilkerson, Doxey A. Compensatory Education for the Disadvantaged. College Entrance Examination Board, New York, 1966.

Moore, William, Jr. Against the Odds. Jossey-Bass, Inc. , San Francisco, California, 1970.

Moore, William, Jr. "Opportunity for the Disadvantaged", Stress on Campus, (G. Kerry Smith, editor) Jossey-Bass, Inc. , San Francisco, California, 1968.

Roueche, John E. Salvage, Redirection, or Custody? Remedial Education in the Community Junior College. American Association of Junior Colleges, One Dupont Circle, NW, Washington DC, 1968.

Part Three

# GENERAL REPORT OF THE INTERNATIONAL MEETING ON SHORT-CYCLE HIGHER EDUCATION

Grenoble (France), 15th-17th November, 1971

## THE GRENOBLE MEETING

On the 15th, 16th and 17th November, 1971, the University of Social Sciences of Grenoble was host to a meeting organised by the OECD to review the problems of short-cycle higher education. The meeting was attended by some 50 participants from 18 countries,* consisting of:

- directors or presidents of short-cycle and non-university institutions, especially those in charge of new types of programmes;
- senior officials of ministries of education or of other central agencies responsible for the planning and reform of non-university and short-cycle higher education;
- academics or experts with particular interest and experience in the study of problems relating to short-cycle and non-university higher education and its links with universities.

The purpose of the meeting was:

- to confront and review different national experiences in non-university and short-cycle higher education, in particular with regard to a number of specific issues which these forms of education are facing;
- to identify alternative solutions to these issues and to formulate broad policy suggestions for development and/or reform of short-cycle and non-university higher education within the overall system of higher education and for more effective links with the universities as well as with society at large;
- to examine areas which could benefit from closer international contact between different institutions of short-cycle higher education and between national or regional groups responsible for

* See list of Participants in Annex II.

their development, and to suggest specific topics where further investigation on a cross-national basis might be of particular relevance.

The meeting discussed in plenary session the place and role of SCIs within the global system of post-secondary education. In addition, three working groups were set up to consider respectively:

- Problems of the teaching staff;
- The content and structure of studies;
- Problems of employment of SCI graduates.

The discussions were based on a series of reports prepared by individual participants,* using as a framework the paper on short-cycle higher education** and the guidelines for discussion prepared by the OECD Secretariat.

* See Part Two and List of Documents (Annex III of Part Three).

** See Part One of this volume.

## GUIDELINES FOR DISCUSSION

# I. THE PLACE AND ROLE OF SCIs IN THE GLOBAL SYSTEM OF POST-SECONDARY EDUCATION

## A. Functions and objectives of SCIs

### a) Basic functions

In most countries, short-cycle higher education institutions (SCIs) are primarily expected to fulfill the following basic function: to provide vocationally oriented education of post-secondary level, leading directly to entry into certain types of employment (i.e. short-cycle higher education).

In a limited number of other Member countries they are in addition expected to provide the first part of long-cycle university studies (i.e. the first-cycle higher education).

### b) Emerging functions

In recent years a number of SCIs started to organise a variety of courses and activities designed to serve particular needs of society so far not provided by formal educational establishments. Four types of functions seem to be gaining increasing importance ("outreach programm in the American terminology):

i) provision of courses in view of retraining and upgrading the economically active population ("permanent", "life-long", "adult" education);

ii) serving some of the cultural and recreational needs of the surrounding community;

iii) providing special (remedial) education to those whose secondary schooling is incomplete, insufficient, or who show basic educational deficiencies, in order to allow them to be admitted to regular higher education studies;

iv) contributing towards solutions of local or regional, economic and social, problems.

## B. Pressures on SCIs

The various functions enumerated in the preceding paragraphs constitute a response to certain demands and pressures of society:

i) the growing need for a wide and diversified range of qualified manpower resulting from rapid technological progress and developments of the labour market;

ii) the increasing pressure of individual demand for higher education and of the demand for greater equality of educational opportunity, and more particularly of the aspirations of students entering SCIs to transfer to university-type education and qualification;

iii) the need for change and innovation in the post-secondary system as a whole, SCIs being expected to cope with a number of educational, economic, social and cultural problems which traditional universities are often reluctant to face.

The main question which arises is whether the actual functions of SCIs, as defined under (A), match the general pressures and demands of society as enumerated under (B), or whether any major imbalances have to be faced.

## C. SCIs and universities: emerging models of overall structures of higher education

A basic Secretariat report on structures of post-secondary education* identifies four models of higher education structures as emerging in different countries, each of which represents a particular type of articulation between the university and non-university sectors.

i) the comprehensive university model which encompasses practically all post-secondary education under the "umbrella" of the university. Various solutions can be envisaged under this

* "Towards new structures of post-secondary education: a preliminary statement of issues" - OECD documents, Paris, June 1971.

model, from a loose federation of different higher education institutions to a complete integration of all types of post-secondary education;

ii) the binary model, implying separate development of the university and non-university sectors. The latter increasingly fulfills many of the functions previously assigned only to universities;

iii) the combined development model, which continues to differentiate universities from non-university institutions but envisages new means designed to improve the linkages and articulation between the two types of establishment;

iv) the intermediary multipurpose model, in which short-cycle and first cycle higher education are under the full responsibility of SCIs while universities concentrate on the second and third (postgraduate) stages of post-secondary education.

Clearly, all these models have their advantages and drawbacks, and the extent to which each of them may be developed and implemented will depend on the countries' context and traditions, as well as on their social and educational objectives. In any case, the advent of mass higher education will most probably create a situation in which European countries will have either to:

a) develop a polyvalent type (Junior College) of SCI representing the open sector of the higher education system (the universities becoming increasingly selective); or

b) continue the traditional open-door policy in universities, in which case universities will have to assume the functions which SCIs are actually fulfilling in other mass higher education countries (USA, Canada), while SCIs will focus their activities mainly on vocational training.

D. Specific issues

Each of the four models mentioned above must provide solutions to a number of problems common to countries with emerging systems of mass higher education. Three such problems (teachers, curricula, employment) will be discussed in working groups; additional issues for discussion are suggested below:

a) SCIs as tools of democratization of higher education

Practically all SCIs are expected to contribute to the equalization of educational opportunity; in certain cases they might even represent the major tool by which access to higher education is more widely opened to social groups and classes which in the past were heavily under-represented in post-secondary institutions.

- To what extent, and under what conditions, is this policy effective? What measures should be taken in order to avoid increasing institutional status differences leading to a dangerous split and a certain kind of pseudo-democratization of the higher education system?

b) Linkages with upper secondary education and admission policies

Questions and solutions related to this issue are probably the most decisive for the development of SCIs, as they will greatly influence their future place and role in the overall system of post-secondary education.

i) How will an increasingly generalized and comprehensive system of upper secondary education influence the admission policies of post-secondary institutions (both of SCIs and of universities)?

ii) Once graduates from all types of secondary schools have access to long-cycle university studies - which have more prestige and usually lead to a better position and higher salaries in industry and administration - will not the SCIs risk losing part of their potential clientele?

iii) Can or should SCIs have the same admission criteria as universities? If not, what should, in this respect, be the appropriate differentiation and for what type of students will SCIs constitute the "first choice"?

iv) What consequences should be drawn from the fact that in some countries SCIs are, in their admission policies, selective, and universities open? Can and should this situation continue?

c) Flexibility and open-ended nature of short-cycle higher education

If it is agreed that future post-secondary education should be organised in such a way that it allows maximum flexibility and student mobility and eliminates blind-alleys, all four models will have to meet at least two basic requirements:

a) graduates from short-cycle courses should have "appropriate" possibilities to pursue further studies;

b) those unable or unwilling to terminate long university studies should be given the possibility to receive vocational education preparing them for immediate employment.

In relation to (a):

i) Who should have the main responsibility for the further training of SCI graduates - SCIs themselves, universities, employers, special "adult training" centres?

ii) What types of rules can be established for transfer of SCI graduates to long-cycle university studies and is there an optimum or maximum value of SCI→university transfer? What measures should be taken if student demand to pursue further studies is such that the main objective (i. e. terminal vocational education) of SCIs risks being endangered or neglected?

iii) What are the structural arrangements (credit point system, Baukasten-system) which, together with curricular solutions, would allow wider permeability and closer co-operation between the different institutions concerned?

iv) Should SCI graduates be required or stimulated to spend a period of full-time employment before being allowed to pursue further studies?

v) What specific measures should SCIs take in order to facilitate the access to and organisation of studies for those who want to re-enter after a period of employment?

vi) In general, can and should the SCIs become a strategic element in the development of a general recurrent (life-long) education system? What other conditions would have to be fulfilled on the SCI side?

In relation to (b):

i) Should SCIs assume the main responsibility for providing vocational training of those unable to finish long university studies? What facilities should be given to these students and on which conditions should they be admitted to SCIs?

ii) What effect will this university→SCI transfer have on the status and prestige of the SCIs?

d) <u>Location of SCIs</u>

A wider geographic distribution and location of SCIs in areas which have up to now been lacking in higher education facilities is often considered an urgent necessity. However, the trend towards the decentralization of the system is counter-balanced by pressures towards a regional concentration of SCI activities, probably resulting from the need to find a "critical mass" without which SCIs cannot fulfil functions assigned to higher education.

i) What strategies are proposed to favour co-operation and/or integration of small specialized and widely dispersed institutions into large polyvalent regionally oriented establishments?

ii) Have any objective criteria on the optimum location of these regionally oriented SCIs been identified and implemented?

iii) Should SCIs be established preferably in the neighbourhood of universities (which might facilitate the co-operation between the two sectors) or, on the contrary, in places where no universities exist (which might strengthen their specific functions and local orientation)?

e) Participation of SCIs in local and/or regional development

This is one of the emerging new functions (see A(a) above) of SCIs which raises several questions:

i) To what extent should the curricula and programme of studies be adapted to specific regional needs in an increasingly mobile society?

ii) How can SCIs respond, on the one hand, to the national standards of education set for them and, on the other, to the immediate manpower needs of regions with very different levels of development?

f) Autonomy and control of SCIs

A large degree of autonomy is often considered as an attribute of prestige and an indispensable condition towards fulfilling some of the basic functions of higher education. Consequently, most SCIs are fighting for an increasing academic, financial and administrative autonomy, which many governments are reluctant to grant because they fear that this may tempt SCIs to emphasize activities leading to university status, thus neglecting some of their specific functions.

i) Should SCIs be subject to the same type and level of control as universities?

ii) How should regional, national and university interests be reflected in SCI government and control?

iii) What are the advantages and drawbacks of different forms of control and government of SCIs?

g) Planning mechanisms and co-ordination of SCIs on the national level

Planning and co-ordination of SCIs must be closely related to the overall planning and co-ordination of higher education. A major problem arises in those countries where up to now different planning and co-ordination bodies were competent for the various categories of post-secondary institutions (usually one for the university and one for the non-university sector).

i) What mechanisms should be established in order to develop an integrated planning system which will help to ensure a better co-operation between SCIs and universities and which will, at the same time, respect their different functions?

ii) Are certain planning approaches and methodologies (e. g. manpower projections) of particular relevance to SCIs?

iii) What should be the role of inter-institutional (Inter-SCI) organisations and associations?

## II. PROBLEMS OF THE TEACHING STAFF

### ISSUES FOR DISCUSSION

On the basis of numerous studies and discussions, it appears that in the majority of countries the issue underlying most of the specific problems concerning teachers in short-cycle and non-university higher education can be stated in the following terms: How can these teachers achieve a status comparable to their university counterparts and at the same time adequately serve specific different purposes, use different methods and respond to the needs, aspirations and attitudes of a different clientele?

It is suggested that this dilemma could be discussed under a number of sub-headings related to its various operational aspects.

a) Qualifications and recruitment

Parity of esteem will hardly ever be achieved if qualifications of SCI teachers are evaluated by purely academic standards. Clearly, a different set of criteria must be used: such personnel must be more teaching than research oriented, more emphasis must be put on their past experience outside the education sector (especially in certain fields) than on academic performance. Otherwise the discrepancy observed in many countries, where the proportion of higher university degree-holders (doctorates, masters) among teachers of SCI is much lower than among those teaching in long-cycle higher education and universities, will always be considered as evidence for a lower status and level of these teachers.

i) Is this discrepancy due simply to the lack of candidates with prestigeful qualifications or to deliberate recruitment policy?

ii) To what extent can appropriate qualifications for SCI teachers be defined more precisely than in the past both in purely educational terms, as well as in terms of practical and pedagogical experience?

iii) What should these qualifications be?

iv) Can any equivalences be established between these various kinds of qualifications?

v) Could the introduction of formal recruitment procedures similar to those applied in universities (e.g. participation of teachers in the selection of their peers) contribute to improving the status of SCI teachers?

vi) In general, what, if any, specific procedures can be considered as particularly appropriate to the recruitment of SCI teachers (e.g. open contest)?

b) Training

If it is agreed that teachers of SCIs, or at least certain categories of these teachers, should have a particular kind of qualification, it follows that they should also receive training distinct from university or secondary school teachers. However, practically nowhere is such a training institutionalized, except on a limited scale, and the question remains wide open as to what its exact patterns and content should be.

i) Could the new "teaching doctorate" as recently introduced on an experimental scale in the USA serve as a model?

ii) Do the Technical Teachers' Colleges in the UK provide a useful example?

iii) Or should it be assumed that short-term courses aimed at providing specific skills to already practising teachers (e.g. concerning use of new media or of new pedagogical approaches to different categories of students) represent the most appropriate solution?

iv) What special training is necessary for part-time or full-time teachers of vocational subjects without any pedagogical experience?

v) Should university departments be mainly responsible for the various types of SCI teacher training or should SCIs set up their own teacher training schemes and centres? What are the advantages and disadvantages of each of these solutions? What should be the content, length and methods of this special training?

c) Salary scales and career prospects

This is certainly the most tangible aspect of the whole SCI teacher problem: a certain feeling of inferiority will always remain if these teachers are paid substantially less than those in universities. In fact, it seems that in many countries the actual salaries, including fringe benefits, of SCI teachers are not widely different from those in universities; sometimes they are even slightly better, in particular when considering the junior teaching staff. The real problem is often linked to the patterns of promotion and advancement which, in most cases, are substantially better in universities than in SCIs. The top positions in the latter are almost always paid significantly less than the top positions in the former.

i) Can this disparity be overcome, given the existing financial constraints on higher education?

ii) If not, can some kind of compensation be provided? (see (d) and (e) below).

d) Working conditions

In the past, working conditions of SCI teachers were often more similar to those of their secondary school counterparts than to working conditions of university teachers, in terms of teaching load, degree of independence towards the institution's governing bodies, degree of academic freedom, etc.

i) Which of these inequalities can be eliminated, and which ones will have to stay due to the particular, and different, role of SCI teachers?

ii) Can some clear guidelines in this respect be established? (It may be, for example, that a higher teaching load in SCIs than in universities is justified, but it could be that possibilities for involvement in outside consultant work should be even greater than in universities, which might represent a compensation for relatively lower salaries at the top level (see (c) above)).

iii) What should be the relation of the teaching staff in SCIs to the authority controlling the institution?

iv) How can the requirement of academic freedom for SCI teachers be reconciled with the need for involvement by the surrounding community in matters such as curriculum, in places where it is expected that the SCIs should also respond to specific local and regional needs?

Another crucial aspect under this heading is the problem of research activities for SCI teachers. To many of them, SCIs are not attractive enough, or of a relatively lower status, because research, especially fundamental research, is not one of their objectives. This might be due to financial reasons or simply to the desire for an appropriate division of labour among institutions of the higher education system.

i) If this is so, can at least certain types of research activities be envisaged by the SCIs in which their teachers could participate (e.g. applied research or research connected with the "social involvement of the SCI")?

ii) If the institution as such does not enter into any research activity, can SCI teachers as individuals be provided with some possibilities for research work within or outside their institution (e.g. appropriate free time, participation in postgraduate and research programmes of universities in their neighbourhood and/or in industry?

iii) What appropriate mechanisms can be devised without endangering the specificity of the SCI objectives?

e) Mobility of SCI teachers

It is recognized that a high degree of horizontal mobility of SCI teachers is indispensable to ensure at least two major objectives of these institutions: adaptation of curricula to actual requirements of the labour market, and their response to broader educational, social and cultural needs of the surrounding - local, regional or national - community. This close contact of the SCIs with society will clearly be favoured if their teachers are not only recruited in non-educational sectors (e.g. industry, social services, administration) but also if they can relatively easily move out into these sectors, either temporarily or for longer periods, after a certain period of work in an SCI.

i) Can this mobility be seen also as serving as a substitute for an inadequate internal promotion policy?

ii) To what extent can mobility of SCI teachers into university positions be facilitated? What are the conditions of reforms necessary in this respect (e.g. recognizing their experience in the SCI as equivalent to university teaching and work)?

iii) Does not a too high mobility of SCI teachers constitute an obstacle to the development of an institutional identity and loyalty indispensable to the status of the establishment and to its attractiveness for both teachers and students? If so, what should be the appropriate balance?

iv) How can the need and advantage of horizontal mobility of SCI teachers be reconciled with the imperative of job security considered as essential by many of these teachers?

f) Diversity of SCI teachers

The heterogeneity and diversity of the teaching staff in some types of SCI raises a number of different problems: part-time and full-time teachers, those involved in vocational courses and those in academic subjects, teachers with and without high-level university degrees, with or without previous experience in non-educational jobs, etc.

i) To what extent do social status (if not salary) differences among these various categories create internal tensions leading to institutional instability and general dissatisfaction?

ii) How can these tensions be overcome and a feeling of common identity created in spite of these differences?

iii) Can a system of differentiated incentives help to solve problems posed by the diversity of the staff?

g) Teachers' attitudes towards the institution

In a certain sense, this problem integrates all the others and could therefore be considered as a synthesis of the discussions on this topic. As stated in the concluding remarks of the report on Teachers in non-university higher education* it seems that there are two camps among teachers in SCIs: "those who would like to be more equal than different (in relation to university teachers) and those who are determined to be different". The quest for equality is comprehensible, but its dangers must also be understood; it can deprive the SCI of its specific innovative character without succeeding in creating more than a second- or third-rate university.

To what extent does the SCI teacher identify himself with his institution and which of the factors previously discussed contribute more or less to this identification or to its rejection?

* Cf. "Teachers in non-university higher education", Part Two of this volume.

## III. STRUCTURE AND CONTENT OF STUDIES

### ISSUES FOR DISCUSSION

Curricula in short-cycle higher education have to fulfil two basic objectives:

1) To enable the short-cycle graduate to enter employment on completion of his studies;

2) to enable the short-cycle student to continue his studies if desired.

It is proposed that certain problems connected with devising appropriate curricula to attain these two objectives should be considered and that an attempt should be made to determine to what extent and in what circumstances the two types of curricula might be reconciled.

### I. Curricula and teaching methods in short-cycle vocationally oriented higher education

#### a) Specialization versus breadth

Almost by definition the idea of vocational training implies preparation for a specific occupation, i.e. a certain specialization. However, several factors militate against excessive specialization and in favour of breadth ("polyvalence"). A redefinition of certain traditional concepts might perhaps help to resolve this apparent contradiction;

- What exactly should be understood by "vocational education" - in the past, at present and with the prospect of continuing education? How should specialization and breadth ("polyvalence") be defined, with particular reference to the situation in the different branches of study?

b) Problems of breadth: clusters of study and common core curriculum

If it is agreed that the guiding principle of vocational education should be breadth, practical procedures must be defined. The solution usually advocated is a common core curriculum, i. e. the division of vocational training into two parts, i. e. a general course common to several types of training and a more specialized course.

i) Should the common core curriculum be based on the traditional relations between disciplines, and in that case, which are the most appropriate associations, e. g. applied social sciences, applied arts, training of different types of engineers?

ii) Or should preference be given to a common core curriculum based on common problem orientation (e. g. health professions, environment, transport), thus on an interdisciplinary common core?

iii) Can this interdisciplinarity be envisaged at the level of short-cycle studies in the same way as within long-cycle or even postgraduate studies?

iv) Can training for several more or less related occupations be based on a single short-cycle higher education course, specialized training being offered only later within industry? (Such a system would take into account the fact that in any case a large proportion of people have jobs for which their formal education, often very specialized, did not prepare them).

c) Problems of a balance between theoretical and practical and between general and specialized training in short-cycle higher education

Even if it is agreed that short-cycle higher education which implies a terminal and vocational orientation must give a large place to practical and specialized training, the question of the relative importance of theoretical and general education has to be faced.

i) Can at least some general guidelines be established in order to determine the appropriate balance?

ii) What should be the content of theoretical education in different fields of short-cycle higher education? Does this imply essentially teaching of basic disciplines corresponding to the desired vocational training (e. g. mathematics and physics for middle level engineers, sociology and psychology for social workers) and/or teaching concerned mainly with scientific concepts and methods?

iii) What should be understood by general education in SCIs? "Languages" (mathematics, the mother tongue and foreign languages) and "general culture" (history, literature, techniques of expression)?

iv) Should new classifications be envisaged to escape from the traditional dichotomies, i. e. theoretical/practical, general/specialized?

d) Teaching methods in vocationally-oriented short-cycle higher education

The problem of appropriate teaching methods is undoubtedly bound up with each of the above questions. Some general questions may, however, be discussed in this connection:

i) Are these or should these methods be essentially the same in short- and long-cycle higher education?

ii) Are certain teaching approaches (old or new) more or less desirable and efficient in SCIs (work in small groups, audio-visual aids, programmed instruction, alternation of study and work periods)?

## II. Links between short- and long-cycle higher education

Where short-cycle education merely represents the first stage of higher education (i. e. the first two or three years of the long cycle) the curricular problems involved are actually the same as those of the long cycle in general (although this first-stage course may be provided in institutions which are more or less independent of the universities). The situation is different and more complex where short-cycle higher education is designed to fulfil the two functions at the same time, i. e. the first stage of higher education and the terminal vocational training. In that case the problem of the pedagogical compatibility of the two functions has to be posed. The problem may be approached from several angles:

a) Structure of studies in short- and long-cycle higher education

The traditional sequence of almost all long-cycle higher education implies an abstract and theoretically-oriented education in the first stage of studies, followed by a more practically-oriented and specialized training in the subsequent stages. In these circumstances it is difficult to envisage a graduate of the short-cycle vocational course switching to the second cycle of a long university course.

i) From the pedagogical standpoint, is it possible to reverse this traditional sequence?

ii) Is it necessary to devise a structure of studies in which the practical and theoretical components would be linked otherwise than in chronological sequence?

iii) In this case what curricular reforms would be required in both the short and the long cycle?

b) The "cost" of transfer

The replies to the above questions will probably show the impossibility of "absolute transferability" and the fact that most transfers of short-cycle vocational graduates to long-cycle university courses and of long-cycle graduates and students to short-cycle courses are only possible at the cost of a certain period of additional study:

i) In view of the position in the different fields of study, what practical procedures might be adopted for this kind of "conditional transferability"?

ii) To what extent are special complementary courses for transferees organised by the receiving institution possible and necessary?

iii) How might the situation be facilitated by a system of credits transferable from one institution to another which no doubt would require special conversion keys?

c) Common core curricula and common courses for short- and long-cycle higher education

Common core curricula - or at least common courses - for short- and long-cycle higher education are no doubt an interesting solution in terms of a more effective utilization of resources, and would also probably help to raise the status of SCIs.

i) Could common core curricula or common courses be envisaged from the pedagogical standpoint and in which sectors (for example: common core curricula for university medical students and for SCI students preparing for para-medical professions)?

ii) What might be the duration and content of such common core curricula and, if only common courses were involved, should they necessarily be placed at the beginning of studies (university and SCI)?

iii) Must common core curricula be based on the grouping of related disciplines and/or on the association of branches of study which represent different aspects of a specific problem or activity? What in practice would be the nature of common core curricula designed for both short-cycle and long-cycle students?

d) Links between short- and long-cycle higher education in the perspective of recurrent education

This prospect will probably change (and facilitate) the nature of the solutions considered. However, it must be realized that a generalized system of recurrent education is a fairly long-term objective.

- In these circumstances and pending the establishment of a system of recurrent education, what pedagogical solutions should be considered which would both facilitate and expedite its introduction?

## IV. EMPLOYMENT PROBLEMS OF GRADUATES

### ISSUES FOR DISCUSSION

The creation and expansion of short-cycle higher education institutions (SCIs) have almost always been justified by the need to train middle-level qualified personnel of whom there was a particularly marked shortage about ten years ago. However, as several documents show, SCI graduates have in recent years run into difficulties, both in finding suitable employment and with regard to starting levels. * The central issue seems to be:

What is the nature and what are the causes of the difficulties encountered by SCI graduates? Which of these difficulties are due to the structure of the labour market and which to inadequate contacts between SCIs and employers? What action may be proposed to meet these difficulties?

a) Problems of graduate unemployment or under-utilization

In several Member countries a considerable proportion of former SCI students are unemployed or do not hold jobs corresponding to their qualifications or their expectations.

i) Is this situation more or less general? If so, is it due to:

- a temporary and localized decline in the demand for qualified personnel of this level due to adverse market conditions (regional or national) or to a lack of flexibility of the labour market ?

* It is obvious that these problems are not specific to SCI graduates but also concern university graduates for example. However, the present note will be confined to aspects of the problem directly relating to the employment of SCI graduates.

- changes in the labour market characterized in the last four or five years by the end of the shortage and by an increase (or a slight sectoral or local surplus) in the supply of SCI graduates (and university graduates)? (Any surplus tending to be absorbed by recruiting these graduates for posts previously occupied by personnel with lower qualifications.

ii) Is this under-utilization, which is frequently referred to, due to an inefficient manpower distribution or to a divergence between graduates' expectations and actual available jobs?

iii) To what extent is it also due to a certain policy (desirable in itself) whereby posts suitable for SCI graduates are reserved for in-service promotion? What generally is the relationship between the requirements of this internal promotion policy and the employment of SCI graduates?

b) Comparative salaries of SCI graduates

The remuneration of SCI graduates is often considerably lower than the salaries paid to university graduates. Even if this is not the case, it would seem that the possibilities of in-career increases are much smaller.

i) Do these disparities largely represent the difference in "intellectual investment" in this type of education as compared with university education or are they due to the fact that the access of SCI graduates to managerial functions is very limited?

ii) To what extent and in what way is the decision of young people to enter or not to enter an SCI influenced by the comparative level of the salaries paid to graduates of these institutions?

iii) What practical measures are likely to improve the comparative salaries of SCI graduates and is this, generally speaking, a matter for priority action?

c) Social status and career prospects

Differences of status and prestige between SCI graduates and university graduates are often due to differences in their social status and career prospects. They are reflected in a rather rigid professional hierarchy (technician - engineer, programmer - analyst, primary school teacher/secondary school teacher, etc.), in differences of function (the SCI graduate performing more subsidiary tasks defined by others and often being excluded from the decision-making function) and in differences in working conditions, e.g. rules of discipline, working hours, insurance systems.

i) What measures are likely to improve status and working conditions of SCI graduates and enhance their chances of in-career promotion?

ii) How far do the various forms of retraining or further training make it possible to achieve these objectives?

d) The position of SCI graduates by economic sector

The position of SCI graduates with reference to the problems mentioned under (a) and (c) above varies considerably from one economic sector to another. It is, for example, often unsatisfactory in the public sector and particularly in the civil service where there is no job category corresponding to the level of training offered by SCIs and where SCI graduates are recruited for jobs requiring a lower level of education. Moreover, in some sectors SCI graduates are appointed to posts which carry a relatively high degree of responsibility, whereas in other sectors they are employed on subordinate tasks only.

i) What is the nature and what are the causes of these sectoral disparities?

ii) Can they be used as a guide in planning the sectoral demand for SCI graduates and what are the limitations of this type of sectoral planning?

iii) In which sector should priority action be taken to facilitate the entry of SCI graduates into working life?

e) Curricula and structures of studies desired by employers

Employers often criticize SCIs on the grounds that their curricula are not adequately adjusted to the functions which graduates have to perform, particularly as regards the degree of specialization or general education required or the relative importance of theoretical and practical instruction. Whether such criticism is justified will at least partly depend on the employment sector, the size of the firm concerned and the opportunities for in-service training.

i) What is the content and what are the limits of this concept of adapting curricula to the requirements of economic sectors or firms? Does it imply direct preparation for a specific job or a more general training which would be supplemented in the firm and would be designed to facilitate adaptability, mobility or conversion?

ii) In what way and to what extent should the employers' influence be exerted? Are employers to be asked to make proposals on SCI curricula through the college boards, for example; what weight should be given to these proposals and what are the risks of adapting SCI curricula too closely to specific needs (sectoral or local)?

iii) What prospects are offered by the creation of joint work-study programmes or of "co-operative" programmes?

f) SCIs and further training

The provision of life-long educational structures for SCI graduates should make it possible to improve their career prospects (see item c), but these structures should also be an instrument for the adaptation and adjustment of the training received to the function or functions offered. It is, therefore, a question of acquiring a specialized in-service training as a supplement to the more general knowledge provided by SCIs and improving or updating this knowledge.

i) Should this function be largely performed by industry or also by the SCI, which would in that case provide the necessary structure (evening classes or intensive courses, seminars, etc.) for former graduates?

ii) What type of co-operation should be established in this field between SCIs and employers?

g) Arrangements for information and co-ordination between SCIs and the employment sectors

The establishment of permanent institutionalized relations between the SCIs and employers in the public or private sector is certainly one of the essential factors in adjusting (quantitatively and qualitatively) available qualifications to employment. These arrangements, which should make it possible to "integrate the SCI into the economic community" and facilitate the entry of graduates into the labour market are probably of three kinds:

- those offering students entering the SCIs the fullest possible information on existing employment outlets (type of job offered, salary scales, prospects of promotion, etc.);
- those providing for a regular information feedback between the labour market and the SCIs, on the utilization of graduates in the various economic sectors;
- those associating employers with SCI directors and administrators in SCI consultative or executive bodies.

i) What specific procedures might be considered with regard to each of these arrangements?

ii) What relevant bodies should be set up (college boards, consultative committees) and what should their responsibilities and functions be?

iii) What is the nature of the relationships which teachers should maintain with the employment sectors (period to be spent in firms, or part-time employment) and what direct role can they play in finding jobs for graduates?

iv) How should graduate placement be organised: in conjunction with the general employment services or by bodies specifically serving the SCIs?

## V. SUMMARY CONSIDERATIONS

The following are some of the main considerations on the place and role of SCIs in the global system of higher education, as formulated in the course of the general discussion held in plenary session.

Short-cycle and/or non-university higher education has developed in most Member countries very rapidly during the past decade (and often well before) as an alternative and/or complement to traditional university education. This development has been of particular importance and magnitude in countries which have reached or are approaching the stage of mass higher education.

The objectives for the development of this form of higher education, and of higher education in general, were more or less clearly formulated in the early sixties: manpower needs, meeting of social demand, democratization, etc. It was often also expected that the new forms of higher education would be cheaper in terms of financial costs. It is now opportune to undertake an evaluation of the new institutions in terms of the objectives originally set for them in order to assess both achievements and failures. In many cases, for example, these institutions have not proved to be less costly than traditional higher education nor have they led to any increase in the democratization of the educational system. In this context, it is now clear that equality of educational opportunity is dependent mainly on measures taken at the lower levels of the educational system, and that those taken at the higher education level can have but a marginal effect. The one clear objective to which they have contributed seems to be that of bringing about a greater diversification in the educational system, which is in itself an important step towards progress in the other areas.

Participants noted that in many countries short-cycle or non-university higher education has been formally assigned a purely vocational function. This exclusivity gives rise to many negative effects, and it becomes obvious that the dichotomy between vocational and academic (general) education must be eliminated, or at least largely attenuated. Both types of education must be provided at all levels, and no distinction need be made between the educational and human development goals which should guide them. Thus short-cycle and non-university institutions have a particularly important role to play in providing, in addition to preparation for immediate entry into the labour market, general education contributing to the building up of a cultural community and to bridging the traditionally prevalent gap between the purely utilitarian and the purely intellectualistic value scales.

The articulation between short-cycle and long-cycle, university and non-university higher education will depend to a large extent on the specific socio-economic and educational context and traditions of each country and no single model of relations between the two sectors can be established. It seems clear, however, that in all circumstances a large permeability between different types of institutions is indispensable. This means, for example, that universities should give appropriate credit for studies pursued in short-cycle and/or non-university establishments even if these establishments have a mainly vocational orientation. In this context, participants noted with interest the experiments or actual plans in certain Member countries for the setting up of a new type of post-secondary institution, designed, through its comprehensive character, to eliminate the traditional division between university and non-university institutions. Experience has further shown that the provision of transfer possibilities from short to long-cycle higher education does not necessarily diminish the demand for short vocational courses, provided that these courses do not represent a blind alley without any possibility for further studies.

In the long run, the latter condition can probably best be fulfilled by the development of a system of life-long (recurrent) education, which thus appears as an essential element for a more rational organisation of both short and long-cycle higher education.

The development of short-cycle higher education cannot be considered separately from the development of universities. The former might often try to adopt traditional values of universities in order to gain more respectability, but it must not be forgotten that universities, on the other hand, are already giving to their education more professional relevance and orientation. Thus innovations taking place within short-cycle institutions should and can serve as a model to universities in several respects, such as content and nature of courses, contact with the outside world, or use of resources. Consequently, short-cycle establishments should not be regarded as a "counter-university", but as a new dimension of all higher education.

# REPORTS OF THE WORKING GROUPS

## I. PROBLEMS OF THE TEACHING STAFF

Traditionally higher education has meant "university", and is characterized by the autonomy of teachers and the self-contained, self-governing nature of the institutions. Teaching and research are given equal weight and knowledge is sought for its own sake. Certain current problems can be identified within this sector:

a) universities have adapted to changing socio-economic needs slowly and with difficulty;

b) they are very expensive in terms of human and financial resources;

c) they are unable and perhaps unwilling to achieve mass involvement.

Consequently, countries are developing "non-university" structures of higher education which are being made relevant and responsive to current social and technological needs. In some countries these new programmes were developed in the expectation that greater efficiency would result in both lower unit costs to the system and reduced cost to the students.

Specific manifestations of these problems differ from country to country, but two main types of institutional structures have emerged as solutions: a "junior" cycle with different degrees of integration with the universities (a two- or three-year cycle, self-contained, that can lead to university studies or give a qualification for direct entry into the labour market) and "alternative structures" (self-contained cycle of higher education, the objectives of which are to give a different type of qualification with traditional higher education status). Each of these systems presents different roles and problems for their respective teaching staffs, and requires the recruitment of different types of staff.

Despite current criticism, the university system has maintained its prestige in its own eyes, in the assessment of the community, and in the opinion of many "new" institutions. Consequently, teachers of the non-university sector are tempted to identify with the traditional university value structure, and expect the status and working conditions of their university colleagues. However, it is questionable how far non-university structures should be compared to universities. The purpose of the new structures should be seen as being different: their curricula, their functions, and their teaching roles should be valued in their own light and not in comparison with traditional institutions. "Alternative" structures are closer to universities in certain important respects (length of courses, nature of final qualifications, etc.) than "junior cycles", and thus permit closer comparison with universities. But even in these institutions, the differences between the traditional and new structures of higher education need to be emphasized and judged in their own right.

Clearly if the non-university establishments are to function properly, they need an effective faculty. This means that their salaries and conditions of employment should be comparable with those current in universities for equivalent personnel. Because of the function of these institutions, recruitment from outside the educational system is essential; this means recruiting teaching staff from business and industry, public administration, social welfare, professions and the arts - in fact from the range of activities that constitute the complex socio-economic structures of contemporary communities which are served by this sector of education. If these new structures are to realize their full potential, different types of teaching contract must be developed for part-time teachers who will retain a firm footing in the non-academic world. It is also desirable that some appointments should be temporary so that interchanges of personnel between teaching and the economy are facilitated, and so that faculty members should have renewed experience with the ways in which knowledge and skills are being used. As a result, salaries and conditions of work in short-cycle structures of higher education must reflect not only university conditions but also conditions in relevant sectors of the economy.

Faculty members should make a contribution to the research effort, but this effort should be mainly related to the practical and vocational role of the institutions and their students, and the problems of the community in general and the local area in particular. To achieve this, teaching commitments should allow free time for the communal, scholarly, and research efforts of the staff, and the necessary technical and material means should be made available. Staff should give priority to keeping in touch with advances in their field of interest in order to achieve high levels of teaching. Furthermore, a crucial part of the teacher's role must be service to the region by active participation in the community. These are more important roles for the faculty than traditional research activities, and for certain faculty members service may even replace the practical types of research outlined earlier.

It is questionable whether the hierarchical nature of universities is relevant to these new institutions and whether it might not be more appropriate for all teachers to have the same status. In any case, in these new institutions it is desirable to examine carefully questions of hierarchy of the profession, in order that non-university institutions do not simply duplicate the universities' system and copy their structure and values. Furthermore, the status of individual faculty members should reflect the complex role of the institution, with its emphasis upon teaching and the need for advanced scholarships to maintain teaching standards, community activities, and research with a practical orientation, rather than the current practice of emphasizing lists of publications.

Despite the variety of short-cycle higher education structures and the importance of seeing them in the context of the socio-economic structure of which they are a part, three points seem common to most innovations and significant for the role of the faculty:

- the emphasis within the new institutions of their role as places for teaching and the impact this has on the role and commitment of the faculty, their training and interests, their relative involvement in teaching and research;
- the emphasis on preparing students for initial entry to the labour market as well as on various types of retraining and upgrading programmes, and on designing the content of their educational experience with specific reference to its relevance to occupational life. This requires a faculty with "broader" recruitment patterns and experiences than is customary in higher education. Further, the faculty has a responsibility to contribute to the development of the students' critical mind and their understanding of the relationship between their vocational training and the wider society;
- the importance of applied rather than basic research in these institutions, and the emphasis upon translating and making relevant the findings of fundamental research to immediate practical socio-economic problems of the community generally and the local area in particular.

These new institutions are not only innovational, but in a sense experimental, both in their general role in the community and the educational system, and in the detail of their course content and teaching methods. As a result these changes require continual evaluation and assessment if a more rational system of education and utilization of resources is to be achieved. A system of continuous assessment of institutional as much as student progress is essential if the new roles for the institution and its staff are to be effectively performed. Given the critical importance of the teaching skills and values of the faculty, special attention should be placed upon methods of recruiting and training staff. In particular, specific in-service training and orientation programmes should be developed and evaluated.

## II. STRUCTURE AND CONTENT OF STUDIES

The subject of this group, the structure and content of studies in short-cycle higher education, was central to the active theme of the meeting:

- The deliberations of the group essentially depended on the definition of the objectives of short-cycle higher education and on the way in which the problem of vocational training was being dealt with in the various national education systems;
- the definition of content and structure should normally have implications for the recruitment of teachers, their job profile, their training where applicable, and their career possibilities;
- it is quite clear that training has an effect on employment possibilities and, in particular, that the possibility of transfer to long-cycle higher education or to traditional higher education provides an outlet in itself; in any event it is a factor in the analysis of employment problems;
- in this way, the problem of curricula, which was our assignment, to some extent determines the work of the other two working groups, but is at the same time determined by them.

The basic documents prepared for the meeting presented either analyses or theoretical "models" for which conditions of implementation had to be determined, or national case-studies from which it was necessary to derive general principles and conditions of applicability in other national educational situations.

The guidelines for discussion proposed consecutively in linear form a number of issues which were clearly inter-related. For example, the definition of the curriculum for short-cycle higher education was inevitably linked to the problem of the impossibility, possibility, or even necessity of liaison with long-cycle higher education and, conversely, the analysis of links between these types of education presupposed definite answers to the curriculum problem.

Notwithstanding these difficulties, which sometimes gave rise to some confusion, the group managed to follow the proposed guidelines quite closely.

Lastly, the working group realized that it was simultaneously discussing several dichotomies which did not have the same meaning for all participants:

- Short-cycle education: long-cycle education;
- Post-secondary education: university education;
- Vocationally oriented education: non-vocationally oriented education.

Several attempts were made to avoid this difficulty by dealing with the problem of changing structures and content in higher education in general and disregarding existing institutions and differences between countries.

However, a number of clarifications, definitions, or even solutions were proposed which should lead to a more satisfactory statement of the problems of new structures of post-secondary education. The group focused its attention essentially on the concepts of breadth ("polyvalence") and specialization, on the definition of what is generally understood by "common core" of studies, on the content of this common core and on the relevant practical teaching methods.

As regards links with long-cycle education, the group considered what type of structure provided maximum flexibility and in particular, what were the advantages and drawbacks of credit point systems.

This analysis provided the basis for discussion of specific cases of transfer from one type of education to another and their implications for the post-secondary systems as a whole.

On the other hand, except for some brief and quick references, the group did not discuss the specific meaning of vocational or specialized training, nor, in particular, the role of on-the-job training and the implications which such training has on the structure of the educational institutions.

Only if clear answers had been given to these questions would it have been possible to deal coherently with the problem of balance between theoretical and practical training.

The group did not discuss in detail the possibility of a generalized system of recurrent education, but took the view that this subject should serve as a reference for all its work since all initial training must be defined in relation to a clear perspective of subsequent further training, i. e. what can and should be introduced into training during or after actual professional practice. From an institutional point of view, it seems that in many respects short-cycle higher education provides a better and more flexible framework for recurrent education.

## KEY ISSUES

The group agreed on the following general principles which provided a framework for the discussion as a whole.

a) The establishment of education systems bringing students together in a prolonged common educational experience is essential for both vocational and pedagogical purposes.

b) The traditional education system has failed to provide equality of opportunity. It has contributed to the basic dichotomy between vocational training and academic education. This dichotomy is socio-cultural in origin and assumes its most dramatic manifestations at the end of the period of compulsory schooling.

c) It is therefore essential that, while pursuing such specific functions as are assigned to it in different educational systems, short-cycle higher education should not represent a blind-alley or provide training totally different from other post-secondary education. It would be contrary to the objective of democratization to reduce theoretical education in short-cycle training.

Thus, if it is not to aggravate the inequality mentioned above, short-cycle higher education should encourage individual development by facilitating possibilities of transfer to other types of education. Furthermore, this double role of short-cycle education - general education/vocational education - should be extended to apply to all higher education.

Specialization and breadth ("polyvalence")

The solution to this problem in fact depends on the values on which the education system is based and on the objectives which are set for it:

- To train individuals who can be integrated into existing structures and make a positive contribution to the economic and technological development of society. In this case a broad education is no more than a refined form of specialization since it facilitates adaptation and occupational mobility;

- to train individuals with a wider knowledge than purely vocational practice and who will therefore possess, in addition to their specialized training, a "good general education" in the humanist tradition;
- to train citizens capable of acquiring suitable frames of reference for analysing and questioning the system in which they are working. The education provided in addition to specialized training is therefore of a "socio-critical" nature, and breadth is no longer confused with adaptability.

Breadth and specialization can therefore be defined either in relation to economic requirements alone, or in terms of educational criteria, in which case they comprise an ethical dimension and the ability to analyse the social system.

These distinctions are clearly fundamental, especially for determining the content of the "common core" and the teaching methods to be used.

The "common core" of studies

The concept of the "common core" is ambiguous. Most members of the groups even considered that this term should only be used as a frame of reference. If "common core" is understood to mean a compact system of one or two years of general education, it merely reinforces the most traditional concept of education and the monolithic structure of the university. Thus, irrespective of the duration of short- or long-cycle higher education, the common core should be considered as a body of knowledge which differs according to the individual and the specialization selected. This common core is rather a "common axis", because it must exist through the whole duration of studies, because it may be taken in a different order according to the individual and because it does not therefore correspond to a chronological division of the education process. The scope of this common core and the form of its integration obviously depend on the characteristics of the secondary education systems in the various countries.

Most members of the group seemed inclined to adopt the second view.

The "content" of this "common axis" is itself extremely complex and may comprise:

- general education, understood in its widest sense, i.e. covering a broad range of subject matter and not implying any internal system of organisation;
- a number of instrumental training courses which form the subject of a "sequential education" and lead to attainments that can be tested;
- training in communication, expression, teamwork, etc. ;
- general knowledge of the discipline to which the specialization belongs;
- a range of specialized knowledge which serves to place the selected specialization in perspective and thus provides a general basis.

This diversity shows that flexibility is essential to such training, which is not directly vocational, and that it should be introduced only in relation to individual needs. (For example, learning communication techniques may very well follow an on-the-job training period which indicated the need for this type of knowledge.)

Teaching methods should be consistent with the flexibility of the proposed model and might cover:

- interdisciplinary projects involving discovery and intellectual output rather than the transmission of knowledge;
- "simulation" techniques;
- intensive seminars attended by beginners, together with skilled personnel requiring refresher courses, etc. ;
- practical training courses, which may be the best incentives for general education;
- direct contact with research through the requirements of the surrounding society.

Links between short- and long-cycle higher education

The group considered the problem (perhaps too narrowly) in terms of transfer from short-cycle vocationally oriented training to the long-cycle traditional education.

In reality, other systems can be envisaged either in the form of an appropriate extension parallel to the traditional system (United Kingdom binary model) or in the form of specific training courses within contexts to be decided after a period of work. In any case, the answer to this problem must presuppose:

- a coherent conception of the general system of post-secondary education;
- a type of structure of studies which facilitates comparison and definition of equivalences, therefore allowing transfer immediately after the short-cycle or after a period on the job.

This transfer is facilitated by the unity of the education system (comprehensive model), by a system of credit points, or by a combination of the two.

Two situations should also be distinguished: one in which the problem is to set up new institutions of higher education, in which case it was agreed by many people that the basis of a global and coherent model should be used; and the other, in which the problem is the reform of existing institutions and where the regulations on transfer conditions would be considered as essential.

In both cases, as it is impossible to determine a priori ideal solutions common to all countries, the condition for any future reforms to be recommended to Member governments is the setting up of institutions characterized basically by their flexibility.

The group gave particular consideration to the credit point system, which can be more readily adapted to any national system.

Credit point system

The group noted that it was essential to distinguish between a number of specific concepts related to this point:

a) Very generally speaking, credit points can be regarded as a system of capitalizing the qualifications acquired during training and as providing a kind of common language among several institutions based on bilateral agreements or more formal arrangements, and thus enabling transfers to be made with minimum complications;
b) credit points may sometimes correspond to the actual practice of an activity, irrespective of the subject matter. In this case the problem of equivalence is easily dealt with, as it is based on the acquisition of specific knowledge or information which it should be possible to define and test;
c) thus, credit points may be a way of expressing the qualifications acquired or of structuring the education itself. They can accordingly allow for a very large number of types of training (intensive training - spread over a year or a term, acquisition

of several points for one important activity, etc.). The instruments of evaluation of these credit points may guarantee the flexibility and relevance of the system.

Irrespective of the system adopted, it is difficult to conceive of "transfer without loss":

a) Losses will be at a maximum if the individual changes from one institution to another and has not foreseen this transfer during the short-cycle.

   Losses will be at a minimum if the individual remains in the same institution and has based his curriculum on the transfer to the long cycle.

b) Having set out these few principles, however, it appears that only empirical solutions exist at the moment.

The question of the cost of transfer is itself linked to the structure of post-secondary education and, in particular, to the greater or lesser degree of university "imperialism". It also corresponds to the ideas that society in general has of the differences between occupational categories, their hierarchical structure, etc.

## CONCLUSION

This last remark ties up with the problem not discussed by the group, i.e. vocational training in the strict sense. The terms and conditions for the provision of such training would have to be determined, together with the context and teaching methods.

But above all it should be questioned to what extent there are some specific vocational features which make specialization as such a method and form of general training. The problem of links between short- and long-cycle higher education would then arise in completely different terms that would not involve any implicit depreciation of the short-cycle, which is often regarded as non-university simply because it is vocationally oriented post-secondary education.

Having established such curricula, it will then be possible to revert to the problem of credit points and to the various institutional aspects of post-secondary education. This research should involve both theory and field-work. To start with, it implies an exchange of information on the existing situations in the various countries, an exchange which should be intensified as a result of this meeting.

## III. PROBLEMS OF EMPLOYMENT OF SCI GRADUATES

The group discussing employment problems of short-cycle higher education graduates followed the guidelines for discussion, covering all suggested items, but concentrating its attention on the following major topics:

Unemployment/under-utilization

Generally speaking, the situation is not worse for short-cycle higher education graduates than it is for university graduates. The group agreed that in some countries short-cycle higher education graduates had difficulties in finding employment peculiar to their own sector. Where this occurred, it was primarily the result of the lower status accorded by employers to short-cycle higher education graduates, irrespective of their potential value.

Employment/promotion

Where unemployment of short-cycle higher education graduates was a serious problem, this was usually a consequence of the general state of the labour market for highly qualified personnel. Status difficulties were however sometimes made worse by the narrow (not necessarily vocational) character of the education given to short-cycle higher education students; some firms sought more adaptable personnel. The group recognized that there was at present a conflict between the recruitment of personnel qualified at the short-cycle level and a regular promotion procedure for those with lower or no recognized qualifications, whose competence justified higher or wider responsibility. It agreed that only a general system for upgrading and updating the qualifications of both groups but especially the latter group - by "éducation permanente" or recurrent education - preferably on a basis which would allow some credit towards higher qualifications for both previous education and work experience, might obviate this problem.

## Salary and status

The same conclusion was reached when the group considered salary and status differentials. The initial salaries of short-cycle higher education graduates were in general found to be equal, and in some cases superior, to those of university graduates. The rate of economic return on public investment in short-cycle education might even be higher than that on university courses (as measured by medium salaries at the same age compared with initial public investment in the higher education of the individual). Furthermore, there was nothing to suggest that potential salary differentials were a disincentive to short-cycle institution recruitment. Nevertheless, there was no doubt that the ultimate and average career salaries of short-cycle higher education graduates seemed likely to be lower than those of university graduates. This was due in part to the lower status of short-cycle institution qualifications, even where these were precisely comparable in level to university qualifications. Short-cycle higher education graduates were more likely to continue to be used in a purely technical capacity, and less likely to be given opportunities for career development. The major factor was, however, the need to maintain in most areas of work a differential between the salary of the engineer/scientist/manager and that of the higher technician (or under-manager) who worked with him. Merit and competence in the lower group could thus only be rewarded if opportunities for recurrent education, leading to promotion, were freely available. Courses genuinely and permanently terminal at the higher technician level would otherwise always be inferior in status to those leading to higher qualifications.

## Trades unions/professional institutions

In some countries the trade union/professional institution structure might depress the salary and status of short-cycle higher education graduates. Where there was a trade union concerned specifically with the interests of graduates, or where the professional institutions defended the interests of the graduate alone, the short-cycle higher education graduate or higher technician might find that he was unprotected, or, worse, squeezed in the nutcracker formed by the skilled craftsmen on the one hand and the university graduate on the other. This was however not a universal problem, and in some countries the professional institutions now showed signs of wishing to defend the status and the professional standards (though not the salary) of the higher technicians as well as of the fully-qualified graduate.

## The public service

Industry seemed to have accepted short-cycle higher education graduates into its hierarchy more readily than the public service. In many countries, especially in Europe, recruitment in the public service was organised by grades corresponding to a scale of qualifications which antedated the creation of short-cycle institutions, and admission to the highest grade often called for skills more likely to be found in the old-fashioned university arts graduate than in the practically-oriented short-cycle higher education graduate. The public service should set an example in recruitment to the rest of society, possibly by changing classification and grading systems. Despite these difficulties, students do enroll in short-cycle higher education programmes; their motivation for so doing is not easily analysed, but deserves further study.

Determination of curricula

Every country had a system through which the views of employers and the professions could be fed into the determination of curricula. Too often the views of employers varied predictably, by size and age of firm or industry, or according to the level and role in the firm of the person consulted. National chairmen/presidents said that they needed adaptable, broadly educated personnel; local personnel managers saw a requirement for narrow specialists. Educators must in consequence often use their own judgment in fitting curricula to job requirements, and in insisting on a general education content. An important responsibility for the nature of curricula and structure of studies must lie, after due consultation, with national and local governments, which alone can safeguard the right of the citizen to education, and the necessity for mobility of manpower, as well as satisfying the demand for continuing education.* It is the responsibility of the State to ensure that due regard is paid to the need for compatibility of curricula across national boundaries, in order to develop international mobility of labour.

Work experience

The group identified a need for the collection and dissemination of information about the ways in which work experience was built into short-cycle higher education in Member countries. There were many methods of achieving this, some of which were industry-based and some college-based; international comparison should prove helpful. Various schemes of paid education leave seem, in this respect, of particular interest and importance. This was one way in which the gap between the requirements of general education and of training for a specific industry or vocation might be closed. For teachers, too,

* Some participants thought that the final responsibility for determining the curricula must lie with the educational establishment as well as with the student himself, so that the objective of individualized education can be achieved.

work experience could have a valuable updating effect; again, the collection of information about national practices would be useful.

Further training

The group agreed that short-cycle institutions must be concerned in the further training and education of their graduates, and indeed others. If this were left to the individual firm, mobility of labour would be restricted by the resultant incompatibility of qualifications. Industry must however be closely involved in further training; both sides must share responsibility. The process would be made easier by the wider use of credit point or similar systems: the group felt that OECD might usefully collect and distribute information on experiments with such systems.

Information about short-cycle institutions

The group agreed that there was a general need for the distribution of fuller information about short-cycle institutions to school-children, their parents, and employers. Their status would properly reflect the character and quality of the education they gave only when their role was more clearly understood in society. This was one way to improve the match between short-cycle higher education and employment.

Data

The data needed nationally and internationally was partly quantitative (number of jobs now available and projected in forecasts, including technological forecasts), and qualitative (based on job analysis). Data available from statistics bureaux, departments of labour and education, was on the whole scarce, partial, and often out-of-date. The problem was made worse by the lack of a common vocabulary even within the same government; different departments used incompatible classifications and sometimes do not attempt to co-ordinate their efforts. OECD might valuably study national systems of data classification and seek to develop an international system, based on broad job categories, related to short-cycle higher education programmes, in order to establish an international framework within which Member countries could usefully exchange information. Knowledge on the experience and the related statistics from countries already highly developed in a particular area of economic or educational activity would be of use to other Member countries in creating new short-cycle higher education programmes. *

* Some participants thought that rather than concentrating on data and information collection, OECD should organise meetings similar to that held in Grenoble, such meetings representing the most effective means for exchange of opinion and information.

## SOME COMMENTS ON THE GRENOBLE MEETING

by Professor Burton Clark
University of Yale

### The Critical Decision in Organisational Structure

Despite the many differences in the national context of higher education, we may identify certain general patterns emerging among non-university institutions. The two extreme cases are: a) the alternative university, and b) the first-tier college.

The alternative university pattern is found in those institutions that intend to compete with the traditional and recognized universities in training that can lead up to the first major degree or even higher. These institutions intend to be different and even if they offer some programmes that are markedly shorter than those of the universities, they want to develop a different educational track that extends upwards about as far as the university. They want to have their students exit from the educational ladder at the points that permit them to step directly into the high occupational and social strata normally peopled by university graduates. The most typical example of this pattern is the binary system in the United Kingdom, with its Polytechnics which seem committed to provide a new track, often centred on technology, aiming at as full a parity of esteem with the university as possible.

The second pattern - the first-tier college - is intended to be very much different from the university. It does not seek the long cycle of studies nor the privilege of granting a degree at a level parallel to the university degree. It commits itself to the education of students in the first one, two or three years above the secondary level and awards a "short-cycle degree". Within this general pattern, colleges may take all the students entering higher education, serving as the universal first tier; or they may take only short-programme terminal students;

or they may take both students intending to transfer to full university studies and those enrolling for a terminal degree. The countries that have moved farthest into mass higher education have generally adopted the latter form of this pattern (e. g. Canada, the United States).

The most critical decision in the organisation of post-secondary education, whether arrived at consciously or by drift, is choice between these various patterns. This "choice" is constrained by the context of tradition, existing educational structure, and political economy in the individual pattern. Considerations related to costs and to expansion targets might also be of central importance in this respect. Since the alternative university model is as expensive as the traditional university itself, the choice of this route alone probably entails relatively low expansion targets. For systems deep in mass higher education, where the number of students is so huge, the economies of first-tier colleges have argued strongly in their favour.

## The Critical Decision in Sector Relations

The new structural forms of the modern period of educational expansion also entail a basic decision in permeability. Will teachers and students have their chances in career and education entirely within one of the two sectors or will they have the opportunity to transfer from one to the other? Much can be said in favour of either choice. The viability of a new sector may well be best enhanced by a lack of bridges, commiting teachers to a new distinct career line and students to a new form of education. Even as a short-run tactic, the increase in institutional autonomy may help to nurture an initial stepchild into a strong and valued member of the family. The nations that opt for the alternative university pattern usually also have, we note, no permeability or else narrow bridges that sharply limit traffic. In favour of the other choice, we note first the personal gains of more options for teachers and students alike. Transferring from one sector to the other may often be much desired by the person and often necessary to his original or amended career objectives. Certain major types of the first-cycle college are premised on great transferability, e. g. the American community college system. The nations that are deep into mass higher education and possessing a sector of first-tier colleges usually have chosen also for high permeability.

## The Critical Decision of Selectivity

As the secondary level of education in a country shifts from elite to mass, the issue of selection at the doors to higher education becomes critical for the various sectors to which the doors open. Differential selectivity is likely to occur. In the United States, for example, the first-tier college has a completely open door while the university at the same time is more selective and may even increase its selectivity. There the critical decision in selection has already been made. In contrast, Continental countries often have open enrolment to the university for all secondary school graduates - or at least all graduates of certain types of secondary schools. This has been an elite form of openness, since most students left school after the elementary level, or while in high school, and only a small part of the age group were secondary school graduates. This situation has changed, and is changing rapidly, causing a process that, if not faced openly as a fundamental critical decision, will make the traditional university the main instrument of mass higher education while at the same time the new sectors will most likely be the more selective ones. Sooner or later, this decision will probably be forced on a country because of the huge economic cost of the massive university and/or because of sheer overload of structures designed for the small enrolments of the past.

Beyond these three issues there are many others not detailed here. These three are highlighted since they seem fundamental to the nature of the non-university sectors in various countries. One other point that has emerged from our discussion, which goes beyond the guidelines with which we began, is a general wish that new and altered forms of higher education not be defined on purely utilitarian (vocational) grounds. It would be a sad situation for the new institutions, their teachers and their students, if the traditional universities were seen as centres of culture while the non-university institutions became defined as places possessed only by the spirit of the job and the pay check. The new institutions need the touch of the aesthetic and the humane, an effort that in varying degrees seeks to blend general or liberal education with training in vocation. No student in post-secondary institutions should be cut off entirely from the history and ideas of his time.

One other common issue in the revision of post-secondary education in the present period is the location and form of adult or recurrent education. Life-long education has been poorly served thus far by the educational structure of nearly all countries. It has been marginal, fastened on to the periphery of institutions shaped basically by the full-time and continuous education of the young. Again we may expect that the efforts to face the problem will be heavily shaped by specific national contexts. What seems clear at this time is that the problem will be most difficult to solve. Recurrent education deserves institutions and teaching cadres of its own. But the public mind, as well as educational structure, remains fixed on the education of the young and a very great effort will be needed. We recommend that distinctive efforts, with much experimentation and assessment, be mounted in various countries towards the devising of an array of appropriate mechanisms for recurrent education.

In general, the progress of all new non-university institutions should be evaluated, through periodic review, against their objectives. Education has yet to learn how to assess itself, and perhaps appropriate attitudes and useful methods of evaluation will be one lesson that the newer enterprises will be able to teach the older ones.

A final word needs to be said about the identity and status of non-university sectors of higher education. All the new forms share the problem of creating separate and distinctive organisational identities, ones that offer alternative profiles of purpose and practice. For example, a new enterprise may concentrate more on teaching and exhibit a greater sense of relevance to current problems than does the university. The new institutions need to hold themselves somewhat over against the university, cultivating a sense of distinctive character and pride among the teachers and students in that difference.

Central to this effort is the problem of creating new "noble" institutions, avoiding as much as possible a radical bifurcation of the noble and less noble. The new institutions need to differentiate the ground, the criteria, of academic esteem, convincing others as well as themselves that there are many forms of academic excellence. This is obviously difficult to do, and considerably more so in some societies than in others. A full parity of esteem will generally not be achievable. After all, the general status system of society inevitably rubs off on educational institutions that prepare for different occupations and life-chances. But institutions that place their graduates at middle and lower levels can still be well-considered, judged to be very good in doing what they have set themselves to do. Compared to the university they can march to a different drummer. Promoting an alternative institutional profile, they can recruit differently and seek to build a different profile of values and skills in the teaching staff.

Thus the new institutions do not need to chase the rainbow of full equality of status with the universities. The latter have taken some time in history to develop their aura, and even moving at a faster rate the new institutions will need considerable time to develop their own full radiance. What they need in the short run is a level of self-esteem and public legitimacy that allows them to get on with their special work. In most countries, this will prove increasingly possible. But its attainment requires a clear eye and steady nerve in institutional leadership. The non-universities will fail us if they evolve only as carbon copies of the past or as institutions that zig and zag with the opportunism of the moment. A firm self-concept is essential to their promising new role in society.

# Annex I

# STATISTICS ON SHORT-CYCLE HIGHER EDUCATION

Table 1. ENROLMENT TRENDS IN SHORT-CYCLE HIGHER EDUCATION AND IN HIGHER EDUCATION IN THE 1960s

| COUNTRY | SHORT-CYCLE HIGHER EDUCATION | | | TOTAL HIGHER EDUCATION | | | % OF THE SCHE IN TOTAL H.E. | | |
|---|---|---|---|---|---|---|---|---|---|
| | 1960/61 | 1965/66 | 1969/70 | 1960/61 | 1965/66 | 1969/70 | 1960/61 | 1965/66 | 1969/70 |
| Germany ............ | 50,201[1] | 68,833[1] | 71,986[3] | 289,211[2] | 367,684[2] | 419,000[3] | 17.3 | 18.7 | 17.2 |
| Belgium ............ | 21,307 | 35,191 | ... | 51,999 | 83,991 | ... | 41.0 | 41.9 | ... |
| Spain ............ | 40,582 | 71,945 | 73,627 | 109,926 | 197,824 | 265,676 | 36.9 | 36.4 | 27.7 |
| Finland ............ | 4,122 | 7,226 | 9,145 | 27,955 | 47,662 | 65,616 | 14.7 | 15.2 | 13.9 |
| France ............ | 38,574[7] | 74,353[7] | 97,113 | 274,263 | 505,278 | 700,000* | 14.1 | 14.7 | 13.9 |
| Norway ............ | ... | 9,534 | 11,578* | ... | 28,899 | 38,658* | ... | 33.0 | 30.0* |
| Netherlands ............ | 35,686 | 45,857 | ... | 85,558 | 124,011 | ... | 41.7 | 48.1 | ... |
| Sweden ............ | 4,476 | 7,032 | 8,122[3] | 39,981 | 77,623 | 124,161[3] | 11,2 | 9.0 | 6.5 |
| United Kingdom ....... | 142,640 | 223,851 | 292,875*[6] | 286,218 | 431,132 | 500,000* | 49.8 | 51.9 | 58.6* |
| Yugoslavia ............ | 31,662 | 68,650 | 81,074[5] | 140,574 | 184,923 | 261,203[5] | 22.5 | 37.1 | 31.0 |
| Canada ............ | 30,531 | 47,076 | 67,849[4] | 175,800 | 326,976 | 427,849[4] | 17.5 | 14.4 | 15.9 |
| United States .......... | 453,617 | 845,244 | 1,484,000[5] | 3,610,007 | 5,570,271 | 7,608,000[5] | 12.6 | 15.2 | 19.5 |
| Japan ............ | 81,858 | 145,458 | 258,680 | 710,019 | 1,085,119 | 1,613,507 | 11.5 | 13.4 | 16.0 |

* Estimation.

1. Excluding the "Höhere Fachschulen" due to lack of statistics.
2. Including the "Pädagogische Höchschulen" which henceforth are considered as being university level.
3. 1968/69.
4. 1967/68.
5. 1970/71.
6. Estimation for Northern Ireland only.
7. Excluding Medical Sciences and Education.

SOURCES: 1960/61 and 1965/66: Development of Higher Education - Statistical Survey, OECD, 1970. 1969/70: National Statistics.

Table 2. COMPARISON OF GROWTH RATES BETWEEN SHORT-CYCLE AND UNIVERSITY EDUCATION DURING THE 1960s

| COUNTRY | SHORT-CYCLE HIGHER EDUCATION | | | | | | UNIVERSITY EDUCATION | |
|---|---|---|---|---|---|---|---|---|
| | 1965/66 1966/67 | 1966/67 1967/68 | 1967/68 1968/69 | 1968/69 1969/70 | 1960/61 1965/66 | 1965/66 1969/70 | 1960/61 1965/66 | 1965/66 1969/70 |
| Germany[1] | 2.0 | 0.0 | 2.5 | 9.1 | 6.5 | 2.7 | 4.6[6] | 5.1[2,6] |
| Belgium | 5.5 | ... | ... | ... | 10.6 | ... | 9.7 | 9.3 |
| Spain | 1.7 | 0.6 | -2.2 | -1.0* | 4.1[4] | 0.5 | 11.5 | 11.1 |
| Finland | 9.4 | 13.1 | 0.9 | 1.3 | 11.9 | 6.1 | 11.1 | 8.4 |
| France | 3.5 | 9.4 | 9.3 | 4.3 | 10.6 | 6.9 | 13.8 | 11.2 |
| Norway | 9.8 | 5.0* | 4.8* | 0.5* | ... | 5.0* | 15.4 | 8.7 |
| Sweden | 11.9 | 10.0 | -6.6 | 0.6 | 9.5 | 3.9 | 14.7 | 13.0* |
| United Kingdom | 9.0 | 10.6 | 4.0 | 4.4 | 9.4 | 6.8 | 7.6 | 8.5[2] |
| Yugoslavia | 9.7 | 9.6 | 1.7 | -7.2 | 16.7 | 3.4[3] | 1.3 | 8.6 |
| Canada | 21.2 | 18.9 | ... | ... | 9.1 | 20.0[5] | 14.0 | 12.4[2] |
| United States | 12.4 | 13.8 | 19.6 | 8.0 | 13.3 | 11.9[3] | 8.4 | 5.7 |
| Japan | 32.0 | 20.7 | 6.5 | 4.8 | 12.3 | 15.6 | 8.4 | 8.5 |

* Estimation.
1. Excluding the "Höhere Fachschulen" due to lack of statistics.
2. 1968/69.
3. 1970/71.
4. 1964/65: Following a reform in 1965/66, figures are no longer comparable with those of the previous years.
5. 1967/68.
6. Including the "Pädagogische Hochschulen" which henceforth are considered as being university level.

Table 3. ENROLMENTS IN SHORT-CYCLE HIGHER EDUCATION BETWEEN 1960/61 AND 1970/71

| COUNTRY | 1960/61 | 1961/62 | 1962/63 | 1963/64 | 1964/65 | 1965/66 | 1966/67 | 1967/68 | 1968/69 | 1969/70 | 1970/71 |
|---|---|---|---|---|---|---|---|---|---|---|---|
| Germany[1] | 50,201 | 54,750 | 58,898 | 62,441 | 66,723 | 68,833 | 70,203 | 70,237 | 71,986 | 78,535 | ... |
| Belgium | 21,307 | 23,746 | 28,054 | 30,509 | 33,025 | 35,191 | 37,116 | ... | ... | ... | ... |
| Spain | 40,582 | 41,478 | 43,046 | 44,691 | 47,685 | 71,945 | 73,199 | 76,051 | 74,380* | 73,627* | ... |
| Finland | 4,122 | 4,524 | 4,728 | 5,311 | 6,678 | 7,226 | 7,908 | 8,948 | 9,028 | 9,145[4] | ... |
| France[2] | 38,574 | 41,748 | 46,318 | 57,727 | 63,055 | 74,353 | 76,969 | 85,186 | 93,141 | 97,113 | 104,831 |
| Norway | ... | ... | ... | ... | 8,405 | 9,534 | 10,471 | 10,993* | 11,518* | 11,578* | ... |
| Sweden | 4,476 | 5,292 | 6,594 | 7,577 | 6,533 | 7,032 | 7,871 | 8,660 | 8,122 | 8,173 | 9,903 |
| United Kingdom[3] | 142,640 | 164,975 | 189,760 | 203,666 | 213,209 | 223,851 | 244,077 | 269,929 | 280,641* | 292,875* | ... |
| Yugoslavia | 31,662 | 40,898 | 47,782 | 53,381 | 63,073 | 68,650 | 75,344 | 82,570 | 83,947 | 77,901 | 81,074 |
| Canada | 30,531 | 33,691 | 34,841 | 40,838 | 44,229 | 47,076 | 57,084 | 67,849 | ... | ... | ... |
| United States | 453,617 | 521,003 | 592,328 | 627,806 | 713,276 | 845,244 | 950,000 | 1,081,000 | 1,293,487 | 1,397,000 | 1,484,000 |
| Japan | 81,528 | 91,245 | 105,182 | 119,767 | 125,566 | 145,458 | 192,083 | 231,779 | 246,890 | 258,680 | 258,573 |

* Estimation.

1. Excluding "Pädagogische Hochschulen" which are henceforth considered as being university level, and "Höhere Fachschulen" due to lack of statistics.
2. The total includes IUTs, higher technicians' courses, preparatory classes to the "Grandes écoles" and the "Capacité en droit".
3. Only Northern Ireland estimated for 1968/69 and 1969/70.
4. Only "Medical Sciences" estimated.

Table 4. BREAKDOWN BY FIELD OF STUDY OF ENROLMENTS IN SHORT-CYCLE HIGHER EDUCATION

| | BELGIUM | | SPAIN | | FINLAND | | JAPAN | | UNITED KINGDOM[3] | | SWEDEN | | YUGOSLAVIA | |
|---|---|---|---|---|---|---|---|---|---|---|---|---|---|---|
| | 1960/61 | 1966/67 | 1960/61 | 1968/69 | 1960/61 | 1969/70 | 1960/61 | 1968/69 | 1964/65 | 1969/70 | 1960/61 | 1969/70 | 1960/61 | 1966/67 |
| Technology ......... | 27.5 | 28.0 | 49.5 | 77.9 | 8.6 | 23.9 | 11.3 | 8.7 | 38.0 | 22.3 | - | - | 12.7 | 16.0 |
| Agriculture ......... | 1.3 | 1.3 | - | - | - | - | 1.7 | 1.4 | 0.0 | 0.4 | 1.6 | 0.7 | 3.9 | 2.4 |
| Medical sciences .... | 10.9 | 26.9 | 8.8 | 7.6 | 15.0 | 14.9 | 0.6 | - | 1.3 | 2.9 | 9.5 | 10.0 | 2.1 | 2.6 |
| Humanities ......... | - | - | - | - | 0.1 | 4.3 | 19.8 | 18.9 | 1.0 | 1.4 | - | - | - | - |
| Education .......... | 43.5 | 20.6 | - | - | 45.6 | 17.4 | 7.2 | 15.6 | 32.6 | 40.5 | 48.5 | 75.1 | 31.0 | 37.5 |
| Fine arts ........... | 6.3 | 11.0 | 25.3 | 6.0 | 5.0 | 5.9 | 3.8 | 4.4 | 3.6 | 5.3 | 11.1 | 9.5 | - | - |
| Social sciences ...... | 5.1 | 11.6 | 16.4 | 8.5 | 13.1 | 25.4 | 55.4 | 51.0 | 12.6 | 18.4 | 18.8 | - | 46.8 | 39.2 |
| Others ............. | 5.4[1] | 0.6 | - | - | 12.6 | 8.2 | 0.2[2] | - | 10.9[4] | 8.8[5] | 10.5 | 4.7 | 3.5 | 2.3 |
| Total .............. | 100.0 | 100.0 | 100.0 | 100.0 | 100.0 | 100.0 | 100.0 | 100.0 | 100.0 | 100.0 | 100.0 | 100.0 | 100.0 | 100.0 |

1. Including Architecture.
2. Pure Science.
3. England and Wales only.
4. Including "Pure Science": 6.1%.
5. Including "Law": 1.2 and "Pure Science": 5.1.

SOURCES: See Table 1.

<u>Table 5.</u> SHORT-CYCLE HIGHER EDUCATION: PROPORTION OF FEMALE STUDENTS

| COUNTRY | SCHE | | | UNIV. EDUCATION |
|---|---|---|---|---|
| | 1960/61 | 1965/66 | 1969/70 | 1965/66 |
| Germany[1] ........... | 7.3 | 6.2 | 6.5[2] | 20.6 |
| Belgium ........... | 37.0 | 45.0 | ... | 24.0 |
| Spain .............. | 24.4 | 10.8 | 10.7[3] | 21.3 |
| Finland ............ | ... | ... | 49.6 | 48.6 |
| France ............ | 34.0 | 34.6 | ... | 43.4 |
| Sweden ............ | 54.1 | 67.3 | 67.0 | 36.9 |
| United Kingdom ..... | ... | 36.4[5] | 38.5 | 25.4 |
| Yugoslavia .......... | 29.9 | 35.2 | 41.7[4] | 32.6 |
| Canada[4] ............ | 46.1 | 35.5 | ... | 33.5 |
| United States ....... | 37.5 | 38.1 | 40.0[4] | 39.2 |
| Japan ............. | 67.3 | 74.7 | 81.7[2] | 16.4 |

1. See note (1), Table 3.
2. 1968/69.
3. 1967/68.
4. 1970/71.
5. 1966/67.

<u>SOURCES:</u> See Table 1.

Table 6. NEW ENTRANTS IN SHORT-CYCLE HIGHER EDUCATION BETWEEN 1960/61 AND 1970/71

| COUNTRY | 1960/61 | 1961/62 | 1962/63 | 1963/64 | 1964/65 | 1965/66 | 1966/67 | 1967/68 | 1968/69 | 1969/70 | 1970/71 |
|---|---|---|---|---|---|---|---|---|---|---|---|
| Germany[1] .......... | 19,325 | 19,933 | 22,091 | 23,090 | 25,901 | 25,672 | 25,722 | 27,613* | 29,461* | 28,772* | 24,658 |
| Belgium ............ | 10,473 | 11,812 | 13,805 | 15,008 | 16,058 | 16,936 | ... | ... | ... | ... | ... |
| Spain ............. | 11,403 | 9,360 | 11,285 | 15,022 | 15,190 | 39,429 | 37,812 | 38,281 | 38,978 | 39,249 | ... |
| Finland ............ | 2,605 | 2,786 | 2,810 | 3,201 | 3,900 | 4,137 | 4,700* | 5,176* | 5,017 | 4,777 | ... |
| France[2] ............ | ... | ... | ... | ... | ... | 44,389 | 45,784 | 50,297 | 54,409 | ... | ... |
| Norway ............ | ... | ... | ... | 4,593 | 5,125 | 5,729 | 5,834 | 5,888* | 6,092* | ... | ... |
| Sweden ............. | ... | ... | ... | ... | ... | ... | ... | ... | ... | ... | ... |
| United Kingdom[3] ..... | ... | ... | ... | ... | ... | 121,875 | ... | 135,521 | 139,519 | 145,821 | ... |
| Yugoslavia .......... | 22,682 | 27,619 | 31,184 | 34,487 | 40,886 | 42,305 | 43,643 | ... | ... | ... | ... |
| Canada ............. | ... | ... | ... | ... | ... | ... | ... | ... | ... | ... | ... |
| United States ........ | 215,383 | 245,577 | 261,768 | 273,117 | 323,466 | 402,357 | 393,000 | 447,000 | 555,469 | 574,000 | 621,000 |
| Japan ............. | 42,318 | 47,278 | 55,613 | 61,417 | 61,070 | 80,563 | 108,052 | 121,263 | 124,949 | 128,124 | 126,659 |

* Estimation.
1 and 2. See table on Enrolments.
3. Figures have been estimated for Northern Ireland for the years 1968/69 and 1969/70. The same has been done for Teacher Training in England and Wales, for 1968/69 only.

Table 7. DEGREES AWARDED IN SHORT-CYCLE HIGHER EDUCATION BETWEEN 1960/61 AND 1970/71

| COUNTRY | 1960/61 | 1961/62 | 1962/63 | 1963/64 | 1964/65 | 1965/66 | 1966/67 | 1967/68 | 1968/69 | 1969/70 | 1970/71 |
|---|---|---|---|---|---|---|---|---|---|---|---|
| Germany[1,3] | 10,886 | 12,898 | 13,855 | 14,712 | 15,658 | 16,651 | 18,121 | 17,543 | 13,322 | ... | ... |
| Belgium | 6,010 | 7,038 | 8,089 | 8,367 | ... | ... | ... | ... | ... | ... | ... |
| Spain | 5,187 | 5,237 | 4,862 | 5,988 | 7,357 | 7,317 | 7,288 | 9,370 | 8,789 | ... | ... |
| Finland | 2,527 | 2,472 | 2,605 | 2,715 | 3,568 | 3,665 | 4,250* | 4,586 | 4,579 | 4,198 | ... |
| France[2] | 2,606 | 2,905 | 4,194 | 4,734 | 6,199 | 7,592 | 9,336 | 13,653 | 15,921 | ... | ... |
| Norway | ... | ... | ... | ... | 4,462 | 5,132 | 5,445 | 5,732* | ... | ... | ... |
| Sweden | ... | ... | ... | ... | ... | ... | ... | ... | ... | ... | ... |
| United Kingdom[4] | 33,368 | ... | 33,813 | 37,378 | 40,451 | 41,668 | 45,615 | 52,954 | 54,008 | ... | ... |
| Yugoslavia | 5,815 | 7,226 | 7,727 | 8,650 | 9,278 | 10,518 | 12,128 | 14,370 | 16,046 | 15,785 | ... |
| Canada | 15,776 | 16,007 | 12,135 | 14,052 | 14,408 | 14,829 | 15,692 | 16,187* | ... | ... | ... |
| United States | ... | ... | ... | ... | ... | ... | ... | ... | ... | ... | ... |
| Japan | 32,893 | 38,348 | 42,761 | 50,995 | 55,728 | 55,371 | 74,695 | 100,166 | ... | ... | ... |

* Estimation.
1. and 2. See Table on Enrolments.
3. Excluding "Fine Arts".
4. Figures have been estimated for Northern Ireland for 1967/68 and 1968/69.

Table 8. COMPARISON OF SOCIAL ORIGIN OF STUDENTS IN SCHE AND UNIVERSITY EDUCATION IN CERTAIN COUNTRIES (IN PERCENTAGES)

| FRANCE (1968) | PROFESSIONS | INDUS-TRIALISTS TRADESMEN | MIDDLE LEVEL EMPLOYEES | OTHER EMPLOYEES | FARMERS | WORKERS IN INDUSTRY | OTHERS | TOTAL |
|---|---|---|---|---|---|---|---|---|
| IUTs ......... | 12.3 | 15.7 | 17.1 | - | 10.7 | 24.2 | 20.0 | 100.0 |
| Faculties ..... | 32.1 | 14.3 | 16.1 | 8.8 | 5.7 | 11.9 | 11.1 | 100.0 |

SOURCE: Enseignement supérieur - no. 3596, MEN, 1969.

| YUGOSLAVIA (1966) | PROFESSIONS | EMPLOYEES | FARMERS | INDUSTRIAL WORKERS AND ARTISANS | NON-ACTIVE | OTHERS | TOTAL |
|---|---|---|---|---|---|---|---|
| Više Škole ............. | 10.7 | 21.1 | 25.4 | 15.6 | 19.5 | 7.7 | 100.0 |
| Faculties .............. | 22.0 | 24.6 | 14.6 | 13.6 | 20.3 | 4.9 | 100.0 |

SOURCE: Visoke Škole 1965/66 - no. 439.

| CANADA: ONTARIO (1967/68) | PROFESSIONS | EMPLOYEES | INDUSTRIAL WORKERS AND ARTISANS | UNSKILLED WORKERS | TRANSPORT AND COM-MUNICATIONS WORKERS | OTHERS | TOTAL |
|---|---|---|---|---|---|---|---|
| CAAT: | | | | | | | |
| - Applied arts ...... | 25.0 | 18.2 | 38.7 | 4.5 | 4.5 | 9.1 | 100.0 |
| - Commerce ....... | 24.0 | 13.6 | 32.5 | 6.5 | 14.3 | 9.1 | 100.0 |
| - Technology ....... | 14.1 | 8.6 | 39.8 | 5.1 | 15.2 | 17.2 | 100.0 |
| Universities: (Arts and Sciences) .. | 40.4 | 11.1 | 23.7 | 3.0 | 9.4 | 12.4 | 100.0 |

SOURCE: Survey of Ontario Post-Secondary Student Finances, 1967/68.

| UNITED STATES (1966) INCOME CLASS ($) | 15,000 AND OVER | 10,000 TO 15,000 | 7,500 TO 10,000 | 5,000 TO 7,500 | 3,000 TO 5,000 | LESS THAN 3,000 | NOT DETERMINED | TOTAL |
|---|---|---|---|---|---|---|---|---|
| 2-year establishments .. | 8.9 | 21.4 | 21.9 | 22.5 | 11.4 | 4.8 | 9.1 | 100.0 |
| 4-year establishments .. | 16.8 | 26.4 | 17.1 | 17.7 | 8.3 | 3.5 | 10.2 | 100.0 |

SOURCE: US Bureau of the Census, Population Characteristics, Series P.20, no. 183, 1969.

| UNITED STATES (1966) FAMILY OCCUPATIONAL LEVEL | VERY HIGH | HIGH | MODERATE | LOW | TOTAL |
|---|---|---|---|---|---|
| Outside higher education .................. | 11 | 18 | 39 | 32 | 100 |
| 2-year establishments ...................... | 22 | 27 | 33 | 18 | 100 |
| 4-year establishments ...................... | 33 | 29 | 27 | 11 | 100 |

SOURCE: L. Medsker and D. Tillery: Breaking the Access Barriers, Series of the Carnegie Commission, McGraw-Hill, 1971.

## Table 9. UNIT COST COMPARISON BETWEEN SHORT-CYCLE HIGHER EDUCATION AND UNIVERSITY EDUCATION IN CERTAIN COUNTRIES

| COUNTRY | YEARS | SCHE | UNIV. EDUCATION |
|---|---|---|---|
| France (Fr.) ........ | 1968 | 1,388[1] | 3,981 |
| Norway (Kr) ......... | 1970 | 8,000 | 15,000 |
| United Kingdom (£) .. | 1967 | 874[2] | 1,076 |
| Yugoslavia (dinars) ... | 1961 | 51 | 114.5 |
| Canada (Can. $) ...... | 1969 | - | 3,210 |
| - Ontario .... | | 1,728[3] | |
| - Quebec ..... | | 1,150[4] | |
| United States ($) ..... | 1969 | | |
| - Public ...... | | 535 | 1,714 |
| - Private ..... | | 860 | 1,968 |

1. Technical Higher Education (excluding IUTs).
2. Further education.
3. CAAT.
4. CEGEP.

SOURCES:
- France : Statistiques financières, MEN, 1968.
- Norway : Country-Reports, OECD, Document DAS/EID/70.24/14.
- United Kingdom : G. Brosan: Patterns and Policies in Higher Education, p. 37.
- Yugoslavia : Reforms in Yugoslavia, OECD, 1970, p. 55.
- United States : US Office of Education, Higher Education - Finance, 1968.
- Canada : C. Watson: New College Systems in Canada, OECD 1973.

## Annex II

# LIST OF PARTICIPANTS

Mr. J. Aguilar Peris
General Sub-Director of
University Centres
Madrid
Spain

Mr. H. Aigner
Federal Ministry for Education
and Art
Vienna
Austria

Mr. S. Bendor
Ministry of Education and
Culture
Jerusalem
Israel

M. Guy Berger — Rapporteur, Working Group on the Content and Structure of Short-Cycle Higher Education Studies
Professeur à l'Université de
Vincennes
Paris
France

M. Yves Bernard — Chairman, Working Group on the Problems of the Teaching Staff
Professeur au Conservatoire
national des Arts et Métiers
Paris
France

M. Eugenio Bertorelle
Directeur
Institut technique de Varèse
Varèse
Italy

M. H. Bonneville
Président
Université des langues et lettres
Grenoble
France

M. Bothello
Direction du Cabinet
des études et planification
de l'action éducative
Lisbon
Portugal

M. Jean Le Bot
Directeur de l'IUT de Rennes
Rennes
France

Mr. Gianpaolo Bonani
Ufficio della Programmazione
scolastica
Ministerio della Pubblica
Istruzione
Roma
Italy

M. André Casadevall
Directeur
Délégué adjoint aux
Enseignements supérieurs et
à la recherche
Ministère de l'Education nationale
Paris
France

Mr. Burton Clark
Chairman, Department of
Sociology
Yale University
New Haven
Connecticut
USA

M. Jacques Dodu
Directeur de l'IUT "A"
Grenoble
France

Mr. U. Fornstedt
Office of the Chancellor of
the Universities
Stockholm
Sweden

M. Jacques Fournier
Association des Collèges
Communautaires du Canada
Montreal
Quebec
Canada

Mr. Gerald Fowler
Deputy Director
Huddersfield Polytechnic
Huddersfield
Yorkshire
United Kingdom

Chairman of the Second Plenary Session

Mrs. Anne-Marie Furumark
U 68 Commission on Education
Stockholm
Sweden

M. Frédéric Gaussen
"Le Monde"
Paris
France

Mr. Rh. Glatz
Director
Karlsruhe Fachhochschule
Karlsruhe
Germany

Mr. Gieseke
Bundesministerium für Bildung
und Wissenschaft
Bonn
Germany

M. Claude Giverdon
Directeur de l'IUT "B"
Grenoble
France

Mr. Brian Holmes
Professor, Institute of Education
University of London
London
United Kingdom

Mr. Arvo Jäppinen
Ministry of Education
Helsinki
Finland

Mr. Hans Christian Johansen
Director, School of Social Workers
Odense University Centre
Odense
Denmark

Mrs. Irene Kehler
Arbeitsgruppe für empirische
Bildungsforschung
Heidelberg
Germany

Mr. B. Klemmensen
Roskilde University Centre
Roskilde
Denmark

Mr. Hugh De Lacy
Headmaster
College of Technology
Dublin
Ireland

Mr. Alan Little
Inner London Education
Authority
London
United Kingdom

Rapporteur, Working Group
on the Problems of the Teaching
Staff

Mrs. Marie Y. Martin
Director, Community College
Education
Bureau of Higher Education
Office of Education
Washington DC
USA

Mr. Robert H. McCabe
Executive Vice President
Miami-Dade Junior College
Miami
Florida
USA

Mr. W. T. Newnham
President
Seneca College of Applied Arts
and Technology
Willowdale
Ontario
Canada

Mr. Oberle
Professor at the College of
Technology
Winterthur
Switzerland

M. Louis Paoli
Chef du Service des enseignements
supérieurs et de la recherche
Ministère de l'Education nationale
Paris
France

M. Leo Paré
Directeur général de
l'enseignement collégial
Quebec
Canada

Rapporteur, Working Group on
Problems of Employment of
Short-Cycle Higher Education
Graduates

M. Jean-Louis Quermonne
Président
Université des Sciences
sociales de Grenoble
Grenoble
France

Chairman of First Plenary
Session

M. Lambert Radoux
Direction générale
Enseignement provincial
Seraing
Belgium

M. Marc Salesse
Président
Alliance universitaire de Grenoble
Grenoble
France

Mrs. Sonja Šarič
Institute of Social Research
University of Zagreb
Zagreb
Yugoslavia

Mr. W. G. Shannon
Executive Director
American Association of Junior Colleges
Washington DC
USA

Chairman, Working Group on Problems of Employment of Short-Cycle Higher Education Graduates

Mr. Raymond E. Schultz
American Association of Junior Colleges
Washington DC
USA

Mr. Ingjald Ø. Sørheim
Regional Colleges Section
Ministry of Education
Oslo
Norway

M. M. Soutif
Président
Université scientifique et médicale de Grenoble
Grenoble
France

Mr. Hans Tangerud
Director
Hedmark Oppland Distrikthogskole
Lillehammer
Norway

Mr. E. U. von Weizsächer
Arbeitsgruppe für empirische Bildungsforschung
Heidelberg
Germany

Mr. Gareth Williams
Higher Education Unit
London School of Economics and Political Science
London
United Kingdom

M. Milorad Zakič
President
Association of Two-Year Post-Secondary Technical Schools
Visa Tehnicka Masinska Skola
Zemum Beograd
Yugoslavie

SECRETARIAT

| | |
|---|---|
| Mr. George Papadopoulos | Chairman, Working Group on the Structure and Content of Short-Cycle Higher Education Studies |
| Mr. Ladislav Cerych | |
| Miss Dorotea Furth | |
| M. Jean-Pierre Pellegrin | |
| M. Pierre Duguet | |

## Annex III

# LIST OF DOCUMENTS

In addition to the papers presented in Part Two of this volume, the following documents provided a basis for discussions:

| | |
|---|---|
| "Towards New Structures of Post-Secondary Education: A Preliminary Statement of Issues" | OECD, Paris 1971 |
| "Models of Short-Cycle Higher Education envisaged in the Netherlands" by W. van Leishout | DAS/EID/71.70 |
| "Control of Two-Year Colleges in the United States" by L. L. Medsker and J. Beckham | DAS/EID/71.40 |
| "Teaching Staff in American Junior Colleges" by J. H. Nelson | DAS/EID/71.38 |
| "Curricular Implications of Developments in Short-Cycle Higher Education" by B. Holmes | DAS/EID/71.69 |
| "A Swedish Approach to Short-Cycle Higher Education: Combination of Vocational Training and Academic Education" by Mrs. A. M. Furumark and Mrs. L. Kim | DAS/EID/71.54 + Corrigendum |
| "The Curriculum of the American Junior College" by Dr. R. McCabe | DAS/EID/71.39 |
| "The Linkage of Short- and Long-Cycle, Theoretically and Practically Oriented Studies in the "Baukasten-Gesamthochschule" by Mrs. I. Kehler | DAS/EID/71.73 |
| "Problems of Employment for Graduates of Short-Cycle Higher Education in Canada: CAATs in Ontario and CEGEPs in Quebec" by the OECD Secretariat, based on a report by J. Fournier, Quebec and W. T. Newnham, Ontario | DAS/EID/71.50 |

"Employment for Occupational Programme Graduates" by Dr. R. H. Hagemeyer — DAS/EID/71.51

"Short-Cycle Higher Education in Japan" by Y. Shimizu — DAS/EID/71.78

## REFERENCE PUBLICATIONS

Development of higher education 1950-1967 - Analytical Report, OECD, Paris, 1971.

Development of higher education 1950-1967 - Statistical Survey, OECD, Paris, 1970.

## OECD SALES AGENTS
## DEPOSITAIRES DES PUBLICATIONS DE L'OCDE

**ARGENTINE**
Libreria de las Naciones
Alsina 500, BUENOS AIRES.

**AUSTRALIA – AUSTRALIE**
B.C.N. Agencies Pty, Ltd.,
178 Collins Street, MELBOURNE 3000.

**AUSTRIA – AUTRICHE**
Gerold and Co., Graben 31, WIEN 1.
Sub-Agent: GRAZ: Buchhandlung Jos. A. Kienreich, Sackstrasse 6.

**BELGIUM – BELGIQUE**
Librairie des Sciences
Coudenberg 76-78 et rue des Eperonniers 56,
B 1000 BRUXELLES 1.

**BRAZIL – BRESIL**
Mestre Jou S.A., Rua Guaipá 518,
Caixa Postal 24090, 05000 SAO PAULO 10.
Rua Senador Dantas 19 s/205-6, RIO DE JANEIRO GB.

**CANADA**
Information Canada
OTTAWA.

**DENMARK – DANEMARK**
Munksgaard International Booksellers
Nørregade 6, DK-1165 COPENHAGEN K

**FINLAND – FINLANDE**
Akateeminen Kirjakauppa, Keskuskatu 2,
HELSINKI.

**FORMOSA – FORMOSE**
Books and Scientific Supplies Services, Ltd.
P.O.B. 83, TAIPEI,
TAIWAN.

**FRANCE**
Bureau des Publications de l'OCDE
2 rue André-Pascal, 75775 PARIS CEDEX 16
Principaux sous dépositaires :
PARIS : Presses Universitaires de France,
49 bd Saint-Michel, 75005 Paris.
Sciences Politiques (Lib.)
30 rue Saint-Guillaume, 75007 Paris.
13100 AIX-EN-PROVENCE : Librairie de l'Université.
38000 GRENOBLE : Arthaud.
67000 STRASBOURG : Berger-Levrault.
31000 TOULOUSE : Privat.

**GERMANY – ALLEMAGNE**
Deutscher Bundes-Verlag G.m.b.H.
Postfach 9380, 53 BONN.
Sub-Agent : HAMBURG : Reuter-Klöckner ; und in den massgebenden Buchhandlungen Deutschlands.

**GREECE – GRECE**
Librairie Kauffmann, 28 rue du Stade,
ATHENES 132.
Librairie Internationale Jean Mihalopoulos et Fils
75 rue Hermou, B.P. 73, THESSALONIKI.

**ICELAND – ISLANDE**
Snæbjörn Jónsson and Co., h.f., Hafnarstræti 9,
P.O.B. 1131, REYKJAVIK.

**INDIA – INDE**
Oxford Book and Stationery Co. :
NEW DELHI, Scindia House.
CALCUTTA, 17 Park Street.

**IRELAND – IRLANDE**
Eason and Son, 40 Lower O'Connell Street,
P.O.B. 42, DUBLIN 1.

**ISRAEL**
Emanuel Brown :
9, Shlomzion Hamalka Street, JERUSALEM.
35 Allenby Road, and 48 Nahlath Benjamin St.,
TEL-AVIV.

**ITALY – ITALIE**
Libreria Commissionaria Sansoni :
Via Lamarmora 45, 50121 FIRENZE.
Via Bartolini 29, 20155 MILANO.
sous-dépositaires :
Editrice e Libreria Herder,
Piazza Montecitorio 120, 00186 ROMA.
Libreria Hoepli, Via Hoepli 5, 20121 MILANO.
Libreria Lattes, Via Garibaldi 3, 10122 TORINO.
La diffusione delle edizioni OCDE è inoltre assicurata dalle migliori librerie nelle città più importanti.

**JAPAN – JAPON**
Maruzen Company Ltd.,
6 Tori-Nichome Nihonbashi, TOKYO 103,
P.O.B. 5050, Tokyo International 100-31.

**LEBANON – LIBAN**
Redico
Immeuble Edison, Rue Bliss, B.P. 5641
BEYROUTH.

**THE NETHERLANDS – PAYS-BAS**
W.P. Van Stockum
Buitenhof 36, DEN HAAG.

**NEW ZEALAND – NOUVELLE-ZELANDE**
Government Printing Office,
Mulgrave Street (Private Bag), WELLINGTON
and Government Bookshops at
AUCKLAND (P.O.B. 5344)
CHRISTCHURCH (P.O.B. 1721)
HAMILTON (P.O.B. 857)
DUNEDIN (P.O.B. 1104).

**NORWAY – NORVEGE**
Johan Grundt Tanums Bokhandel,
Karl Johansgate 41/43, OSLO 1.

**PAKISTAN**
Mirza Book Agency, 65 Shahrah Quaid-E-Azam,
LAHORE 3.

**PORTUGAL**
Livraria Portugal, Rua do Carmo 70, LISBOA.

**SPAIN – ESPAGNE**
Mundi Prensa, Castelló 37, MADRID 1.
Libreria Bastinos de José Bosch, Pelayo 52,
BARCELONA 1.

**SWEDEN – SUEDE**
Fritzes, Kungl. Hovbokhandel,
Fredsgatan 2, 11152 STOCKHOLM 16.

**SWITZERLAND – SUISSE**
Librairie Payot, 6 rue Grenus, 1211 GENEVE 11
et à LAUSANNE, NEUCHATEL, VEVEY,
MONTREUX, BERNE, BALE, ZURICH.

**TURKEY – TURQUIE**
Librairie Hachette, 469 Istiklal Caddesi, Beyoglu,
ISTANBUL et 12 Ziya Gókalp Caddesi, ANKARA.

**UNITED KINGDOM – ROYAUME-UNI**
H.M. Stationery Office, P.O.B. 569, LONDON
SE1 9NH
or
49 High Holborn
LONDON WC1V 6HB (personal callers)
Branches at: EDINBURGH, BIRMINGHAM, BRISTOL, MANCHESTER, CARDIFF, BELFAST.

**UNITED STATES OF AMERICA**
OECD Publications Center, Suite 1207,
1750 Pennsylvania Ave, N.W.
WASHINGTON, D.C. 20006. Tel.: (202)298-8755.

**VENEZUELA**
Libreria del Este, Avda. F. Miranda 52,
Edificio Galipan, CARACAS.

**YUGOSLAVIA – YOUGOSLAVIE**
Jugoslovenska Knjiga, Terazije 27, P.O.B. 36,
BEOGRAD.

Les commandes provenant de pays où l'OCDE n'a pas encore désigné de dépositaire peuvent être adressées à :
OCDE, Bureau des Publications, 2 rue André-Pascal, 75775 Paris CEDEX 16
Orders and inquiries from countries where sales agents have not yet been appointed may be sent to
OECD, Publications Office, 2 rue André-Pascal, 75775 Paris CEDEX 16

**OECD PUBLICATIONS, 2, rue André-Pascal, 75775 Paris Cedex 16 - No. 31.015 1973**

**PRINTED IN FRANCE**